WILLIAM BYRD

Routledge Music Bibliographies

SERIES EDITOR: BRAD EDEN

COMPOSERS

Isaac Albéniz (1998)
Walter A. Clark

C. P. E. Bach (2002)
Doris Bosworth Powers

Samuel Barber (2001)
Wayne C. Wentzel

Béla Bartók, Second Edition (1997)
Elliott Antokoletz

Vincenzo Bellini (2002)
Stephen A. Willier

Alban Berg (1996)
Bryan R. Simms

Leonard Bernstein (2001)
Paul F. Laird

Johannes Brahms (2003)
Heather Platt

Benjamin Britten (1996)
Peter J. Hodgson

William Byrd, Second Edition (2005)
Richard Turbet

Elliott Carter (2000)
John L. Link

Carlos Chávez (1998)
Robert Parker

Frédéric Chopin (1999)
William Smialek

Aaron Copland (2001)
Marta Robertson and Robin Armstrong

Frederick Delius (2005)
Mary Christison Huismann

Gaetano Donizetti (2000)
James P. Cassaro

Edward Elgar (1993)
Christopher Kent

Gabriel Fauré (1999)
Edward R. Phillips

Christoph Willibald Gluck, Second Edition (2003)
Patricia Howard

G. F. Handel, Second Edition (2005)
Mary Ann Parker

Paul Hindemith (2005)
Stephen Luttmann

Charles Ives (2002)
Gayle Sherwood

Scott Joplin (1998)
Nancy R. Ping-Robbins

Zoltán Kodály (1998)
Mícheál Houlahan and Philip Tacka

Franz Liszt, Second Edition (2003)
Michael Saffle

Guillaume de Machaut (1995)
Lawrence Earp

Felix Mendelssohn Bartholdy (2001)
John Michael Cooper

Giovanni Pierluigi da Palestrina (2001)
Clara Marvin

Giacomo Puccini (1999)
Linda B. Fairtile

Maurice Ravel (2004)
Stephen Zank

Gioachino Rossini (2002)
Denise P. Gallo

Camille Saint-Saëns (2003)
Timothy S. Flynn

Alessandro and Domenico Scarlatti (1993)
Carole F. Vidali

Heinrich Schenker (2003)
Benjamin Ayotte

Jean Sibelius (1998)
Glenda D. Goss

Giuseppe Verdi (1998)
Gregory Harwood

Tomás Luis de Victoria (1998)
Eugene Casjen Cramer

Richard Wagner (2002)
Michael Saffle

Adrian Willaert (2004)
David M. Kidger

GENRES

American Music Librarianship (2005)
Carol June Bradley

Central European Folk Music (1996)
Philip V. Bohlman

Chamber Music (2002)
John H. Baron

Choral Music (2001)
Avery T. Sharp and James Michael Floyd

Church and Worship Music (2005)
Avery T. Sharp and James Michael Floyd

Ethnomusicology (2003)
Jennifer C. Post

Jazz Scholarship and Pedagogy, Third Edition (2005)
Eddie S. Meadows

Music in Canada (1997)
Carl Morey

The Musical (2004)
William Everett

North American Indian Music (1997)
Richard Keeling

Opera, Second Edition (2001)
Guy Marco

The Recorder, Second Edition (2003)
Richard Griscom and David Lasocki

Serial Music and Serialism (2001)
John D. Vander Weg

String Quartets (2005)
Mara E. Parker

Women in Music (2005)
Karin Pendle

WILLIAM BYRD
A GUIDE TO RESEARCH
SECOND EDITION

RICHARD TURBET

ROUTLEDGE MUSIC BIBLIOGRAPHIES

Routledge
Taylor & Francis Group
New York   London

Published in 2006 by
Routledge
Taylor & Francis Group
270 Madison Avenue
New York, NY 10016

Published in Great Britain by
Routledge
Taylor & Francis Group
2 Park Square
Milton Park, Abingdon
Oxon OX14 4RN

Printed in the United States of America on acid-free paper
10 9 8 7 6 5 4 3 2 1

International Standard Book Number-10: 0-415-94301-9 (Hardcover)
International Standard Book Number-13: 978-0-415-94301-7 (Hardcover)
Library of Congress Card Number 2005013599

Library of Congress Cataloging-in-Publication Data

Turbet, Richard.
    William Byrd, a guide to research / Richard Turbet.-- 2nd ed.
        p. cm. -- (Routledge music bibliographies)
    Includes index.
    ISBN 0-415-94301-9 (hardback : alk. paper)
    1. Byrd, William, 1542 or 3-1623--Bibliography. I. Title. II. Series.

ML134.B96T9 2005
016.78'092--dc22   2005013599

Taylor & Francis Group
is the Academic Division of Informa plc.

Visit the Taylor & Francis Web site at
http://www.taylorandfrancis.com

and the Routledge Web site at
http://www.routledge-ny.com

Contents

"At least he works in a library," Bertha murmured, "one does feel that is *something.*"

—Barbara Pym, *An Unsuitable Attachment*

Preface

This edition is a new book, surveying writings published 1987–2004, and discs released 1995–2003. It is an independent book with its own contents. The same remains true of its predecessor, the first edition. That book contains material up to 1986, some of which remains unique, and it will not be superceded by its successor. The two are complementary but different books on the same topic, separated by time and circumstances, with a limited amount of material in common. Everything that is worth preserving in the first edition and that has not been incorporated into this new edition is cited here so that reference may easily be made to the first edition, which remains a source of some significant research. The aspiration behind these two volumes is that everything that is worth knowing about Byrd should be available in, or accessible through, their pages.

The material they share occurs mainly in the first two chapters: much of the catalogue of Byrd's works, and part of the checklist of all identified literature devoted to Byrd, which complements the histories of Byrd literature that introduce it in the two editions. The criteria for inclusion in the checklist are that the item should have in its title Byrd's name or something that is unique to Byrd, or be entirely about Byrd. Many new items from the period covered by the first edition have subsequently been identified, so for the sake of completeness and continuity, the complete checklist is appended to the introductory survey which, in the present volume, carries on from 1986, when the survey in the first edition ended. Its *terminus ad quem,* and that of the annotated bibliography that follows it, is the end of 2004; however, one completed project of major significance, with a definite date of publication early in 2005, has been included in both the checklist and the annotated bibliography, not the least because there was at one time the possibility that it would be published late in 2004. The annotated bibliography of significant writings about Byrd, which includes many items not eligible for the checklist, consists of writings about but not necessarily devoted to Byrd, which contain material of value in the study and understanding of his life, music, and reputation. The earliest entry, hitherto overlooked in Byrd literature, dates from Byrd's own lifetime. This new annotated bibliography carries on from when its predecessor left off at the end of 1986, but it includes the small number of writings from before 1987 that emerged subsequently. It also includes listings of those items from the bibliography in the first edition that remain recommended. The next two chapters of the first edition were rendered redundant in 1997 by John Harley's monograph and his subsequent researches and discoveries. Similarly, the selective discography of chapter VI has been superseded by Michael Greenhalgh's complete discography of 1992 and its supplement in 1996; however, it has been replaced in this new edition by a further supplement, now Chapter IV, compiled by the same author, the doyen of British discographers. An intervening chapter about the *Annual Byrd newsletter* is an innovation, and the concluding chapter contains perspectives on the future for Byrd and his music, covering anticipated developments and projections for the longer term. The two images (see Photos 1A and 1B) are unique in Byrd literature and depict the current condition of the site of Thorndon Hall.

There is a substantial amount of significant material that remains unique to the first edition. Of great importance are the transcriptions of three original sources, none of which has been published elsewhere. These are "The tercentenary of William Byrd" by E.H.L. Reeve, the full original text of the Queen's letters patent to Tallis and Byrd for printing music, and Anthony Wood's notes on Byrd: respectively chapter VIII and appendices A and B. (Appendix C, the third of the three, has been superseded by my article "Coste not Byrd," 1998Tc.) In the case of the letters patent, it is worth repeating and emphasizing that this remains the only published source of the full original text, as distinct from the widely disseminated, cited, and quoted "extract and effect."

The ample quantity of fresh material in this new edition is a reflection of the gratifying increase in published Byrd literature. *The Byrd edition* is now complete, and discussion continues about the admission, retention, and rejection of attributed and anonymous works on the fringes of the Byrd canon. The number of new books and articles about Byrd has greatly extended the checklist and, although some superseded or outdated writings have not been carried over from the first bibliography into the lists of continued recommendations, a greater number of subsequent writings have been selected for comment in the new edition, including all articles from the ten years of the *Annual Byrd newsletter.* Respect for the discarded is shown by their being listed at the end of Chapter III.

That Byrd's music has flourished on compact disc is reflected in the extent of Chapter IV, Michael Greenhalgh's further supplementary discography, which covers the period from not long after the origins of the compact disc to date. This substantial contribution to Byrd scholarship includes listings of such projects as the complete keyboard music and the continuing complete Latin music, to add to the complete consort music listed in his previous supplement in 1996.

A unique forum, dedicated to the expansion of knowledge about Byrd, came into being when the *Annual Byrd newsletter* was launched in 1995. Still the only periodical to have been devoted to an early English, indeed British, composer (before Elgar), it was created to increase the amount of informed writing about Byrd through articles shorter than those in mainstream musicological journals, and to add as much information as possible by means of sections listing new writings and disseminating miscellanea. Partly in view of the imminent publication of the present volume, it ceased publication in 2004. It is described and indexed in Chapter V.

There is still insufficient material being written about Byrd, but the situation is better at the time of this writing than it was when the first edition was being written. At that time, much information about Byrd was awaiting rediscovery and publication, whereas much else was either not being disseminated (sometimes deliberately) or was being disseminated without discipline. It was appropriate and necessary to try to bring such disparate sources of information into a disciplined format, and also to include items of original research—Chapter VIII and the appendices mentioned earlier—not yet (nor since) published elsewhere. Subsequently, such has been the improvement in the development of Byrd literature that it is appropriate and necessary to refine the content of this new edition, focusing on those areas that have expanded: catalogue (with the completion of *The Byrd edition*), checklist, bibliography, discography, and the *Newsletter.*

Acknowledgments

I am most grateful to the Music Libraries Trust for a grant that expedited the preparation of this book. In this context I wish to thank Ann Yardley for her fine and heroic typing, Rosemary Firman, Christopher Jackson, and the Trustees.

I renew my thanks to all whose assistance I acknowledged in the first edition of this book. The legacy of their help lives on. Most significantly, this applies to my late parents and to the late Donald Francombe, who had the thankless task of being both Second Master and Music Master when I was a pupil at Bancroft's School, Woodford, Essex, and who continues to receive my eternal thanks for introducing me to the music of Byrd.

At Routledge I had the pleasure of corresponding with Richard Carlin, Brad Eden, and Sarah Blackmon.

In no particular order, and with apologies to any who feel they should have been included, I now thank the following: Carol Wakefield (Stainer and Bell), Jonathan Martin (Primary Source Microfilm), Martin Monkman (Amphion Recordings), Simon Perry (Hyperion Records), Peter Berg (Lindum Records), Clifford Bartlett (King's Music), the International Association of Music Libraries (United Kingdom and Ireland Branch), David J. Smith (Music Research Group, University of Aberdeen) and Cantores ad Portam, Timothy Storey (my oldest friend) and the Choir of St Botolph's Church Bishopsgate in the City of London, John Harley, Dennis Townhill, David Pinto, Janet Clayton, Joseph Kerman, The Squair Mile Consort, Iain Beavan (Head of Special Libraries and Archives, University of Aberdeen), John Easton (my successor as Head of Arts and Divinity, Queen Mother Library, University of Aberdeen), Kerry McCarthy (Duke University), Rachelle Taylor (Magill University), Richard Rastall (University of Leeds), Gilbert Blount (Thornton School of Music, University of South California), Esther Jones (Editor, *Church Music Quarterly*), Irene Wears (Administrator, The Cardinall's Musick), David Humphreys (Cardiff University) and Adrian Yardley (Guildhall School of Music and Drama).

Finally, but finest, my family: Lynda Turbet (Robert Gordon's College), William Turbet (Napier University), Rory Turbet (University of Edinburgh), and Rowan (University of East London, Barking Campus).

Frontispiece

Photo 1A. The site of the original Thorndon Hall, now in Thorndon Country Park, West Horndon, Essex, England. (See I.CLv.)
Photographed by Janet Clayton, 1997. Reproduced by permission.

Photo 1B. Surviving foundations of Thorndon Hall, demolished during the eighteenth century, now protected by barbed wire, and overgrown. (See I.Clv.)
Photographed by Janet Clayton, 1997. Reproduced by permission.

1

Catalogue of Byrd's Works

This catalogue consists of all known works accepted as Byrd's, with an appendix containing dubious attributions. It is followed by "The Byrd Apocrypha," which consists of all known spurious attributions. The catalogue is in a broadly classified order based on A, except for the keyboard music, which is based on J, and the consort music, which is partially based on L. The apocrypha is alphabetical. There is an index to titles of all pieces including separate sections and contrafacta, with versions of those titles that survive in significantly varied forms.

The catalogue provides references to the appearances of Byrd's works in the complete or partial editions A–H and lists J–L; in the six publications from Byrd's lifetime containing, but not devoted to, his works, a–f; and in a variety of printed sources BMS-WI containing apocryphal items not in the editions of Byrd's music. References are given for all Byrd's works in FVB as F was intended to complete the then-published corpus of Byrd's keyboard music begun in FVB, H and e: see F p. xi.

One or more of the following pieces of information are provided: the number of the item if it occurs in one of Byrd's own publications; the key letter or letters to indicate printed editions or lists; in Roman, the volume number; in Arabic, the number of the first page; the section of the edition or list in which the item occurs; the number of the item in the edition or list; and the title given to the item where it differs substantially from the one in the catalogue. Any appropriate annotations are placed at the end of the entry. A lone letter indicates the presence of the item with no deviations of title or allotted section in one of the lists. Unnecessary duplication of any verbiage and numeration is avoided. Only a Byrd source or the most recent source is usually provided for apocryphal material.

The purpose of the catalogue and of its arrangement is twofold: first, to provide unification in respect of the inconsistent and unsatisfactory numerations among existing editions and lists; and, second, to provide published sources for all works associated with Byrd, especially when these sources have attempted to publish all of Byrd's works or all of a section of his works, such as the keyboard music.

The criterion for a work's inclusion in the main catalogue is that, having weighed the opinions, alongside my own, of appropriate authorities—bibliographical, executive, historical, analytical—I consider the balance of evidence favourable. In the absence of conclusive evidence and when there is a difference of opinion, it is my policy to be inclusive. Appendant and apocryphal items are provided with references that explain their status when this is not obvious from the editions in which they appear.

THE EDITIONS

A and B represent the latest research and have substantial introductory material. C has now been rendered obsolete by A and B but remains historically important; recent findings (see 1995Tf) have made it possible to revise several dates of publication within the edition. D represents an even earlier attempt to publish all of Byrd's church music. E consists of contemporary transcriptions as Byrd never composed for the lute. F brought into print all of Byrd's hitherto unpublished keyboard works. G consists of three anonymous pieces for keyboard which analysis suggests were probably composed by Byrd. H is the modern printed edition of a contemporary manuscript devoted to Byrd. An introduction to A is given in 1980Be.

A   *The Byrd edition.* General editor Philip Brett. London: Stainer & Bell, 1970–2004.

   1.   *Cantiones sacrae (1575),* edited by Craig Monson. 1977.
   2.   *Cantiones sacrae I (1589),* edited by Alan Brown. 1988.
   3.   *Cantiones sacrae II (1591),* edited by Alan Brown. 1981.
   4.   *The masses [1592–1595],* edited by Philip Brett. 1981.
   5.   *Gradualia I (1605): the Marian masses,* edited by Philip Brett. 1989.
   6a.   *Gradualia I (1605): All Saints and Corpus Christi, with hymns to the Blessed Sacrament and other motets,* edited by Philip Brett. 1991.
   6b.   *Gradualia I (1605): other feasts and devotions,* edited by Philip Brett. 1993.
   7a.   *Gradualia II (1607): Christmas to Easter,* edited by Philip Brett. 1997.

7b.   *Gradualia II (1607): Ascension, Pentecost and the feasts of Saints Peter and Paul*, edited by Philip Brett. 1997.

8.   *Latin motets I (from manuscript sources)*, edited by Warwick Edwards. 1984.

9.   *Latin motets II (from manuscript sources)*, edited by Warwick Edwards. 2000.

10a.   *The English Services*, edited by Craig Monson. 1980.

10b.   *The English Services II (the Great Service)*, edited by Craig Monson. 1982.

11.   *The English anthems*, edited by Craig Monson. 1983.

12.   *Psalmes, sonets and songs (1588)*, edited by Jeremy L. Smith. 2004.

13.   *Songs of sundrie natures (1589)*, edited by David Mateer. 2004.

14.   *Psalmes, songs, and sonnets (1611)*, edited by John Morehen. 1987.

15.   *Consort songs for voice & viols*, edited by Philip Brett. 1970.

16.   *Madrigals, songs and canons*, edited by Philip Brett. 1976.

17.   *Consort music*, edited by Kenneth Elliott. 1971.

Vols. 15 and 17 originally bore series title *The collected works of William Byrd*. Vol. 15 reissued in *The Byrd edition* 1995. Vol. 17 reissued in *The Byrd edition* 1985.

B   *William Byrd: keyboard music*, edited by Alan Brown. Musica britannica 27–28. London: Stainer & Bell, 1969–71. 2v. 2nd ed. 1976; rev. repr. of vol. 2, 1985. 3rd ed. of vol.1, 1999. 3rd ed. of vol. 2, 2004.

C   *The collected works of William Byrd*, edited by Edmund H. Fellowes. London: Stainer & Bell, 1937–50.

I.   *Masses. Cantiones sacrae (1575)*. 1937.

II.   *Cantiones sacrae (1589)*. 1937. Rev. by Thurston Dart, 1966.

III.   *Cantiones sacrae (1591)*. 1937. Rev. by Thurston Dart, 1966.

IV.   *Gradualia (1605) (part i)*. 1938.

V.   *Gradualia (1605) (parts ii and iii)*. 1938.

VI.   *Gradualia (1607) (part i)*. 1938.

VII.   *Gradualia (1607) (part ii)*. 1938.

VIII.   *Motets for three, four and five voices (recovered from manuscript)*. 1939.

IX.   *Motets for six, eight and nine voices (recovered from manuscript).* 1939.

X.   *English liturgical music.* 1948 [i.e., 1949].

XI.   *English anthems.* 1949.

XII.   *Psalmes, sonets and songs (1588).* 1948 [i.e., 1949]. Revised by Philip Brett, 1965.

XIII.   *Songs of sundrie natures (1589).* 1949. Revised by Philip Brett, 1962.

XIV.   *Psalmes, songs and sonnets (1611).* 1949. Revised by Thurston Dart, 1964.

XV.   *Songs.* 1948 [i.e., 1949].

XVI.   *Additional madrigals, canons and rounds. Appendix: fragments of text.* 1948 [i.e., 1949].

XVII.   *Chamber music for strings.* 1948 [i.e., 1949].

XVIII.   *Keyboard works (part i).* 1950.

XIX.   *Keyboard works (part ii).* 1950.

XX.   *Keyboard works (part iii).* 1950.

Vols I–XVI bear the series title *The collected vocal works of William Byrd.* Vol. XVII "(Supplementary)." The eventual official title of the series is confirmed in 1995Tf.

D   *Tudor church music,* editorial committee P. C. Buck, E. H. Fellowes, A. Ramsbotham, R. R. Terry, S. Townsend Warner. London: Oxford University Press, 1922–29; reprint ed., New York: Broude, 1963.

II.   *William Byrd: English church music: part I: 1543–1623.* 1922.

VII.   *William Byrd, 1543–1623: Gradualia, books I and II.* 1927.

IX.   *William Byrd, 1543–1623: masses, Cantiones, and motets.* 1928.

Vol. IX contains all three masses, the *Cantiones* of 1575 and all unpublished motets then known. Terry was no longer on the editorial board for vols. VII and IX.

V.   *Robert White, d. 1574.* 1926.

VI.   *Thomas Tallis, c. 1505–1585.* 1928.

Appendix, with supplementary notes, by Edmund H. Fellowes. London: Oxford University Press, 1948.

E   *William Byrd,* edited by Nigel North. Music for the lute, 6. London: Oxford University Press, 1976.

F   *William Byrd: forty–five pieces for keyboard instruments,* edited by Stephen Tuttle. Paris: Oiseau-Lyre, 1939.

G   *Three anonymous pieces attributed to William Byrd,* edited by Oliver Neighbour. London: Novello, 1973.

H   *My Ladye Nevells booke of virginal music, by William Byrd,* edited by Hilda Andrews. London: Curwen, 1926; reprint ed., with a new introduction by Blanche Winogron, New York: Dover, 1969.

J   Fellowes, Edmund H. *William Byrd.* See 1948Fw. Instrumental music only: "Chamber music for strings," pp. 198–200, or "List of keyboard music," pp. 212–20.

K   Neighbour, Oliver. *The consort and keyboard music of William Byrd.* See 1978Nc.

L   Dodd, Gordon. *Thematic index of music for viols.* London: Viola da Gamba Society of Great Britain, 1980–2002. 7 instalments.
"William Byrd (1543–1623)" pp. 31–45/BYRD-1-BYRD-15.
Pages BYRD-5, 9 and 11 revised for 7th instalment, which is on CD-ROM only.

M   Fellowes, Edmund H. *William Byrd: a short account of his life and work.* See 1923Fw. Numerations of individual pieces refer to "Instrumental music by William Byrd," p. 117: (c) "Miscellaneous." [No. 2:] "Twenty-one compositions, in short score, made 'upon the Fa burden of these playne Songs' (Brit. Mus. Add. MS. 29996)."

N   Byrd, William. *Fantasia a 4 no. 3 for viols or recorders,* reconstructed by Warwick Edwards. Wyton: King's Music, 1995.

P   *A paven of Mr Byrds,* edited by Richard Turbet. Lincoln: Lindum Desktop Music, 1993.

Q   Byrd, William. *Five-part consort music,* edited by George Hunter. Urbana: Northwood, 1994.

R   Byrd, William. *Pavans and galliards in five parts,* edited and recon-
        structed by Richard Rastall. Leeds: four-fifteen press, 1998.

a   *Musica transalpina,* compiled by Nicholas Yonge. London: Thomas East,
        the assigne of William Byrd, 1588.

b   Byrd, William and Watson, Thomas. *A gratification unto Master John
        Case, for his learned booke, lately made in the praise of musicke.* Lon-
        don: Thomas East, the assigne of William Byrd, 1589.

c   *The first sett, of Italian madrigalls englished,* compiled by Thomas Wat-
        son. London: Thomas Este, the assigne of William Byrd, 1590.

d   Morley, Thomas. *A plaine and easie introduction to practicall musicke.* Lon-
        don: Peter Short, 1597; reprint eds, Shakespeare Association facsimiles, 14.
        London: Oxford University Press, 1937; Farnborough: Gregg, 1971.

e   *Parthenia or the maydenhead of the first musicke that ever was printed
        for the virginalls. Composed by three famous masters: William Byrd, Dr.
        John Bull, & Orlando Gibbons.* London: Dor: Evans, [1612/13]; reprint
        ed., Harrow replicas, 3. Cambridge: Heffer, 1942.

f   *The teares or lamentacions of a sorrowful soule,* compiled by William
        Leighton. London: William Stansby, 1614.

BMSJ   Turbet, Richard. "*I am weary of my groaning:* a hitherto unpublished
        round attributed to Morley or Byrd." *British Music Society journal* 8
        (1986): 10–11.

CC   *The catch club or merry companions. A collection of favourite catches
        for three and four voices.* London: Walsh, 1762. 2 bks; reprint ed.,
        Farnborough: Gregg, 1965. 2 bks in 1.

CCC   *Catch that catch can, or a choice collection of catches, rounds,
        & canons for 3 or 4 voyces,* edited by John Hilton. London: Benson
        & Playford, 1652; reprint ed., Da Capo Press music reprint series.
        New York: Da Capo, 1970.

CCL   *Church choir library,* no 577, edited by Thurston Dart. London:
        Stainer & Bell, 1955.

CO   *Cantantibus organis: Sammlung von Orgelstucken alter Meister.*
        Regensburg: Pustet, 1958–.

        16. *Altenenglische Orgelmusik,* edited by Eberhard Kraus. 1968.

DVB   *Dublin virginal book.* New ed., edited by John Ward. London: Schott,
        1983.

EECM   *Early English church music.* London: Stainer & Bell, 1963.

> 6. *Early Tudor organ music: I. Music for the office,* edited by John Caldwell. 1965.

> 13. *Thomas Tallis: English sacred music: II. Service music,* edited by Leonard Ellinwood, revised by Paul Doe. 1974.

> Supplementary vol. 1. Daniel, Ralph T. and le Huray, Peter. *Sources of English Church music 1549–1660.* 1972.
> 2 pts paginated consecutively.

> Supplementary vol. 2. Hofman, May and Morehen, John. *Latin music in British sources c1480–c1610.* 1987.

EMR   *Early music review* 61 (2000): 14–17.

EMRD   *Early music review* 91 (2003): 28, Diary p. 35.

EMV   Fellowes, E.H. *English madrigal verse, 1588–1632.* 3rd ed., revised and enlarged by Frederick W. Sternfeld and David Greer. Oxford: Clarendon, 1967.

FVB   *The Fitwilliam virginal book,* edited by J.A. Fuller Maitland and W. Barclay Squire. Leipzig: Breitkopf & Hartel, 1894–99. 40 fascicles; reissue, 2 vols, 1899; reprint ed., rev. by Blanche Winogron, 2 vols, New York: Dover, 1979.

> Complete listing and dating of fascicles in XI.Tt.

HYP   Moroney, Davitt. *William Byrd: the complete keyboard music.* Booklet accompanying Hyperion compact discs CDA66551/7: see Chapter 4.

JM   Blount, Gilbert Lee. "The sacred vocal music of John Mundy: a critical edition." 2 vols. Ph.D. dissertation, University of California, Los Angeles, 1974.

KM   Byrd, William [attrib.]. *Haec est dies,* edited by Brian Clark. Wyton: King's Music, 1996.

MAS   *Publications of the Musical Antiquarian Society.* London: Musical Antiquarian Society, 1841–48.

> 1. Byrd, William. *A mass for five voices, composed between 1553 & 1558, for the old Cathedral of Saint Paul; now first printed in score, and preceded by a life of the composer,* edited by Edward F. Rimbault. 1841.

> 14. *A collection of anthems,* edited by Edward F. Rimbault. 1846.

MB *Musica britannica: a national collection of music.* London: Stainer & Bell, 1951.

   V. *Thomas Tomkins: keyboard music,* edited by Stephen D. Tuttle. 2nd ed., 1973.

   XXII. *Consort songs,* edited by Philip Brett. 1967.

   XLIV–XLV. *Elizabethan consort music,* edited by Paul Doe. 1979–88.

   LV. *Elizabethan keyboard music,* edited by Alan Brown. 1989.

   LXVI. *Tudor keyboard music, c.1520–1580,* edited by John Caldwell. 1995.

   LXXIV. Watson, Thomas. *Italian madrigals englished (1590),* edited by Albert Chatterley. 1999.

MCC McCoy, Stewart. "Lost lute solos revealed in a Paston manuscript." *Lute* 26 (1986): 21–39.

MCL *The first book of consort lessons, collected by Thomas Morley, 1599 and 1611,* edited by Sydney Beck. The New York Public Library music collections. New York: Peters, 1959.

MM *Music manuscripts from the great English collections.* London: Primary Source Microfilm, 1999. 9 ser. Orig. pub. Brighton: Harvester Microform, 1979–91.

   (a) Ser. 1: *The music collection of the Bodleian Library, Oxford.* Pt 4: "Unpublished English music manuscripts before c. 1850, section A."

   (b) Ser. 3: *The music collection of Christ Church Oxford.* Pt 2: "Unpublished English music manuscripts of the 16th and 17th centuries."

   (c) Ser. 4: *The music manuscript collection of the British Library, London.* Pt 2: "Polyphonic music before c. 1640. Section B."

   (d) Ser. 4: *The music manuscript collection of the British Library, London.* Pt 4: "English music manuscripts c. 1640–c. 1714. Section B."

   (e) Ser. 6: *The music collections of the Cambridge libraries.* Pt 1: "Music manuscripts before 1850 from Cambridge University Library and Ely Cathedral."

MS   *Musical sources.* London: Boethius, 1973–.

            21. *The Hirsch lute book,* edited by Robert Spencer. Clarabricken,
            1982.

NOA   *Novello's octavo anthems,* no 1297, edited by Philippe Oboussier.
            London: Novello, 1954. See also:
            http://www.millertheat.com/parsons/englishpdf/deliverme12_5.pdf

NPCB   *Novello's parish choir book,* no 892, edited by Francis Burgess and
            Royle Shore. London: Novello, 1913.

OCS   *Oxford choral songs from the old masters,* no 360, edited by Peter
            Warlock. London: Oxford University Press, 1927.

PS   *Psalms, hymns & anthems, used in the chapel of the Hospital for the
            Maintenance & Education of Exposed & Deserted Young Children.*
            London [: Foundling Hospital], 1774, pp. 32–33; facsim. ed., *Annual
            Byrd newsletter* 5 (1999): 12.

SD   L[owe], E[dward]. *A short direction for the performance of cathedrall
            service. Published for the information of such persons, as are ignorant
            of it, And shall be call'd to officiate in cathedrall, or collegiate
            churches, where it hath formerly been in use.* Oxford: Richard Davis,
            1661; photolithographic facsimile ed.: Oxford: J. Guggenheim,
            [1882].

TM   Turbet, Richard. *Tudor music.* See 1994Tt, p. 238 and plates 1–8.

VV   Monson, Craig. *Voices and viols in England, 1600–1650: the sources
            and the music.* Studies in musicology, 55. Ann Arbor: UMI Research
            Press, 1982.

WI   Inglott, William. *The short Service,* edited and reconstructed by
            Michael Walsh from transcriptions by Richard Turbet. Wyton: King's
            Music, 1989. 3 vols.

THE CATALOGUE

Latin Church Music

Masses published separately without title pages or imprints 1592–95: see
1966Cp.

    T 1   Mass a4
            (a) Kyrie
            (b) Gloria
            (c) Credo

(d) Sanctus
(e) Agnus
    A iv 24 no 2
    C i 30
    D ix 17

T 2   Mass a3
    (a)–(e) as T 1
        A iv 1 no 1
        C i 1
        D ix 3

T 3   Mass a5
    (a)–(e) as T 1
        A iv 63 no 3
        C i 68
        D ix 36

Tallis, Thomas and Byrd, William. *Cantiones, quae ab argumento sacrae vocantur.* Londinensis: Excudebat Thomas Vautrollerius, 1575; facsim. ed., Early music reprinted, 3. Leeds: Boethius, 1976.

T 4   *Emendemus in melius* a5
    Adiuva nos (2nd section)
        4
        A i 1 no 1
        C i 119 no 1
        D ix 61
        J (Arrangement for keyboard; in 1st ed. only)

T 5   *Libera me Domine et pone* a5
    Dies mei transierunt (2nd section)
        5
        A i 8 no 2
        C i 124 no 2
        D ix 64

T6   *Peccantem me quotidie* a5
        6
        A i 25 no 3
        C i 138 no 3
        D ix 72

T7   *Aspice Domine quia facta* a6
      10
      A i 39 no 4
      C i 149 no 4
      D ix 86

T8   *Attollite portas* a6
      11
      A i 52 no 5
      C i 159 no 5 (includes underlay for T 192e)
      C xvi 142 *Let us arise* (fragment of contrafactum)
      D ix 92
      Adapted for T 186e.

T9   *O lux beata trinitas* a6
      Te mane laudem (2nd section)
      Deo Patri sit gloria (3rd section)
      12
      A i 69 no 6
      C i 170 no 6
      D ix 99

T 10   *Laudate pueri* a6
      17
      A i 82 no 7
      C i 181 no 7
      C xvi 138 *Behold now praise the Lord* (fragment of contrafactum)
      D ix 105
      Adaptation of T 386

T 11   *Memento homo* a6
      18
      A i 97 no 8
      C i 194 no 8
      C xi 80 no 12 *O Lord give ear to the prayer* (contrafactum)
      D ii 262 *O Lord, give ear* (contrafactum)
      D ix 112

T 12   *Siderum rector* a5
      19
      A i 104 no 9
      C i 199 no 9
      D ix 78

T 13   *Da mihi auxilium* a6
   23
   A i 113 no 10
   C i 206 no 10
   D ix 115

T 14   *Domine secundum actum meum* a6
   Ideo deprecor (2nd section)
   24
   A i 132 no 11
   C i 218 no 11
   D ix 122

T 15   *Diliges Dominum* a8
   25
   A i 151 no 12
   C i 232 no 12
   D ix 149

T 16   *Miserere mihi* a6
   29
   A i 161 no 13
   C i 240 no 13
   D ix 129

T 17   *Tribue Domine* a6
   Te deprecor (2nd section)
   Gloria Patri qui creavit (3rd section)
   30–32
   A i 167 nos 14–16
   C i 245 nos 14–16
   D ix 132

T 18   *Libera me Domine de morte* a5
   33
   A i 213 no 17
   C i 275 no 17
   D ix 81

Liber primus sacrarum cantionum. Londini: Excudebat Thomas Est ex assignatione Guilielmi Byrd, 1589.

T 19   *Defecit in dolore* a5
       Sed tu Domine refugium (2nd section)
        1–2
        A ii 1 no 1
        C ii 1

T 20   *Domine praestolamur* a5
       Veni Domine (2nd section)
        3–4
        A ii 15 no 2
        C ii 14

T 21   *O Domine adiuva me* a5
        5
        A ii 32 no 3
        C ii 29

T 22   *Tristitia et anxietas* 5
       Sed tu Domine qui non (2nd section)
        6–7
        A ii 42 no 4
        C ii 37

T 23   *Memento Domine* a5
        8
        A ii 62 no 5
        c ii 55

T 24   *Vide Domine afflictionem* a5
       Sed veni Domine (2nd section)
        9–10
        A ii 73 no 6
        C ii 65

T 25   *Deus venerunt gentes* a5
       Posuerunt morticinia (2nd section)
       Effuderunt sanguinem (3rd section)
       Facti sumus opprobrium (4th section)
        11–14
        A ii 89 no 7
        C ii 80
       4th section listed as "Opprobrium facti sumus" in M 55, 1st ed.
       only (1st and 3rd voices begin with "Opprobrium").

T 26   *Domine tu iurasti* a5
    15
    A ii 124 no 8
    C ii 110

T 27   *Vigilate* a5
    16
    A ii 135 no 9
    C ii 120

T 28   *In resurrectione tua* a5
    17
    A ii 150 no 10
    C ii 134

T 29   *Aspice Domine de sede* a5
    Respice Domine (2nd section)
    18–19
    A ii 156 no 11
    C ii 139

T 30   *Ne irascaris* a5
    Civitas sancti tui (2nd section)
    20–21
    A ii 169 no 12
    C ii 151
    L 45 Arrangement for 2 Lyra Viols (incipit of tablature)

T 31   *O quam gloriosum* a5
    Benedictio et claritas (2nd section)
    22–23
    A ii 187 no 13
    B ii 195 nos 119–20 (incipits)
    C ii 166
    MB lv 140 no 48 (keyboard arrangement)

T 32   *Tribulationes civitatum* a5
    Timor et hebetudo (2nd section)
    Nos enim pro peccatis (3rd section)
    24–26
    A ii 202 no 14
    C ii 180
    C xvi 142 *Let not our prayers* (fragment of contrafactum of 3rd section)

T 33   *Domine secundum multitudinem* a5
      27
      A ii 221 no 15
      C ii 198

T 34   *Laetentur coeli* a5
     Orietur in diebus (2nd section)
      28–29
      A ii 229 no 16
      C ii 206

     Liber secundus sacrarum cantionum. Londini: Excudebat Thomas Este ex assignatione Guilielmi Byrd, 1591.

T 35   *Laudibus in sanctis* a5
     Magnificum Domini (2nd section)
     Hunc arguta (3rd section)
      1–2
      A iii 1 no 1
      C iii 1
      2nd section unnumbered in 1591 ed.

T 36   *Quis est homo* a6
     Diverte a malo (2nd section)
      3–4
      A iii 21 no 2
      C iii 18

T 37   *Fac cum servo tuo* a5
      5
      A iii 37 no 3
      C iii 33

T 38   *Salve regina* a5
     Et Iesum benedictum (2nd section)
      6–7
      A iii 47 no 4
      C iii 42

T 39   *Tribulatio proxima est* a5
     Contumelias et terrores (2nd section)
      8–9
      A iii 63 no 5
      C iii 58

T 40 *Domine exaudi orationem meam inclina* a5
Et non intres (2nd section)
    10–11
    A iii 74 no 6
    C iii 68

T 41 *Apparebit in finem* a5
    12
    A iii 89 no 7
    C iii 83

T 42 *Haec dicit Dominus* a5
Haec dicit Dominus (2nd section)
    13–14
    A iii 97 no 8
    C iii 90

T 43 *Circumdederunt me* a5
    15
    A iii 111 no 9
    C iii 102

T 44 *Levemus corda* a5
    16
    A iii 121 no 10
    C iii 110

T 45 *Recordare Domine* a5
Quiescat Domine (2nd section)
    17–18
    A iii 132 no 11
    C iii 120

T 46 *Exsurge Domine* a5
    19
    A iii 144 no 12
    C iii 132

T 47 *Miserere mei* a5
    20
    A iii 157 no 13
    C iii 144
    C viii 29 (Fellowes's arrangement a4 from recomposition in organ
        score)
    MB lv 172 no 60 (recomposition in organ score)

T 48   *Descendit de coelis* a6
         Et exivit per auream (2nd section)
              21–22
              A iii 163 no 14
              C iii 150

T 49   *Domine non sum dignus* a6
              23
              A iii 174 no 15
              C iii 160

T 50   *Infelix ego* a6
         Quid igitur faciam (2nd section)
         Ad te igitur (3rd section)
              24–26
              A iii 180 no 16
              C iii 166

T 51   *Afflicti pro peccatis* a6
         Ut eruas nos (2nd section)
               27–28
               A iii 212 no 17
              C iii 193

T 52   *Cantate Domino* a6
              29
              A iii 223 no 18
              C iii 203

T 53   *Cunctis diebus* a6
              30
              A iii 232 no 19
              C iii 211

T 54   *Domine salva nos* a6
              31
              A iii 245 no 20
              C iii 222

T 55   *Haec dies* a6
              32
              A iii 251 no 21
              C iii 228

Gradualia: ac cantiones sacrae. Londini: Excudebat Thomas Este, 1605; 2nd ed., Excudebat H.L. Impensis Ricardi Redmeri, 1610; facsim. ed., Wyton: King's Music, 1991.

In festo Purificationis.

T 56   *Suscepimus Deus* a5
        Magnus Dominus (2nd section)
            1
            A v 2
            C iv 1
            D vii 3

T 57   *Sicut audivimus* a5
            2
            A v 12
            C iv 10
            D vii 8

T 58   *Senex puerum portabat* a5
            3
            A v 16
            C iv 14
            D vii 10

T 59   *Nunc dimittis servum tuum* a5
        Quia viderunt (2nd section)
        Lumen ad revelationem (3rd section)
            4
            A v 19
            C iv 17
            D vii 11

T 60   *Responsum accepit Simeon* a5
            5
            A v 31
            C iv 28
            D vii 17

In Nati: S. Mariae Virginis.

T 61   *Salve sancta parens* a5
        Eructavit cor meum (2nd section)

6
A v 40
C iv 35
D vii 21

T 62 *Benedicta et venerabilis* a5
7
A v 50
C iv 43
D vii 25

T 63 *Virgo Dei genetrix* a5
8
A v 53
C iv 45
D vii 26

T 64 *Felix es* a5
9
A v 56
C iv 49
D vii 28

T 65 *Beata es* a5
10
A v 60
C iv 53
D vii 30

T 66 *Beata viscera* a5
11
A v 65
C iv 57
D vii 32

Pro Adventu:

T 67 *Rorate coeli* a5
Benedixisti Domine (2nd section)
12
A v 70
C iv 61
D vii 34

T 68   *Tollite portas* a5
     Quis ascendit (2nd section)
        13
        A v 78
        C iv 70
        D vii 38

T 69   *Ave Maria* a5
        14
        A v 83
        C iv 75
        D vii 40

T 70   *Ecce virgo concipiet* a5
        15
        A v 87
        C iv 78
        D vii 42

Post Nativitatem Do:

T 71   *Vultum tuum* a5
        16
        A v 94
        C iv 82
        D vii 45

T 72   *Speciosus forma* a5
     Lingua mea (2nd section)
        17
        A v 101
        C iv 88
        D vii 49

T 73   *Post partum* a5
        18
        A v 108
        C iv 94
        D vii 53

T 74   *Felix namque* a5
        19
        A v 113

C iv 98

D vii 56

Post Septuagesima.

T 75   *Alleluia. Ave Maria* a5
      Virga Iesse floruit (2nd section)
        20
        A v 117
        C iv 101
        D vii 58

T 76   *Gaude Maria* a5
        21
        A v 127
        C iv 109
        D vii 63

In Annunti: B. Maria.

T 77   *Diffusa est gratia* a5
      Propter veritatem (2nd section)
      Audi filia (3rd section)
      Vultum tuum (4th section)
      Adducentur regi (5th section)
      Adducentur in laetitia (6th section)
        22
        A v 136
        C iv 116
        D vii 67

In Assump: B Mariae vir:

T 78   *Gaudeamus omnes* a5
      Assumpta est Maria (2nd section)
        23
        A v 156
        C iv 134
        D vii 76

T 79   *Assumpta est Maria* a5
          24
          A v 166
          C iv 144
          D vii 81

T 80   *Optimam partem elegit* a5
          25
          A v 170
          C iv 148
          D vii 83

[Non-liturgical pieces]

T 81   *Adoramus te Christe* a1 + 4 viols
          26
          A via 1 no 1
          C iv 152
          D vii 85

T 82   *Unam petii a Domino* a5
          Ut videam voluntatem (2nd section)
          27
          A via 4 no 2
          C iv 155
          D vii 87

T 83   *Plorans plorabit* a5
          Dic regi (2nd section)
          28
          A via 15 no 3
          C iv 165
          D vii 92

In festo omnium Sanctorum

T 84   *Gaudeamus omnes* a5
          Exultate iusti (2nd section)
          29
          A via 27 no 4
          C iv 175
          D vii 98

T 85   *Timete Dominum* a5
       Inquirentes autem (2nd section)
          30
          A via 37 no 5
          C iv 185
          D vii 104

T 86   *Iustorum animae* a5
          31
          A via 48 no 6
          C iv 195
          D vii 109

T 87   *Beati mundo corde* a5
          32
          A via 53 no 7
          C iv 199
          D vii 112

FINIS.

T 88   *Cibavit eos* a4
       Exultate Deo (2nd section)
          1
          A via 61 no 8
          A viia 137 no A1
          C v 1
          D vii 116

T 89   *Oculi omnium* a4
       Aperis tu manum (2nd section)
       Caro mea (3rd section)
          2
          A via 67 no 9
          A viia 142 no A2
          C v 8
          D vii 119

T 90   *Sacerdotes Domini* a4
          3
          A via 75 no 10
          A viia 149 no A3
          C v 18
          D vii 123

T 91   *Quotiescunque manducabitis* a4
        4
        A via 77 no 11
        A viia 151 no A4
        C v 21
        D vii 124

T 92   *Ave verum corpus* a4
        5
        A via 82 no 12
        C v 27
        D vii 127

T 93   *O salutaris hostia* a4
        6
        A via 87 no 13
        C v 31
        D vii 129

T 94   *O sacrum convivium* a4
        7
        A via 92 no 14
        C v 37
        D vii 132

T 95   *Pange lingua* (chant)
      Nobis datus nobis natus a4
      Verbum caro (2nd section)
      Tantum ergo (3rd section)
        8
        A via 97 no 15
        C v 43 *Nobis datus nobis natus*
        D vii 134 *Nobis datus nobis natus*

T 96   *Ecce quam bonum* a4
      Quod descendit (2nd section)
        9
        A vib 1 no 1
        C v 53
        D vii 139

T 97   *Christus resurgens* a4
      Dicant nunc Judaei (2nd section)

10
A vib 9 no 2
C v 64
D vii 143

T 98   *Visita quaesumus* a4
11
A vib 19 no 3
C v 76
D vii 148

T 99   *Salve regina* a4
Eia ergo (2nd section)
12
A vib 26 no 4
C v 84
D vii 151

T 100   *Alma redemptoris* a4
13
A vib 35 no 5
C v 93
D vii 155

T 101   *Ave regina* a4
14
A vib 44 no 6
C v 103
D vii 159

T 102   *In manus tuas* a4
15
A vib 51 no 7
C v 111
D vii 163
Adaptation of T 382.

T 103   *Laetania* a4
16
A vib 56 no 8
C v 118
D vii 166

T 104 *Salve sola Dei genetrix* a4
      17
      A vib 67 no 9
      C v 123
      D vii 169

T 105 *Senex puerum portabat* a4
      18
      A vib 73 no 10
      C v 130
      D vii 172

T 106 *Hodie beata virgo* a4
      19
      A vib 77 no 11
      C v 134
      D vii 174

T 107 *Deo gratias* a4
      20
      A vib 82 no 12
      C v 139
      D vii 176

FINIS.

T 108 *Quem terra pontus* a3
      Cui luna (2nd section)
      Beata mater (3rd section)
      Beata coeli nuncio (4th section)
      Gloria tibi Domine (5th section)
         1
      A vib 83 no 13
      C v 140
      D vii 177

T 109 *O gloriosa domina* a3
      Quod Eva tristis (2nd section)
      Tu regis alti (3rd section)
      Gloria tibi Domine (4th section)
         2
      A vib 89 no 14
      C v 150
      D vii 181

T 110 *Memento salutis auctor* a3
       Maria mater gratia (2nd section)
       Gloria tibi Domine (3rd section)
           3
           A vib 93 no 15
           C v 156
           D vii 183

T 111 *Ave maris stella* a3
       Sumens illud (2nd section)
       Solve vincla reis (3rd section)
       Monstra te esse (4th section)
       Virgo singularis (5th section)
       Vitam praesta (6th section)
       Sit laus Deo (7th section)
           4
           A vib 97 no 16
           C v 162
           D vii 186

T 112 *Regina coeli* a3
       Quia quem meruisti (2nd section)
       Resurrexit (3rd section)
       Ora pro nobis (4th section)
           5
           A vib 109 no 17
           C v 176
           D vii 192

T 113 *Alleluia. Vespere autem sabbathi* a3
       Quae lucescit (2nd section)
           6
           A vib 117 no 18
           C v 185 *Alleluia. Quae lucescit*
           D vii 196 *Alleluia. Quae lucescit*
           See 1963Jl p. 25 concerning conflicting titles.

T 114 *Haec dies* a3
           7
           A vib 121 no 19
           C v 189
           D vii 198

T 115 *Angelus Domini descendit* a3
     8
     A vib 123 no 20
     C v 192
     D vii 199

T 116 *Post dies octo* a3
     Mane nobiscum (2nd section)
     9
     A vib 125 no 21
     C v 195
     D vii 200

T 117 *Turbarum voces* a3
     10
     A vib 128 no 22
     C v 198 (subtitled *In Passione Domini secundum Joannem*)
     D vii 202 (subtitled as above . . . *Ioannem*)

T 118 *Adorna thalamum tuum* a3
     Subsistit virgo (2nd section)
     11
     A vib 136 no 23
     C v 207
     D vii 205

FINIS.

Gradualia: seu cantionum sacrarum. Liber secundus. Londini: Excud-
ebat Thomas Este . . . ex assignatione Gulielmi Barley, 1607; 2nd ed.,
Excudebat H.L. Impensis Ricardi Redmeri, 1610; reprint ed., Wyton:
King's Music, 1991.

In nativitate Domini.

T 119 *Puer natus est nobis* a4
     Cantate Domino (2nd section)
     1
     A viia 2
     C vi 1
     D vii 210

T 120 *Viderunt omnes* a4
     Notum fecit Dominus (2nd section)

```
            2
            A viia 9
            C vi 11
            D vii 213

T 121  Dies sanctificatus a4
            3
            A viia 14
            C vi 16
            D vii 216

T 122  Tui sunt coeli a4
            4
            A viia 17
            C vi 20
            D vii 218

T 123  Viderunt omnes a4
            5
            A viia 20
            C vi 24
            D vii 219

T 124  Hodie Christus natus est a4
            6
            A viia 22
            C vi 26
            D vii 220

T 125  O admirabile commercium a4
            7
            A viia 28
            C vi 33
            D vii 223

T 126  O magnum misterium a4
            8
            A viia 34
            C vi 40
            D vii 226

T 127  Beata virgo a4
       Ave Maria (2nd section)
            9
```

A viia 38
C vi 45
D vii 228

In Epiphania Domini.

T 128 *Ecce advenit* a4
       Deus iudicium (2nd section)
       10
       A viia 42
       C vi 48
       D vii 230

T 129 *Reges Tharsis* a4
       11
       A viia 49
       C vi 57
       D vii 234

T 130 *Vidimus stellam* a4
       12
       A viia 54
       C vi 64
       D vii 237

T 131 *Ab ortu solis* a4
       13
       A viia 64
       C vi 69
       D vii 239

T 132 *Venite comedite* a4
       14
       A viia 71
       C vi 77
       D vii 242

T 133 *Surge illuminare* a4
       15
       A viia 58
       C vi 82
       D vii 244

Post Pascha

T 134 *Alleluia. Cognoverunt discipuli* a4
            16
            A viia 75
            C vi 87
            D vii 247

T 135 *Ego sum panis vivus* a4
            17
            A viia 82
            C vi 96
            D vii 251

T 136 *O quam suavis* a4
            18
            A viia 86
            C vi 101
            D vii 253

T 137 *Iesu nostra redemptio* a4
            Quae te vicit (2nd section)
            Inferni claustra (3rd section)
            Ipsa te cogat (4th section)
            Tu esto nostrum gaudium (5th section)
            19
            A viia 93
            C vi 111
            D vii 257

In tempore Paschali.

T 138 *Resurrexi* a5
            Domine probasti me (2nd section)
            20
            A viia 102
            C vi 123
            D vii 262

T 139 *Haec dies* a5
            21
            A viia 111

    C vi 132
    D vii 267

T 140 *Victimae paschali* a5
    Dic nobis Maria (2nd section)
      22
      A viia 117
      C vi 137
      D vii 270

T 141 *Terra tremuit* a5
      23
      A viia 129
      C vi 150
      D vii 277

T 142 *Pascha nostrum* a5
      24
      A viia 132
      C vi 152
      D vii 278

In Ascensione Domini.

T 143 *Viri Galilaei* a5
    Omnes gentes plaudite (2nd section)
      25
      A viib 2
      C vii 1
      D vii 281

T 144 *Alleluia. Ascendit Deus* a5
      26
      A viib 11
      C vii 10
      D vii 286

T 145 *Dominus in Sina* a5
      27
      A viib 15
      C vii 14
      D vii 288

T 146 *Ascendit Deus* a5
       28
       A viib 19
       C vii 17
       D vii 290

T 147 *Psallite Domino* a5
       29
       A viib 23
       C vii 20
       D vii 292

T 148 *O rex gloriae* a5
       30
       A viib 26
       C vii 23
       D vii 294

In festo Pentecostes

T 149 *Spiritus Domini* a5
       Exsurgat Deus (2nd section)
       31
       A viib 34
       C vii 28
       D vii 297

T 150 *Alleluia. Emitte Spiritum* a5
       32
       A viib 42
       C vii 37
       D vii 302

T 151 *Veni Sancte Spiritus reple* a5
       33
       A viib 46
       C vii 41
       D vii 304

T 152 *Confirma hoc* a5
       34
       A viib 49

          C vii 44
          D vii 306

T 153 *Factus est repente* a5
          35
          A viib 53
          C vii 48
          D vii 308

T 154 *Veni Sancte Spiritus et emitte* a5
       O lux beatissima (2nd section)
       Da tuis fidelibus (3rd section)
          36
          A viib 59
          C vii 53
          D vii 311

T 155 *Non vos relinquam* a5
          37
          A viib 73
          C vii 66
          D vii 318

In festo SS. Petri & Pauli.

T 156 *Nunc scio vere* a6
       Domine probasti me (2nd section)
          38
          A viib 80
          C vii 71
          D vii 321

T 157 *Constitues eos* a6
       Pro patribus tuis (2nd section)
          39
          A viib 91
          C vii 82
          D vii 327

T 158 *Solve iubente Deo* a6
          40
          A viib 99
          C vii 90
          D vii 332

T 159 *Tu es Petrus* a6
41
A viib 107
C vii 97
D vii 336

T 160 *Hodie Simon Petrus* a6
42
A viib 114
C vii 104
D vii 340

T 161 *Tu es pastor* a6
43
A viib 125
C vii 114
D vii 346

T 162 *Quodcunque ligaveris* a6
44
A viib 131
C vii 120
D vii 349

T 163 *Laudate Dominum* a6
45
A viib 143
C vii 132
D vii 356

T 164 *Venite exultemus* a6
46
A viib 152
C vii 141
D vii 361

Latin music unpublished during Byrd's lifetime

T 165 *Alleluia. Confitemini Domino* a3
Alleluia. Laudate pueri (2nd section)
A viii 1 no 1
C viii 23 no 2
D ix 181

T 166 *Similes illis fiant* a4
        A viii 4 no 2
        C viii 42 no 6
        D ix 298
        2nd section of *In exitu Israel:* 1st section by Sheppard, 3rd section by William Mundy. See A 189 Appendix. J 107 gives title of first section as "Sit nomen Domini."

T 167 *Audivi vocem* a5
        A ix 51 no 17
        C viii 48 no 7
        D ix 182

T 168 *Ave regina* a5
        A viii 156 no 10
        D Appendix 36 (fragment, attributed to Taverner)

T 169 *Benigne fac* a5
        A ix 45 no 16
        C viii 56 no 8
        D ix 186

T 170 *Christe qui lux* (chant)
        Precamur sancte Domine a5
        A viii 14 no 4
        C viii 63 no 9
        D ix 279

T 171 *De lamentatione Jeremiae* a5
        Heth. Cogitavit Dominus (2nd section)
        Teth. Defixae sunt (3rd section)
        Joth. Sederunt in terra (4th section)
        Jerusalem convertere (5th section)
        A viii 20 no 5
        C viii 1 no 1
        D ix 153 *Lamentationes*

T 172 *Decantabat populus* a5
        A ix 149 no 24
        C viii 68 no 10

T 173 *Domine Deus omnipotens* a5
        Ideo misericors (2nd section)

A ix 58 no 18
C viii 77 no 11
D ix 213

T 174 *Ne perdas cum impiis* a5
       Eripe me (2nd section)
       A viii 168 no 11
       C viii 99 no 12
       D ix 243

T 175 *Omni tempore benedic Deum* a5
       Memor esto fili (2nd section)
       A viii 178 no 12
       C viii 122 no 14
       D ix 257

T 176 *Peccavi super numerum* a5
       A ix 13 no 1
       C viii 133 no 15
       D ix 264

T 177 *Petrus beatus* a5
       Quodcunque vinclis (2nd section)
       Per immensa saecula (3rd section)
       Gloria Deo (4th section)
       A viii 137 no 9
       C viii 145 no 16
       D ix 270

T 178 *Reges Tharsis* a5
       A ix 164 no 26
       C viii 162 no 17
       D ix 295
       D Appendix 50

T 179 *Sacris solemniis* (chant)
       Noctis recolitur a5
       Dedit fragilibus (2nd section)
       Panis angelicus (3rd section)
       A ix 170 no 27
       C viii 110 no 13 *Noctis recolitur*
       D ix 248 *Noctis recolitur*

T 180   *Vide Domine quoniam tribulor* a5
         Quoniam amaritudine (2nd section)
                 A ix 185 no 30
                 C viii 169 no 18

T 181   *Circumspice Hierusalem* a6
         Ecce enim veniunt (2nd section)
                 A ix 84 no 20
                 C ix 1 no 19
                 D ix 190

T 182   *Deus in adiutorium* a6
         Avertantur retrorsum (2nd section)
         Exultent et laetentur (3rd section)
         Et dicant semper (4th section)
         Ego vero egenus (5th section)
                 A ix 12 no 14
                 C ix 13 no 20
                 D ix 196
                 4th section omitted in J.

T 183   *Domine ante te* a6
                 A ix 36 no 15
                 C ix 38 no 21
                 D ix 208

T 184   *O salutaris hostia* a6
                 A viii 44 no 6
                 C ix 48 no 22
                 D ix 254

T 185   *Ad Dominum cum tribularer* a8
         Heu mihi (2nd section)
                 A viii 50 no 7
                 C ix 54 no 23
                 D ix 164

T 186   *Quomodo cantabimus* a8
         Si non proposuero (2nd section)
                 A ix 94 no 21
                 C ix 99 no 24
                 D ix 283

T 187 *Domine quis habitabit* a9
        A viii 97 no 8
        C ix 130 no 25
        D ix 223

T 188 *Domine exaudi orationem meam et clamor* a5
        A ix 78 no 19
        C xvi 127 (fragment)
        D Appendix 54 (fragment)

T 189 *Ad punctum in modico* (fragment) a5
      In momento indignationis (2nd section)
        A ix 124 no 22
        C xvi 122
        D Appendix 51

English Church Music

T 190 Preces and Responses a5
        A xa 1 no 1
        C x 7 "(Third version)"
        D ii 45
        Includes Lesser Litany and Versicles

T 191 First Preces and Psalms
      (a) Preces a5
      (b) *O clap your hands* a5 (Ps. XLVII)
      (c) *Save me O God* a7 (Ps. LIV)
        A xa 9 no 2
        C x 1, 18, 27
        D ii 3

T 192 Second Preces and Psalms
      (a) Preces a5
      (b) *When Israel came out of Egypt* a5 (Ps. CXIV)
      (c) *Hear my prayer O God* a5 (Ps. LV)
      (d) *Teach me O Lord* a1, 5 + organ (Ps. CXIX)
      (e) *Lift up your heads* a6 (Ps. XXIV, contrafactum of T 8)
        A xa 28 no 3; alternative version of (d) 163 Appendix II
        C x 4, 36, 38, 46 (alternative version); i 159 provides underlay for (e)
        D ii 13; alternative version ((a)–(c) a4; (d) a1, 5 + organ)
      Magnificat and Nunc dimittis (no. 5) set to Gregorian tones with verses in faux-bourdon

NPCB

Modern contrafactum: Magnificat set to the full sections of T 192d, Nunc dimittis set to T 192c "slightly modified by the Rev. John Jebb and the Editors" (p. 7).

T 193 Litany a5
       A xa 50 no 4

T 194 *Short Service* a6
       (a) Venite
       (b) Te Deum
       (c) Benedictus
       (d) Kyrie
       (e) Creed
       (f) Magnificat
       (g) Nunc dimittis
           A xa 59 no 5
           C x 52 a–d, Apocrypha (a), e, Apocrypha (c), f, g
           D ii 51 a–e, Apocrypha (a)–(c), f, g
           EMR *Jubilate for Mr Bird's Service* (Benedictus arranged by Robert Shenton [c. 1730–98])
           Also entitled *First Service* in one source: see A 174.

T 195 *Second Service* a5, 5 + organ
       (a) Magnificat
       (b) Nunc dimittis
           A xa 121 no 6
           C x 108
           D ii 99
           Referred to as *Verse Service* in 1981Mt.

T 196 *Third Service* a5
       (a) Magnificat
       (b) Nunc dimittis
           A xa 136 no 7
           C x 122
           D ii 111

T 197 *Great Service* a10
       (a) Venite
       (b) Te Deum
       (c) Benedictus
       (d) Kyrie

(e) Creed
(f) Magnificat
(g) Nunc dimittis
    A vb 1
    C x 136
    D ii 123
    Also entitled *Whole, Long* or *New Service:* see A 152–53 and
    EECM Supplementary i 89.

T 198 Jubilate a1, chorus + organ (fragment)
    A xa 162 no 10 (incipit) *Psalm 100*
    C xvi 138

Full Anthems

T 199 *Arise O Lord* a6
    Help us O God (2nd section)
    A xi 1 no 1
    C xi 64 pt I no 10
    D ii 227

T 200 *Exalt thyself O God* a6
    A xi 11 no 2
    C xvi 140 (fragment)
    D Appendix 33 (fragment)

T 201 *How long shall mine enemies triumph* a5
    A xi 25 no 3
    C xi 12 pt I no 4
    D ii 242

T 202 *O God the proud are risen* a6
    A xi 33 no 4
    C xi 72 pt I no 11
    D ii 248

T 203 *O God whom our offences* a5
    A xi 42 no 5
    C xi 25 pt I no 6
    D ii 255

T 204 *O Lord make thy servant Elizabeth* a6
    A xi 51 no 6

C xi 85 pt I no 13
D ii 266

T 205 *O praise our Lord* a5
       Extol the greatness (2nd section)
       Praise him on tube (3rd section)
       The gladsome sound (4th section)
       Let all the creatures (5th section)
           A xi 174 no 21
           C xi 33 pt I no 7

T 206 *Out of the deep* a6
           A xi 57 no 7

T 207 *Prevent us O Lord* a5
           A xi 69 no 8
           C xi 52 pt I no 8
           D ii 277

T 208 *Sing joyfully* a6
           A xi 82 no 10
           C xi 90 pt I no 14
           D ii 288
           Blow up [sic] *the trumpet* listed at J 143 as 2nd section, but insep-
               arable from the 1st.

Verse Anthems with Organ

T 209 *Alack when I look back* a1, 5
           A xi 91 no 11A (a1 + lute), 93 no 11B
           C xi 98 pt I no 15
           D ii 223

T 210 *Behold O God the sad and heavy case* a2, 5
           A xi 104 no 12
           C xi 103 pt I no 16
           C xvi 144 *Now may Israel say* (fragment of contrafactum)
           D ii 233
           T A5 may be contrafactum.

T 211 *Hear my prayer O Lord* a1, 5
           A xi 129 no 14
           C xi 112 pt I no 17
           D ii 238

T212   *O Lord rebuke me not* a1, 5
        A xi 137 no 15
        C xi 119 pt I no 18
        D ii 271

T 213   *Thou God that guid'st* a2, 5
        A xi 148 no 16
        C xi 128 pt I no 19
        D ii 296

T 214   *Let us be glad*
        A xi 190 no 23 (text only)

T 215   *Sing ye to our Lord*
        A xi 191 no 24 (text only)

Secular vocal music

Psalmes, sonets, & songs of sadnes and pietie. London: Thomas East, the assigne of W. Byrd, 1588.

T 216   *O God give ear* a5
        1
        A xii 1
        C xii 2

T 217   *Mine eyes with fervency* a5
        2
        A xii 6
        C xii 10

T 218   *My soul oppressed* a5
        3
        A xii 9
        C xii 14

T 219   *How shall a young man* a5
        4
        A xii 14
        A xvi 73 no 7 (consort song a1 + 4 viols)
        C xii 20

T 220   *O Lord how long* a5
        5

A xii 20
C xii 26
C xv 35 (consort song a1 + 4 viols)

T 221 *O Lord who in thy sacred tent* a5
          6
          A xii 24
          A xvi 77 no 8 (consort song a1 + 4 viols)
          C xii 32

T 222 *Help Lord for wasted are those men* a5
          7
          A xii 28
          C xii 38

T 223 *Blessed is he* a5
          8
          A xii 32
          A xvi 81 no 9 (consort song a1 + 4 viols)
          C xii 44
          C xv 1 (consort song a1 + 4 viols)

T 224 *Lord in thy wrath reprove me not* a5
          9
          A xii 37
          A xvi 85 no 10 (consort song a1 + 4 viols)
          C xii 49

T 225 *Even from the depth* a5
          10
          A xii 40
          C xii 53

          Here endeth the Psalms and beginneth the Sonnets and Pastorals

T 226 *I joy not in no earthly bliss* a5
          11
          A xii 43
          A xvi 88 no 11 (consort song a1 + 4 viols)
          C xii 57

T 227 *Though Amaryllis dance in green* a5
          12
          A xii 46

A xvi 90 no 12 (consort song a1 + 4 viols)
C xii 60

T 228 *Who likes to love* a5
13
A xii 51
A xvi 93 no 13 (consort song a1 + 4 viols)
C xii 64

T 229 *My mind to me a kingdom is* a5
14
A xii 55
A xvi 96 no 14 (consort song a1 + 4 viols)
C xii 69
MB lv 148 no 49 (keyboard arrangement)

T 230 *Where fancy fond* a5
15
A xii 59
A xvi 99 no 15 (consort song a1 + 4 viols)
C xii 74

T 231 *O you that hear this voice* a5
16
A xii 63
A xvi 102 no 16 (consort song a1 + 4 viols)
C xii 78

T 232 *If women could be fair* a5
17
A xii 68
C xii 84

T 233 *Ambitious love* a5
18
A xii 73
C xii 90
Proceed then given as 2nd section in MS source: see 1960Ds
p. 362.

T 234 *What pleasure have great princes* a5
19
A xii 78
C xii 96

T 235 *As I beheld* a5
          20
          A xii 83
          C xii 100

T 236 *Although the heathen poets* a5
          21
          A xii 92
          C xii 110

T 237 *In fields abroad* a5
          22
          A xii 94
          A xvi 106 no 17 (consort song a1 + 4 viols)
          C xii 112
          MB lvi 127 no 82 (keyboard arrangement)

T 238 *Constant Penelope* a5
          23
          A xii 99
          A xvi 110 no 18 (consort song a1 + 4 viols)
          C xii 117

T 239 *La virginella* a5
          24
          A xii 104
          A xvi 114 no 19 (consort song a1 + 4 viols)
          C xii 124
          Adapted for T 318

T 240 *Farewell false love* a5
          25
          A xii 109
          A xvi 118 no 20 (consort song a1 + 4 viols)
          C xii 131

T 241 *The match that's made* a5
          26
          A xii 114
          C xii 137

Here endeth the Sonnets and Pastorals, and beginneth Songs of Sadness and Piety

T 242 *Prostrate O Lord I lie* a5
      27
      A xii 119
      A xvi 122 no 21 (consort song a1 + 4 viols)
      C xii 143

T 243 *All as a sea* a5
      28
      A xii 123
      C xii 150

T 244 *Susanna fair* a5
      29
      A xii 127
      A xvi 127 no 22 (consort song a1 + 4 viols)
      C xii 154
      MB lv 149 no 50 (keyboard arrangement)

T 245 *If that a sinner's sighs* a5
      30
      A xii 132
      A xvi 130 no 23 (consort song a1 + 4 viols)
      C xii 159
      MB lv 150 no 51 (keyboard arrangement)

T 246 *Care for thy soul* a5
      31
      A xii 137
      A xvi 134 no 24 (consort song a1 + 4 viols)
      C xii 165
      MB lv 152 no 52 (keyboard arrangement)

T 247 *Lullaby* a5
      32
      A xii 142 *Lulla lullaby*
      A xvi 138 no 25 (consort song a1 + 4 viols)
      B ii 189 no 110 (incipit of keyboard adaptation)
      C xii 172
      C xx 146 [Keyboard] Adaptations no 1
      E 4 no 1 (arrangement by Francis Cutting for lute)
      F 82 no 27 (keyboard adaptation)
      L 45 Lyra Viol Accompaniment (incipit of tablature)
      MB lv 154 no 53 (keyboard adaptation)

T 248 *Why do I use* a5
        33
        A xii 150
        A xvi 144 no 26 (consort song a1 + 4 viols)
        C xii 183

The funeral songs of that honorable Gent. Sir Philip Sidney

T 249 *Come to me grief* a5
        34
        A xii 155
        A xvi 148 no 27 (consort song a1 + 4 viols)
        C xii 190

T 250 *O that most rare breast* a5
        35
        A xii 158
        A xvi 150 no 28 (consort song a1 + 4 viols)
        C xii 194
        The doleful debt listed as 2nd section in VV 49.

Songs of sundrie natures. London: Thomas East, the assigne of William Byrd, 1589; facsim. ed., Performers' facsimiles, 163. New York: Performers' Facsimiles, [2000].

T 251 *Lord in thy rage* a3
        1
        A xiii 1
        C xiii 1

T 252 *Right blest are they* a3
        2
        A xiii 4
        C xiii 7

T 253 *Lord in thy wrath correct me not* a3
        3
        A xiii 7
        C xiii 14

T 254 *O God which art most merciful* a3
        4
        A xiii 10
        C xiii 20

T 255 *Lord hear my prayer* a3
      5
      A xiii 13
      C xiii 27

T 256 *From depth of sin* a3
      6
      A xiii 15
      C xiii 32

T 257 *Attend mine humble prayer* a3
      7
      A xiii 18
      C xiii 38

T 258 *Susanna fair* a3
      8
      A xiii 22
      C xiii 46

T 259 *The nightingale* a3
      9
      A xiii 27
      C xiii 52

T 260 *When younglings first* a3
      But when by proof (2nd section)
      10–11
      A xiii 32
      C xiii 59

T 261 *Upon a summer's day* a3
      Then for a boat (2nd section)
      12–13
      A xiii 40
      C xiii 68

T 262 *The greedy hawk* a3
      14
      A xiii 47
      C xiii 77

T 263 *Is love a boy* a4
       Boy pity me (2nd section)
              15–16
              A xiii 51
              C xiii 83

T 264 *Wounded I am* a4
       Yet of us twain (2nd section)
              17–18
              A xiii 64
              C xiii 94

T 265 *From Citheron* a4
       There careless thoughts (2nd section)
       If love be just (3rd section)
              19–21
              A xiii 76
              C xiii 105

T 266 *O Lord my God* a4
              22
              A xiii 91
              C xiii 121

T 267 *While that the sun* a4
              23
              A xiii 97
              C xiii 129

T 268 *From virgin's womb* a1 + 4 viols
       Rejoice rejoice a4 (chorus)
              35, 24
              A xiii 102
              C xi 227 pt II no 11
              C xiii 135

T 269 *An earthly tree* a2 + 4 viols
       Cast off all doubtful care a4 (chorus)
              40, 25
              A xiii 109
              C xi 219 pt II no 10 (+ organ)
              C ciii 145
              See T 270.

T 270 *Cease cares* (fragment)
        A xvi 176 no 36 (incipit)
        MM (c) MS 31992 35v.
        Alternative chorus for T 269.

T 271 *Weeping full sore* a5
        26
        A xiii 118
        C xiii 155

T 272 *Penelope that longed* a5
        27
        A xiii 134
        C xiii 168

T 273 *Compel the hawk* a5
        28
        A xiii 145
        C xiii 178

T 274 *See those sweet eyes* a5
    Love would discharge (2nd section)
        29, 34
        A xiii 155
        A xvi 161 no 29 (consort song a1 + 4 viols, 1st section only)
        C xiii 188

T 275 *When I was otherwise* a5
        30
        A xiii 164
        C xiii 194

T 276 *When first by force* a5
        31
        A xiii 172
        A xvi 163 no 30 (consort song a1 + 4 viols with alternative text *I*
          that sometime)
        C xiii 199

T 277 *I thought that love* a5
        32
        A xiii 177

A xvi 167 no 31 (consort song a1 + 4 viols)
C xiii 204

T 278   *O dear life* a5
33
A xiii 181
C xiii 208

T 279   *Of gold all burnished* a5
Her breath is more sweet (2nd section)
36–37
A xiii 185
C xiii 212

T 280   *Behold how good* a6
And as the pleasant morning dew (2nd section)
38–39
A xiii 200
C xiii 225

T 281   *Who made thee, Hob, forsake the plough* a2 + 4 viols
41
A xiii 216
C xiii 241
C xv 162

T 282   *And think ye nymphs* a6
Love is a fit of pleasure (2nd section)
42–43
A xiii 221
C xiii 245

T 283   *If in thine heart* a6
44
A xiii 230
C xiii 253

T 284   *Unto the hills* a6
45
A xiii 238
C xiii 264

T 285 *Christ rising again* a2, 6 + 4 viols
       Christ is risen (2nd section)
           46–47
           A xi 113 no 13 (verse anthem with organ)
           A xiii 251
           C xiii 280

       Psalmes, songs, and sonnets. London: Thomas Snodham, the assigne
       of W. Barley, 1611.

T 286 *The eagle's force* a3
           1
           A xiv 1
           C xiv 1

T 287 *Of flattering speech* a3
           2
           A xiv 4
           C xiv 6

T 288 *In winter cold* a3
       Whereat an ant (2nd section)
           3–4
           A xiv 6
           C xiv 10

T 289 *Who looks may leap* a3
           5
           A xiv 10
           C xiv 18

T 290 *Sing ye to our Lord* a3
           6
           A xiv 13
           C xi 136 pt II no 1
           C xiv 24

T 291 *I have been young* a3
           7
           A xiv 16
           C xiv 31

T 292 *In crystal towers* a3
       8
       A xiv 18
       C xiv 35

T 293 *This sweet and merry month* a4
       9
       c no 8
       A xiv 22
       C xiv 42
       MB lxxiv 24 no 8

T 294 *Let not the sluggish sleep* a4
       10
       A xiv 27
       C xiv 49

T 295 *A feigned friend* a4
       11
       A xiv 30
       C xiv 54

T 296 *Awake mine eyes* a4
       12
       A xiv 33
       C xiv 59

T 297 *Come jolly swains* a4
       13
       A xiv 36
       C xiv 63

T 298 *What is life* a4
       14
       A xiv 39
       C xiv 68

T 299 *Come let us rejoice* a4
       16
       A xiv 47
       C xi 142 pt II no 2
       C xiv 75

T 300 *Retire my soul* a5
      17
      A xiv 51
      C xiv 81

T 301 *Arise Lord into thy rest* a5
      18
      A xiv 57
      C xi 148 pt II no 3
      C xiv 88

T 302 *Come woeful Orpheus* a5
      19
      A xiv 64
      C xiv 98

T 303 *Sing we merrily* a5
      Blow up the trumpet (2nd section)
      20–21
      A xiv 70
      C xi 171 pt II no 6
      C xiv 106

T 304 *Crowned with flowers I saw fair Amaryllis* a5
      22
      A xiv 84
      C xiv 125

T 305 *Wedded to will is witless* a5
      23
      A xiv 91
      C xiv 134

T 306 *Make ye joy to God* a5
      24
      A xiv 97
      C xi 163 pt II no 5
      C xiv 143

T 307 *Have mercy upon me* a1, 6 + 4 viols
      25
      A xiv 105
      C xi 232 pt II no 12 (a2, 6 + organ)
      C xiv 154

T 308 *This day Christ was born* a6
        27
        A xiv 128
        C xi 198 pt II no 8
        C xiv 178
        Subtitled *A Carroll for Christmas day.*

T 309 *O God that guides* a1, 6 + 5 viols
        28
        A xiv 136
        C xiv 189
        Subtitled *A Carroll for New-year's day.*

T 310 *Praise our Lord* a6
        29
        A xiv 144
        C xi 188 pt I no 7
        C xiv 199

T 311 *Turn our captivity* a6
        30
        A xiv 154
        C xi 207 pt II no 9
        C xiv 211

T 312 *Ah silly soul* a1 + 5 viols
        31
        A xiv 165
        C xiv 225
        C xv 69

T 313 *How vain the toils* a1 + 5 viols
        32
        A xiv 171
        C xiv 233
        C xv 8
        Entitled *O vain the toils* and *In vain the toils* in MS sources: see
          EECM supplementary i 85 and VV 117.

Other Madrigals and Partsongs, Sacred and Secular

T 314 *Be unto me* a4
        f songs of four parts no 12

A xi 157 no 17
C xi 1 pt I no 1

T 315 *Look down O Lord* a4
f songs of four parts no 1
A xi 171 no 20
C xi 5 pt I no 2

T 316 *Come help O God* a5
f songs of five parts no 22
A xi 161 no 18
C xi 8 pt I no 3

T 317 *I laid me down* a5
f songs of five parts no 1
A xi 166 no 19
C xi 20 pt I no 5

T 318 *The fair young virgin* a5
But not so soon (2nd section)
a nos 44–45
A xvi 1 no 1
C xvi 1
Adaptation of T 239. Index to a gives title of 2nd section as *Ma non si tosto.*

T 319 *Let others praise* a6
There may the solemn Stoics find (2nd section)
b
A xvi 16 no 2
C xvi 148 (fragment)

T 320 *This sweet and merry month* a6
c no 28
A xvi 33 no 3
C xvi 15
MB lxxiv 114 no 28
Not listed in J, though mentioned pp. 154–55.

T 321 *O sweet deceit* a5
Like Harpias vile (2nd section)
A xvi 46 no 4
C xvi 34

T 322   *What pleasure have great princes* a5
         A xvi 60 no 5

T 323   *What vaileth it to rule* a5
         A xvi 62 no 6
         C xvi 59

Canons

T 324   Canon two in one
         d 103
         A xvi 169 no 32
         C xvi 100

T 325   Canon six in one (and four in two)
         A xvi 171 no 33
         C xvi 101
         For solution to canon four in two see 1975Rb.

Consort Songs

T 326   *O Lord within thy tabernacle* a1 + 4 viols
         A xv 1 no 1
         C xv 44

T 327   *The Lord is only my support* a1 + 4 viols
         A xv 5 no 2
         C xv 56

T 328   *Have mercy on us Lord* a1 + 4 viols
         A xv 8 no 3
         C xv 5
         Have mercy Lord on me I pray, alternative given text, made additional item in J 169.

T 329   *The man is blest* a1 + 4 viols
         A xv 11 no 4
         C xv 59

T 330   *Lord to thee I make my moan* a1 + 4 viols
         A xv 14 no 5
         C xv 12

T 331   *O God but God* a1 + 4 viols
         A xv 17 no 6

C xv 21
MB lv 158 no 54 (keyboard arrangement)

T 332 *O Lord bow down* a1 + 4 viols
A xv 22 no 7
C xv 31

T 333 *O Lord how vain* a1 + 4 viols
A xv 25 no 8
C xv 40

T 334 *O that we woeful wretches* a1 + 4 viols
A xv 28 no 9
C xv 48

T 335 *Out of the orient crystal skies* a1 + 4 viols
A xv 31 no 10
Anonymous but accepted as Byrd's: see 1960Ds.

T 336 *Rejoice unto the Lord* a1 + 4 viols
A xv 37 no 11

T 337 *Triumph with pleasant melody* a1 + 4 viols
What unacquainted cheerful voice (2nd section)
My faults O Christ (3rd section)
A xv 43 no 12
C xv 126, 62, 16

T 338 *Ah golden hairs* a1 + 4 viols
A xv 51 no 13
C xv 66

T 339 *As Caesar wept* a1 + 4 viols
A xv 54 no 14
C xv 74

T 340 *Blame I confess* a1 + 4 viols
A xv 56 no 15
C xv 52 (editorial reconstruction of missing voice part to text
Awake sad heart under original alternative title *Remember Lord*)
C xv 83

T 341 *Come pretty babe* a1 + 4 viols
A xv 59 no 16

T 342 *Content is rich* a1 + 4 viols
        A xv 63 no 17
        Anonymous but accepted as Byrd's: see 1960Ds.

T 343 *E'en as in seas* a1 + 4 viols
        A xv 66 no 18
        C xv 165 (a3 + 2 viols)
        Anonymous but accepted as Byrd's: see A 172.

T 344 *I will not say* a1 + 4 viols
       Let fortune fail (2nd section)
       My years do seek (3rd section)
        A xv 68 no 19
        C xvi 26 (2nd section, a5)

T 345 *Mount hope* a1 + 4 viols
        A xv 73 no 20
        C xvi 30 (a5)

T 346 *My freedom ah* a1 + 4 viols
        A xv 76 no 21 (sets "I thought that love," text of T 277, in absence
           of any words beyond title)
        C xv 102 (sets "In crystal towers," text of T 292: see above)

T 347 *Sith death at length* a1 + 4 viols
        A xv 78 no 22
        C xv 115 *Sithence that death*

T 348 *Sith that the tree* a1 + 4 viols
        A xv 81 no 23
        C xvi 54 (a5)

T 349 *Thou poets' friend* a1 + 4 viols
        A xv 84 no 24
        C xv 121

T 350 *Truce for a time* a1 + 4 viols
        A xv 87 no 25
        C xv 129

T 351 *Truth at the first* a1 + 4 viols
        A xv 90 no 26
        Anonymous but accepted as Byrd's: see 1960Ds.

T 352 *What steps of strife* a1 + 4 viols
      A xv 93 no 27
      C xv 130

T 353 *While Phoebus us'd to dwell* a1 + 4 viols
      A xv 97 no 28
      C xv 135
      Alternative text *The noble famous queen.*

T 354 *Crowned with flowers and lilies* a1 + 4 viols
      O worthy queen (2nd section)
      A xv 100 no 29
      C xv 147 (a2 + 3 viols)

T 355 *Delight is dead* a2 + 3 viols
      A xv 107 no 30
      C xv 156

T 356 *In angel's weed* a1 + 4 viols
      A xv 111 no 31
      Possibly entitled originally *Is Sidney dead.* Anonymous but
      accepted as Byrd's: see A 175–76 and 1960Ds.

T 357 *Ye sacred Muses* a1 + 4 viols
      A xv 114 no 32
      C xv 141 (subtitled *an elegy on the death of Thomas Tallis 1585*)

T 358 *An aged dame* a1 + 4 viols
      A xv 119 no 33
      C xv 77

T 359 *Fair Britain isle* a1 + 4 viols
      A xv 124 no 34
      Anonymous but accepted as Byrd's: see 1960Ds.

T 360 *He that all earthly pleasure scorns* a1 + 4 viols
      A xv 128 no 35
      Anonymous but accepted as Byrd's: see A 176.

T 361 *My mistress had a little dog* a1 + 4 viols
      But out alas (2nd section)
      A xv 131 no 36
      Anonymous but accepted as Byrd's: see 1960Ds.

T 362 *Quis me statim* a1 + 4 viols
    A xv 140 no 37
    C xv 109

T 363 *Though I be brown* a1 + 4 viols
    A xv 144 no 38
    Anonymous but accepted as Byrd's: see A 177–78.

T 364 *Where the blind* a1 + 4 viols
    A xv 146 no 39
    Anonymous but accepted as Byrd's: see 1960Ds.

T 365 *With lilies white* a1 + 4 viols
    A xv 149 no 40
    Anonymous but accepted as Byrd's: see A 178.

T 366 *Wretched Albinus* a1 + 4 viols
    A xv 152 no 41
    Anonymous but accepted as Byrd's: see 1960Ds.

T 367 *Ah youthful years* (fragment)
    A xvi 175 no 34 (incipit)
    C xvi 151 (incipit)
    MM (b) MS 31992 9v.

T 368 *Behold how good* (fragment)
    A xvi 175 no 35 (incipit)
    MM (c) MS 31992 40v.

T 369 *Depart ye Furies* (fragment)
    A xvi 177 no 37 (incipit)
    C xvi 151 (incipit)
    MM (c) MS 31992 47

T 370 *I will give laud* (fragment)
    A xvi 177 no 38 (incipit)
    MM (c) MS 31992 23v.

T 371 *In tower most high* (fragment)
    A xvi 178 no 40 (incipit)
    C xvi 152 (incipit)
    MM (c) MS 31992 11v.

T 372 *Look and bow down* (fragment)
   My soul ascend (2nd section)
   This Joseph's Lord (3rd section)
     A xvi 178 no 41 (incipit)
     C xvi 152 (incipit)
     EMRD (facsimile of arrangement for lute in tablature)
     Title of 3rd section given in one MS source as "'Tis Joseph's
      herd"

T 373 *O happy thrice* (fragment)
     A xvi 180 no 42 (incipit)
     C xvi 153 (incipit)
     MM (a) MS Mus. Sch. e.423 52
     MM (c) MS 31992 12v.

T 374 *What wights are these* (fragment)
     A xvi 181 no 45 (incipit)
     C xvi 153 (incipit)
     MM (c) MS 31992 28v.

T 375 *While that a cruel fire* (fragment)
     A xvi 181 no 46 (incipit)
     C xvi 153 (incipit)
     MM (c) MS 31992 41v.

T 376 *With sighs and tears* (fragment)
     A xvi 182 no 47 (incipit)
     C xvi 153 (incipit)
     MM (c) MS 31992 17v.

Consort Music

T 377 Fantasia a3
     A xvii 2 no 1 I
     C xvii 2 Trios no 1
     J no 1
     K 3/C1
     L no 1

T 378 Fantasia a3
     A xvii 4 no 2 II
     C xvii 4 Trios no 2

        J no 2
        K 3/C2
        L no 2
        MCC (reconstruction of arrangement for lute)

T 379 Fantasia a3
        A xvii 6 no 3 III
        K 3/C3
        L no 3

T 380 Fantasia a4
        A xiv 42 no 15
        A xvii 7 no 4 I
        C xiv 71 no 15
        C xvii 10 Quartets no 1
        C xviii 35 Fantasies no 6 (arrangement in short score for key-
            board)
        J no 1
        K 4/g
        L no 1
        MB lv 161 no 55 (keyboard arrangement)
        MS xxi 21v. no 44 (facsimile of arrangement for lute in tablature)

T 381 Fantasia a4
        A xvii 11 no 5 II
        C xvii 118 Fragments *Fantasy quartet no. 2*
        C xviii 44 Fantasies no 10 (arrangement in short score for key-
            board; fragment)
        F 111 no 33 (arrangement in short score for keyboard; fragment)
        J no 2
        K 4/a
        L no 2

T 382 Fantasia a4
        A xvii 147 no 34 III (single part)
        C xvii 118 Fragments *Fantasy quartet no. 3*
        J no 3
        K 4/G
        L no 3
        N (reconstruction)
        Adapted for T 102.

T 383 Fantasia a5
        A xvii 19 no 8

C xvii 20 Quintets no 1
J no 1
K 5/C
L
Adapted for T 527. Mistitled "In nomine" in one list: see K 26.

T 384 Prelude a5
A xvii 29 no 9 *Prelude [and ground]*
C xvii 38 *Prelude and fantasy*
J *Prelude and fantasy*
K *Prelude and ground*
L *Prelude and ground*

T 385 *Browning* a5
A xvii 39 no 10
C xvii 30 Fantasy Quintet no 2
J no 2
K
L

T 386 Fantasia a6
A xvii 48 no 11 I
C xvii 92 Sextets no 3
J no 3 "for two basses"
K 6/F
L no 1
M 99 *A song of two basses*
Adapted for T 10.

T 387 Fantasia a6
A xvii 53 no 12 II
C xvii 81 Sextets no 2
J n02
K 6/g1
L no 2
CO xvi 33 no 11 (contemporary keyboard reduction entitled *Fantazia 6 voc.*)

T 388 Fantasia a6
A xiv 114 no 26
A xvii 63 no 13 III
C xiv 166 no 26
C xvii 70 Sextets no 1

J no 1
K 6/g2
L no 3
CO xvi 38 no 12 (contemporary keyboard reduction. Title in source *One other fantasi 6 voc.* Title in edition *Another fantazia 6 voc.*)

T 389 Pavan a5
A xvii 73 no 14
K 5/c
L
Q 42 (includes missing part rediscovered since A)
Adapted for T 487.

T 390 Pavan a6
Galliard a6
A xvii 75 no 15
C xvii 99 Sextets
J
K 6/C
L

T 391 In nomine a4
A xvii 80 no 16 I
C xvii 17 Quartets no 2
J no 2
K 4/1
L no 1

T 392 In nomine a4
A xvii 83 no 17 II
C xvii 14 Quartets no 1
J no 1
K 4/2
L no 2

T 393 In nomine a5
A xvii 86 no 18 I
C xvii 49 Quintets no 1
J no 1
K 5/1
L no 1

T 394 In nomine a5
    A xvii 90 no 19 II
    C xvii 62 Quintets no 4
    J no 4
    K 5/2
    L no 2

T 395 In nomine a5
    A xvii 94 no 20 III
    C xvii 66 Quintets no 5
    J no 5
    K 5/3
    L no 5

T 396 In nomine a5
    A xvii 98 no 21 IV
    C xvii 53 Quintets no 2
    J no 2
    K 5/4
    L no 4

T 397 In nomine a5
    A xvii 103 no 22 V
    C xvii 58 Quintets no 3
    J no 3
    K 5/5
    L no 5
    MB lvi 39 no 16 (keyboard arrangement)
    In *Chelys* 13 (1984): 81, Stewart McCoy notes that T 397 gives
     rise to the title of Nicholas Strogers' *In nomine pavan* (MCL 127
     no 13).

T 398 *Sermone blando* a3
    A xvii 108 no 23 verse 1
    C xvii 103 Plainsong Fantasy Trio "Salvator mundi"
    D ix 309 "Salvator Mundi"
    J "Salvator mundi" a3
    K setting 1
    L verse A

T 399 *Sermone blando* a3
    A xvii 109 no 23 verse 2
    K setting 2
    L verse B

T 400 *Christe qui lux* a4
            A xvii 110 no 24 I verse 1
            C viii 40 no 5 verse 4 (vocal) *Precamur sancte Domine*
            D ix 307 verse 3 *Precamur*
            K I setting 1
            L verse A

T 401 *Christe qui lux* a4
            A xvii 111 no 24 I verse 2
            C xvii 121 (fragment; incipit)
            J Lute Tablature
            K I setting 2
            L verse B

T 402 *Christe qui lux* a4
            A xvii 112 no 24 I verse 3
            K I setting 3
            L verse C

T 403 *Christe qui lux* a4
            A viii 9 no 3 verse 2 (vocal)
            A xvii 114 no 25 II verse I
            C viii 34 no 5 verse 1 (vocal) *Precamur sancte Domine*
            D ix 306 verse 1 *Precamur*
            J Motets *Precamur sancte Domine*
            K II setting 1
            L verse D

T 404 *Christe qui lux* a4
            A viii 11 no 3 verse 4 (vocal)
            A xvii 115 no 25 II verse 2
            C viii 38 no 5 verse 3 (vocal) *Precamur sancte Domine*
            J Motets *Precamur sancte Domine*
            K II setting 2
            L verse E

T 405 *Christe qui lux* a4
            A viii 12 no 3 verse 6 (vocal)
            A xvii 116 no 25 II verse 3
            C viii 36 no 5 verse 2 (vocal) *Precamur sancte Domine*
            D ix 306 verse 2 *Precamur*
            J Motets *Precamur sancte Domine*
            K II setting 3
            L verse F

T 406 *Christe qui lux* a4
    A xvii 117 no 26 III
    C xvii 116 Plainsong Fantasy Quartet no 8 "Te lucis ante termi-
    num"
    D ix 311 "Te lucis"
    J "Te lucis" a4
    K III
    L verse G

T 407 *Christe redemptor* a4
    A xvii 118 no 27 verse 1
    C xvii 106 no 2 Plainsong Fantasy Quartet no 2
    D ix 301 no I
    J no 1
    K setting 1
    L verse A

T 408 *Christe redemptor* a4
    A xvii 119 no 27 verse 2
    C xvii 104 no 1 Plainsong Fantasy Quartet no 1
    D ix 302 no II
    J no 2
    K setting 2
    L verse B

T 409 *Miserere* a4
    A xvii 122 no 28 verse 1
    C xvii 109 no 2 Plainsong Fantasy Quartet no 4
    D ix 305 no II
    J no 2
    K setting 1
    L verse A

T 410 *Miserere* a4
    A xvii 123 no 28 verse 2
    C xvii 108 no 1 Plainsong Fantasy Quartet no 3
    D ix 305 no I
    J no 1
    K setting 2
    L verse B

T 411 *Salvator mundi* a4
    A xvii 124 no 29 verse 1
    C xvii 120 no 2 (fragment; incipit)

        J Lute Tablature no 2
        K setting 1
        L verse A

T 412 *Salvator mundi* a4
        A xvii 125 no 29 verse 2
        C xvii 120 no 1 (fragment; incipit)
        J Lute Tablature no 1
        K setting 2
        L verse B

T 413 *Sermone blando* a4
        A xvii 127 no 30 I verse 1
        C xvii 120 no 1 (fragment; incipit)
        J Lute Tablature no 1
        K I setting 1
        L verse C

T 414 *Sermone blando* a4
        A xvii 128 no 30 I verse 2
        K I setting 2
        L verse D

T 415 *Sermone blando* a4
        A xvii 129 no 30 I verse 3
        C xvii 120 no 2 (fragment; incipit)
        J Lute Tablature no 2
        K I setting 3
        L verse E

T 416 *Sermone blando* a4
        A xvii 131 no 31 II verse 1
        C xvii 112 no 1 Plainsong Fantasy Quartet no 6
        D ix 309 no I
        J no 1
        K II setting 1
        L verse F
        Anonymous but accepted as Byrd's: see K 51.

T 417 *Sermone blando* a4
        A xvii 132 no 31 II verse 2
        C xvii 114 no 2 Plainsong Fantasy Quartet no 7

D ix 310 no II
J no 2
K II setting 2
L verse G
Anonymous but accepted as Byrd's: see K 51.

T 418– *Te lucis* a4
T 425   A xvii 134–41 no 32 I verses 1–8
            K I settings 1–8
            L verses A–H

T 426 *Te lucis* a4
            A xvii 143 no 33 II verse 1
            C xvii 121 no 1 (fragment; incipit)
            J Lute Tablature no 1
            K II setting 1
            L verse I

T 427 *Te lucis* a4
            A xvii 144 no 33 II verse 2
            C xvii 110 Plainsong Fantasy Quartet no 5 "Precamur sancte
            Domine"
            D ix 308 "Precamur II"
            J "Precamur sancte Domine"
            K II setting 2
            L verse J

T 428 *Te lucis* a4
            A xvii 145 no 33 II verse 3
            K II setting 3
            L verse K

T 429 *Te lucis* a4
            A xvii 146 no 33 II verse 4
            C xvii 121 no 2 (fragment; incipit)
            J Lute Tablature no 2
            K II setting 4
            L verse L
            T 418–29 may originally have formed one piece, T 426–29 + T
            418–25: see K 57.

Keyboard Music

    T 430 *All in a garden green*
               B ii 28 no 56
               C xx 1 Airs and Variations on Song Tunes no 1
               H 181 no 32
               J
               K Keyboard Variations
               FVB i 411 no 104

    T 431 *Monsieur's alman*
               B ii 151 no 87 I
               C xviii 79 no 1
               J no 1
               K G1
               FVB i 234 no 61

    T 432 *Monsieur's alman*
               B ii 154 no 88 II
               C xviii 83 no 2 *Variatio . . .*
               H 221 no 38
               J no 1 *Variatio*
               K G2
               FVB i 238 no 62 *Variatio*

    T 433 *Monsieur's alman*
               B i 164 no 44
               C xviii 93 no 4
               J no 5
               K C1
               FVB i 245 no 63

    T 434 *The queen's alman*
               B i 39 no 10
               C xviii 90 no 3
               J no 2
               K g1
               FVB ii 217 no 172

    T 435 Alman
               B ii 159 no 89
               C xviii 95 no 5

J no 3
K G3
FVB ii 182 no 156

T 436 Alman
B i 41 no 11
C xviii 96 no 6
J no 4
K g2
FVB ii 196 no 163

T 437 Alman
B ii 195 no 117 (incipit)
G 1 no 1
K C2
MB lv 92 no 30
Anonymous but accepted as Byrd's: see K 169–70.

T 438 *The barley break*
B ii 163 no 92
C xviii 58 Dance Measures no 1
H 43 no 6
J
K Almans [&c.]

T 439 *The battle*
(a) *The soldiers' summons*
(b) *The march of footmen*
(c) *The march of horsemen*
(d) *The trumpets*
(e) *The Irish march*
(f) *The bagpipe and the drone*
(g) *The flute and the drum*
(h) *The march to the fight*
(i) *The retreat*
B ii 174 no 94
C xviii 105 nos 2–10
H 20 no 4
J
K Almans [&c.]
See also T 461, T 483 and Apocrypha.

T 440   *The bells*
        B i 132 no 38
        C xx 96 Airs with Variations on a Ground no 1
        J
        K Grounds
        FVB i 274 no 69

T 441   *Callino casturame*
        B i 126 no 35
        C xx 5 Airs and Variations on Song Tunes no 2
        J
        K Keyboard Variations
        FVB ii 186 no 158

T 442   *The carman's whistle*
        B i 127 no 36
        C xx 7 Airs and Variations on Song Tunes no 3
        H 189 no 34
        J
        K Keyboard Variations
        FVB i 214 no 58
        Also entitled *The carter's whistle, The whistling carman* and
         Ground.

T 443   *Christe qui lux*
        B ii 195 no 121 (incipit)
        EECM vi 67 no 34
        Probably by Byrd: see K 101 and HYP 61–63.

T 444   *Clarifica me Pater*
        B ii 5 no 47 I
        C xviii 41 Fantasies no 8 "Fantasia. mr bird 2 partes"
        F 4 no 2 "Mr. bird 2 parts"
        J Fancies no 9
        K Organ Antiphons 1st setting

T 445   *Clarifica me Pater*
        B ii 6 no 48 II
        C xx 140 Fantasies on Plain-Song Melodies no 4 "Miserere
         (no. 2) of Three Parts"
        J Misereres no 1 "Miserere of 3 Parts"
        K Organ Antiphons 2nd setting
        FVB ii 230 no 176 "Miserere. 3 Parts"

T 446 *Clarifica me Pater*
B ii 8 no 49 III
C xx 137 Fantasies on Plain-Song Melodies no. 2 "Gloria tibi Trinitas . . . called 'In Nomine' . . ."
J Misereres no 2 "Miserere of 4 parts"
K Organ Antiphons 3rd setting
FVB ii 232 no 177 "Miserere. 4 Parts"

T 447 *The first French coranto*
B i 78 no 21a
C xviii 98 no 1
J
K Almans [&c.] a1
FVB ii 305 no 218
See also E 40 no 12.

T 448 *The second French coranto*
B i 79 no 21b
C xviii 99 no 2
F 124 Appendix 5
J
K Almans [&c.] a2
See also E 40 no 12 and Apocrypha.

T 449 *The third French coranto*
B i 80 no 21c
C xviii 100 no 3
F 125 Appendix no 6
J
K Almans [&c.] a3
See also E 40 no 12.

T 450 Coranto
B i 166 no 45
C xviii 101 no 4 . . . *or Mr Bird's gigg*
J (reference from Jigs)
K Almans [&c.] C1 . . . (Jig)
FVB ii 359 no 241

T 451 *A fancy for my Lady Nevell*
B i 86 no 25
C xviii 25 no 4
H 204 no 36

J no 5
K C2
FVB i 406 no 103

T 452 Fantasia
B i 42 no 13
C xviii 4 no 1
J no 4
K a1
FVB i 188 no 52
See also T 514.

T 453 Fantasia
B ii 1 no 46
C xviii 30 no 5
H 237 no 41
J no 8
K d1

T 454 Fantasia
B ii 54 no 62
C xviii 17 no 3
J no 2
K G2
FVB ii 406 no 261

T 455 Fantasia
B ii 59 no 63
C xviii 12 no 2
J no 1
K G3
FVB i 37 no 8

T 456 Fantasia
B i 96 no 27
C xvii 6 Trios no 3 (Fellowes's arrangement for consort)
C xviii 38 no 7
F 92 no 29
J Fantasies a 3 no 3 (Fellowes's arrangement for consort)
J no 6
K C3
L Fantasies a 3 no 4
See also T 528.

T 457 *Fortune*
> B i 24 no 6
> C xx 11 Airs and Variations on Song Tunes no 4 . . . or *Farwell delighte*
> J
> K Keyboard Variations
> FVB i 254 no 65

T 458 *Galliard: Mistress Mary Brownlow*
> *e* no 5
> B i 123 no 34
> C xix 130 no 29
> J no 12
> K C4
> See also T 503.

T 459 *Harding's galliard*
> B ii 25 no 55
> C xix 154 no 39
> J no 16
> K Almans [&c.]
> FVB ii 47 no 122
> Can be paired with T 500.

T 460 Galliard
> B ii 19 no 53
> C xix 141 no 35
> J Almans no 4 [Alman and] Galliard
> K d2
> FVB ii 198 no 164

T 461 *The galliard for the victory*
> B ii 186 no 95
> C xviii 124 *The battell* no 12
> H 40 no 5
> J (unlisted part of *Mr. Bird's Battell;* reference from *Victorie*)

T 462 *Galliard jig*
> B i 66 no 18
> C xix 135 Pavans and Galliards no 32
> H 54 no 7
> J Jigs no 1
> K Almans [&c.]

T 463 *The ghost*
      B ii 110 no 78
      C xviii 66 Dance Measures no 2
      J
      K Almans [&c.]
      FVB ii 193 no 162

T 464 *Gipsies' round*
      B ii 116 no 80 *Gypsies' round*
      C xx 15 Airs and Variations on Song Tunes no 5
      J
      K Keyboard Variations
      FVB ii 292 no 216

T 465 *Gloria tibi Trinitas*
      B ii 10 no 50
      C xx 135 Fantasies on Plain-Song Melodies no 1 I
      F 6 no 3 *Two pts* . . .
      J
      K Organ antiphons

T 466 *Go from my window*
      B ii 112 no 79
      C xx Airs and Variations on Song Tunes no 6
      F 113 Appendix 2
      J
      K Keyboard Variations

T 467 *My Lady Nevell's Ground*
      B ii 32 no 57
      C xx 58 no 1
      H 1 no 1
      J no 1
      K

T 468 *The second ground*
      B i 155 no 42
      C xx 63 no 2
      H 163 no 30
      J no 2
      K
      Also called *Goodnight ground:* see HYP 47.

T 469 *Hugh Ashton's ground*
B i 71 no 20 . . . or *Tregian's ground*
C xx 71 no 3 . . . (or *Tregian's*) . . .
H 194 no 35
J no 3
K *Hugh Aston's ground*
FVB i 226 no 60 *Treg[ian's] ground*
Entitled "Frog ground" in MAS i 5.
See also F 44 no 14.

T 470 Ground
B ii 145 no 86
C xx 78 no 4
F 13 no 7
J no 4
K Short ground in G major

T 471 Ground
B i 162 no 43
C xx 84 no 5
F 22 no 8
J no 5
K Short ground in C major

T 472 Ground
B i 35 no 9
C xx 87 no 6
F 26 no 9
J no 6
K Short ground in G minor

T 473 Hornpipe
B i 137 no 39
C xx 102 Airs with Variations on a Ground no 2
F 31 no 10
J
K Grounds

T 474 *The hunt's up*
B i 143 no 40: version 1; 150 no 41: version 2
C xx 109 Airs with Variations on a Ground no 3 . . . or *Pescodd time* [version 2]
H 58 no 8 [version 2]

J

K Grounds . . . (*Peascod time*)

FVB i 218 no 59 [version 1]

FVB ii 430 no 276 *Pescodd time* [version 2]

T 475 *If my complaints*

B ii 195 no 118 *Galliard: If my complaints* (incipit)

F 80 no 26 . . . or *Pypers gal[liard]*

MB lv 83 no 26 . . . or *Piper's galliard*

Anonymous but accepted as Byrd's by F; see also HYP 81–82.

T 476 *Parsons' In nomine*

B ii 12 no 51

C xx 150 Adaptations no 2

F 131 Appendix 10

FVB ii 135 no 140

See also K 165.

T 477 Jig

B i 81 no 22

C xviii Corantos, Jigs and Lavoltas no 5 *A gigg F. Tr(egian)*

J no 2

K Almans [&c.] Jig a1

FVB ii 237 no 181 *A gigg*

T 478 *John come kiss me now*

B ii 121 no 81

C xx Airs and Variations on Song Tunes no 8

J

K Keyboard Variations

FVB i 47 no 10

T 479 *Lavolta: Lady Morley*

B ii 161 no 90

C xviii 104 Corantos, Jigs and Lavoltas no 7

J no 1 "(T. Morley, set by Byrd)"

K Almans [&c.] Volte G2

FVB ii 188 no 159 "T. Morley [set by] William Byrd"

Dedication to Lord Morley on p. 7 (no 8) of *William Byrd: fifteen pieces,* edited by Thurston Dart. Early keyboard series, 4. London: Stainer & Bell, 1956. Altered to Lady Morley, 2nd ed., 1969.

T 480 Lavolta
    B ii 162 no 91
    C xviii 103 Corantos, Jigs and Lavoltas no 6
    J no 2
    K Almans [&c.] Volte G1
    FVB ii 180 no 155
    See also E 42 nos 13(a) and 13(b) entitled *Curent.*

T 481 *Lord Willoughby's welcome home*
    B i 27 no 7 *Rowland*
    C xx 45 Airs and Variations on Song Tunes no 11 *Rowland*
    E 24 no 6 (arrangement for lute)
    H 186 no 33
    J (reference from *Rowland*)
    K Keyboard Variations . . . (Rowland)
    FVB ii 190 no 160 *Rowland*

T 482 *The maiden's song*
    B ii 126 no 82
    C xx 36 Airs and Variations on Song Tunes no 9
    H 149 no 28
    J
    K Keyboard Variations
    FVB ii 67 no 126

T 483 *The march before the battle*
    B ii 171 no 93 . . . or *The Earl of Oxford's march*
    C xviii 105 *The battell* no 1: *The Earl of Oxford's marche*
    H 15 no 3
    J
    K Almans [&c.] . . . (*The Earl of Oxford's march*)
    FVB ii 402 no 259 *The Earle of Oxfords marche*
    See also *My Lord of Oxenford's masque* (Apocrypha)

T 484 *Miserere*
    B ii 74 no 66 I
    K Organ Antiphons 1st setting
    Anonymous but accepted as Byrd's: see K 101.

T 485 *Miserere*
    B ii 75 no 67 II
    C xx 139 Fantasies on Plain-Song Melodies no 3 I
    F 12 no 6

J no 3
K Organ Antiphons 2nd setting

T 486 *O mistress mine*
       B ii 130 no 83
       C xx 41 Airs and Variations on Song Tunes no 10
       J
       K Keyboard Variations
       FVB i 258 no 66

T 487 *The first pavan*
      The galliard to the first pavan
       B i 100 no 29
       C xix 1 no 1
       E 18 no 5 (Three arrangements for lute of *Galliard,* of which (c)
         is possibly by Edward Collard)
       H 77 nos 10–11
       J
       K c1
       R 2 (consort arrangement of *Pavan,* see also Q 42; modern
         arrangement of *Galliard*)
       FVB ii 204 nos 167–68
       Adaptation of T 389 (*Pavan* only).

T 488 *The second pavan*
      The galliard to the second pavan
       B ii 91 no 71
       C xix 6 no 2
       H 84 nos 12–13
       J
       K G2
       R 7 (modern arrangement for consort)
       FVB ii 398 nos 257–58 *Pavana fant[asia]*
       Entitled *Pavana fant.* (possibly *fantastic:* see K 193, note) in FVB
         ms. May be dedicated to Richard Farrant: see B ii 203; or to
         Byrd's niece Mary Farrant *nee* Byrd or her otherwise unknown
         husband: see 1999Hw p. 25 fn. 75.

T 489 *The third pavan*
      The galliard to the third pavan
       B i 49 no 14
       C xix 10 no 3
       H 90 nos 14–15

J
K a1
R 10 (modern arrangement for consort)
FVB ii 384 nos 252–53

T 490 *The fourth pavan*
       The galliard to the fourth pavan
       B i 105 no 30
       C xix 16 no 4
       H 96 nos 16–17
       J
       K C1
       R 14 (modern arrangement for consort)

T 491 *The fifth pavan*
       The galliard to the fifth pavan
       B i 109 no 31
       C xix 20 no 5
       E 14 no 4 (arrangement for lute of *Pavan*)
       H 102 nos 18–19
       J
       K c2
       L 45 Mixed Consorts E 705 (incipit: only 3 parts of *Pavan* survive)
       P (reconstruction for mixed consort of *Pavan*)
       R 18 (modern arrangement for [viol] consort)

T 492 *The sixth pavan: Kinborough Good*
       The galliard to the sixth pavan
       B i 114 no 32
       C xix 25 no 6
       H 110 nos 20–21
       J
       K C2
       R 22 (modern arrangement for consort)

T 493 *The seventh pavan*
       B ii 102 no 74
       C xix 30 no 7
       H 117 no 22
       J
       K G6

          R 26 (modern arrangement for consort)
          FVB ii 427 no 275 *Pavana. Canon. Two parts on one*

T 494   *The eighth pavan*
          B i 64 no 17
          C xix 33 no 8
          H 121 no 23
          J
          K a4
          R 28 (modern arrangement for consort)

T 495   *The ninth pavan*
       The galliard to the ninth pavan
          B i 1 no 2 *Passamezzo pavan* and *galliard*
          C xix 36 no 9 . . ."Passamezzo"
          H 125 nos 24–25 *The passing measures* . . .
          J
          K g1 Grounds *Passing Measures* . . .
          FVB i 203 nos 56–57 *Passamezzo* . . .

T 496   *The tenth pavan: Mr William Petre*
       The galliard to the tenth pavan
          e nos II–III *Pavan: Sir William Petre*
          B i 11 no 3
          C xix 47 no 10
          H 229 nos 39–40
          J
          K g2

T 497   *Pavan: Bray*
       Galliard
          B ii 40 no 59
          C xix 53 no 11
          E 6 no 2 (Two arrangements for lute by Francis Cutting of pavan)
          J no 11
          K F1
          FVB i 361 nos 91–92

T 498   *Pavan delight*
       Galliard
          B i 19 no 5
          C xix 144 no 37
          J no 14

K Almans [&c.] *Johnson's delight*
FVB ii 436 nos 277–78

T 499 *Echo pavan*
Galliard
     B ii 190 no 114
     K G5
     Anonymous but accepted as Byrd's: see K 215.

T 500 *Pavan lachrymae*
     B ii 21 no 54
     C xix 150 no 38
     J no 17
     K Almans [&c.]
     FVB ii 42 no 121
     Can be paired with T 459.

T 501 *Lady Monteagle's pavan*
     B ii 105 no 75
     C xix 121 no 26
     J no 18
     K G7
     FVB ii 483 no 294

T 502 *The quadran pavan*
The galliard to the quadran pavan
     B ii 79 no 70
     C xix 64 no 14
     J no 20
     K G1 Grounds
     FVB ii 103 nos 133–34

T 503 *Pavan: the Earl of Salisbury*
Galliard
Second galliard
     e nos VI–VIII (Second galliard dedicated to "Mris. Marye
       Brownlo")
     B i 57 no 15
     C xix 58 no 12 (Pavan and galliard only)
     C xix 133 no 30 *Galiardo secundo: 'Mris Marye Brownlo'*
     J no 13 *Galliard secundo. Mris. Marye Brownlo*
     J no 19 (Pavan and galliard only)

K a2
Dedication to Mary Brownlow regarded as mistaken: see B 175
and K 217. See also T 458.

T 504 *Pavan: Philippa Tregian*
Galliard
B i 46 no 60
C xix 59 no 13
J Pieces with Alternative Ascriptions *Pavan Ph. Tr.*
K F2
FVB i 367 nos 93–94
May alternatively be dedicated to Sir Charles Somerset: see K
179.

T 505 Pavan
Galliard
B i 16 no 4
C xix 75 no 15
J no 21
K g3
FVB ii 200 nos 165–66

T 506 Pavan
Galliard
B ii 99 no 73
C xix 78 no 16
F 60 nos 17–18
J no 22
K G4

T 507 Pavan
Galliard
B ii 95 no 72
C xix 82 no 17
F 65 nos 19–20
J no 23
K G3

T 508 Pavan
Galliard
B ii 107 nos 76–77
C xix 124 no 27 (Pavan)
C xix 140 no 34 (Galliard)
F 76 nos 23–24

```
            J nos 24–25
            K G8–9

T 509  Pavan
       Galliard
            B i 59 no 16
            C xix 89 no 19
            F 70 nos 21–22
            J no 29
            K a3

T 510  Pavan
       Galliard
            B i 81 no 23
            C xix 99 no 21
            E 12 no 3 (arrangement for lute and bass viol of Pavan)
            F 118 Appendix 3–4
            J no 31
            K Bb1
            L 45 Mixed Consorts E 704 (incipit)
            R 30 (modern arrangement for [viol] consort)

T 511  Pavan
       Galliard
            B i 118 no 33
            C xix 104 no 22
            F 47 nos 13–14
            J no 33
            K C3

T 512  Pavan
       Galliard
            B ii 14 no 52
            C xix 116 no 25
            J no 36
            K d1
            FVB ii 389 nos 254–55

T 513  Prelude
            e no I
            B i 1 no 1
            C xviii 1 no 1
            J no 1
            K G minor
```

T 514 *Praeludium to the fancie*
        B i 42 no 12
        C xviii 4 no 4
        J no 3
        K A minor
        FVB i 394 no 100
        See also T 452.

T 515 Prelude
        e no IIII
        B i 85 no 24
        C xviii 1 no 2
        J no 4
        K C major
        FVB i 83 no 24

T 516 Prelude
        B ii 195 no 115 (incipit)
        G 3 no 2
        K F major
        MB lv 2 no 3
        Anonymous but accepted as Byrd's: see K 210.

T 517 Prelude
        B ii 195 no 116 (incipit)
        G 4 no 3
        K G major
        FVB ii 40 no 120
        MB lv 3 no 4
        Anonymous but accepted as Byrd's: see K 223–24.

T 518 *Qui passe*
        B i 68 no 19
        C xviii 69 Dance Measures no 3
        H 9 no 2
        J (reference from *Kapassa*)
        K Grounds *Chi passa*

T 519 *Salvator mundi*
        B ii 76 no 68 I
        C xx 142 Fantasies on Plain-Song Melodies no 5 "Veni Creator
           Spiritus (no. 1)"
        F 8 no 4 "Mr. birds upon a plainesong"

  J "Upon a Plainsong, Mr Birds"
  K Organ antiphons 1st setting

T 520 *Salvator mundi*
  B ii 77 no 69 II
  C xx 144 Fantasies on Plain-Song Melodies no 6 "Veni Creator Spiritus (no. 2)"
  F 10 no 5 "Mr. birds (Upon the Same Plainsong)"
  J "Upon the Same Plainsong, 3 Parts"
  K Organ Antiphons 2nd setting
  Listed as "Prelude in G" by Margaret H. Glyn in *Elizabethan virginal music and its composers,* London: Reeves, [1964], p.140.

T 521 *Sellinger's round*
  B ii 135 no 84
  C xx 47 Airs and Variations on Song Tunes no 12
  H 211 no 37
  J
  K Keyboard Variations
  FVB i 248 no 64

T 522 *Ut mi re*
  B ii 69 no 65
  C xx 118 Variations on Notes of the Scale no 1
  J
  K Keyboard Fantasias
  FVB i 401 no 102

T 523 *Ut re mi*
  B ii 64 no 64
  C xx 123 Variations on Notes of the Scale no 2
  H 68 no 9
  J [no 1]
  K Keyboard Fantasias
  FVB i 395 no 101

T 524 *Ut re mi*
  B ii 37 no 58
  C xx 130 Variations on Notes of the Scale no 3
  F 86 no 28
  J [no 2]
  K Grounds

T 525 Verse
        B i 99 no 28
        C xviii 42 Fantasies no 9
        F 1 no 1
        J Fancies no 7
        K Keyboard Fantasias C4

T 526 *Voluntary for my Lady Nevell*
        B ii 51 no 61
        C xviii 45 no 1
        H 140 no 26
        J no 1
        K Keyboard Fantasies G1

T 527 *A lesson of voluntary*
        B i 91 no 26 Fantasia
        C xviii 52 no 3
        H 156 no 29
        J no 2
        K Keyboard Fantasias C1
        Adaptation of T 383.

T 528 Voluntary
        B i 97 no 27 *Fantasia* (bar 46 to end)
        C xviii 49 no 2
        H 243 no 42
        J no 3
        K Keyboard Fantasias C3 (see note to B above)
        See also T 456. Sanctioned by Byrd as individual piece through
          its inclusion in H.

T 529 *Walsingham*
        B i 29 no 8
        C xx 24 Airs and Variations on Song Tunes no 7 *Have with yow*
          to . . .
        H 173 no 31 *Have with yow to . . .*
        J (gives *As I went to . . .* as alternative title)
        K Keyboard variations
        FVB i 267 no 68

T 530 *Wilson's wild*
        B i 131 no 37

C xx 57 Airs and Variations on Song Tunes no 14 *Wolsey's wilde*
J *Wolsey's wilde*
K Keyboard Variations
FVB ii 184 no 157 *Wolsey's wilde*

T 531 *The woods so wild*

B ii 141 no 85
C xx 53 Airs and Variations on Song Tunes no 13 *Will yow walke . . .*
E 26 no 7 (arrangement for lute)
H 144 no 27
J *Will yow walke . . .*
K Keyboard Variations
FVB i 263 no 67

Lost

T 532 *Calui curis*

Mentioned on f.42 of Essex Record Office T/A 174, a typed transcript William Petre's accounts (Folger MS 1772.1). The entry reads "January of 1601 [1601/2] To Mr. Birde for a calui: turis [*recte* curis] 10s." A translation of the title would be "I glow with cares."

T 533 *Medulla musicke*

See A xvi p.vi.
Settings of *Miserere.*

Appendix

T A1 Sanctus a3

A ix 183 no 28
C viii 27 no 3
Very doubtful though attributed to "Mr William Birde": see A 200.

T A2 *Sponsus amat sponsam* (fragment)

A ix 183 no 29
C xvi 128
D Appendix 50
See 1981Km p. 57.

T A3   Litany a4
           A xa 149 no 8
           C x 15
           D ii 49
           See A p. viii.

T A4   *Fourth Service*
       (a) Te Deum
       (b) Benedictus
           A xa 162 no 11 (incipits) *Service in F*
           C x 253 (partial reconstruction a4 of openng of Te Deum)
           C xvi 130
           See A p. ix. Title from 1928Hw.

T A5   *Behold O God with Thy all prosp'ring eye*
           A xi 190 no 22 (text only)
           See p. xi. May be contrafactum of T 210.

T A6   *By force I live* a1 + 4 viols
           A xv 155 no 42
           C xv 86
           See A 178–79.

T A7   *Methought of late* a1 + 4 viols
           A xv 158 no 43
           C xv 98
           See A 179.

T A8   *The day delay'd* a1 + 4 viols
           A xv 161 no 44
           See p. 179.

T A9   *Whom hateful harms* a1 + 4 viols
           A xv 164 no 45
           C xv 138
           See A 179.

T A10 Fantasia a4
           A xvii 14 no 6 IV
           L 45 E 37 no1
           See K 89–90.

T A11 Fantasia a4
　　　　A xvii 16 no 7 V
　　　　L 45 E 38 no 2
　　　　See K 89–90.

T A12 *Malts come down*
　　　　B ii 189 no 107 (incipit)
　　　　C x 116 Airs with Variations on a Ground no 4
　　　　FVB ii 166 no 150
　　　　See B 209 and K 115–16.

T A13 Medley
　　　　B ii 189 no 112 (incipit)
　　　　C xviii 73 Dance Measures no 4
　　　　FVB ii 220 no 173
　　　　See B 210 and K 166.

T A14 Pavan
　　　　B ii 188 no 101 (incipit)
　　　　C xix 126 no 28
　　　　J no 34
　　　　FVB ii 394 no 256
　　　　Unique surviving attribution to Byrd probably erroneous: see B
　　　　　　209 and K 178.

T A15 Pavan
　　　　E 36 no 9
　　　　See p. 53.

T A16 Pavan
　　　　Galliard
　　　　B ii 188 no 100 (incipit)
　　　　C xix 109 no 23
　　　　F 55 nos 15–16
　　　　J no 32
　　　　MB lv 22 no 10
　　　　See MB 178, HYP 101–2 and K 178.

T A17 Pavan
　　　　Galliard
　　　　B ii 188 no 98 (incipit)
　　　　C xix 94 no 20

F 40 nos 11–12
J no 30
Unique surviving attributions to Byrd probably erroneous: see B
208–09 and K 178.

Apocrypha

A solis ortus (keyboard)
EECM vi 44 no 24
Anonymous: see M 111 and 117 no 7, J 211 and EECM pp. xi–xii.

Abradate (see *Ah alas you salt sea gods*)

Aeterne rerum conditor (keyboard)
EECM vi 50 no 27
Anonymous: see M111 and 117 no 15 *Eterne rerum conditor*, J
211 and EECM pp. xi–xii.

Ah alas you salt sea gods
A xv 165 no 46 (annotation)
C xvi 145 (fragment) *Abradate*
J 193 *Abradate*
MB xxii 15 no 7
By Richard Farrant.

Ah silly poor Joas a1 + 4 viols
MB xii 43 no 24
Anonymous. Broadcast on British Broadcasting Corporation's
Radio 3 as by Byrd, and listed as such in *Radio times* 12 July
1965.

Air (see Alman (keyboard) II)

Alman (keyboard) I
B ii 189 no 108 (incipit)
C xix 143 no 36 (fragment) Galliard
F 79 no 25 *A galliard of Mr. Birds [Alman]*
J Almans no 6 *Alman galliard*
"Coranto" by Lever: see B 209 and K 179.

Alman (keyboard) II
B ii 189 no 109 (incipit)
F 126 Appendix 7 "Piece with no title"
J Pavan no 26

MB lv 90 no 28

See B 209–10 and K 165–66, where it is also described as a toy; see also the contents of two of the anthologies mentioned in 1998Tb: p. 10 where it is listed as "Pavan" and p. 11 where it is listed as "Air."

Alman (keyboard) III

MB lv 90 no 29

Anonymous: see B ii 120 (textual commentary on no 117) and K 169.

Alman galliard (see Alman I)

Audi benigne conditor

EECM vi 56 no 20

Anonymous: see M 111 and 117 no 20, J 211 and EECM pp. xi–xii.

Barofostus' dream (keyboard)

FVB i 72 no 18

Anonymous: see 1923HUk p. 944.

The battle

(a) *The burying of the dead*

B ii 189 no 113a (incipit)

C xviii 123 *The battell* no 11

H 38

(b) *The morris*

B ii 189 no 113b (incipit)

C xviii 126 *The battell* no 13

H 39

(c) *The soldiers' dance*

B ii 189 113c (incipit)

C xviii 126 *The battell* no 14

C xviii 127 *The battell* no 15 *The souldiers' delight* (another version)

F 112 Appendix 1 *The souldiers' delight*

H 39

See B 210 and K 166.

Bina caelestis (keyboard) I

EECM vi 58 no 31

Anonymous: see M 111 and 117 no 9, J 211 and EECM pp. xi–xii.

Bina caelestis (keyboard) II
>>> EECM vi 62 no 32
>>> Anonymous: see M 111 and 117 no 10, J 211 and EECM pp. xi–xii.

Bless them that curse you a3
>>> C xvi 114
>>> By John Hilton: see A xvi p. vii.

Bonny sweet Robin (keyboard)
>>> B ii 189 no 106 (incipit)
>>> F 139 Appendix 12
>>> FVB ii 77 no 128
>>> By Bull and/or Giles Farnaby: see B 209.

Born is the babe a1 + 5 viols, chorus a5
>>> MB xxii 74 no 46
>>> Anonymous. Attributed to Byrd on BBC Radio 3 programme *Byrd at Ingatestone* 29 December 1989: see 1990Bm.

The burying of the dead (see *The battle*)

Captain(e) Piper's pavan (see *Piper's pavan*)

Christ rising again a5
>>> A xi 198 no 27 (annotation)
>>> EECM xiii 63 no 2
>>> Possibly by Tallis: see A p. viii but also EECM p.viii and Peter le Huray's article "The Chirk Castle partbooks," *Early music history* 2 (1982): 17–42, especially p. [37].

Christe qui lux (keyboard)
>>> EECM vi 68 no 35
>>> Anonymous: see M 111 and 117 no 18, J 211 and EECM pp. xi–xii.

Christe redemptor (keyboard)
>>> EECM vi 72 no 37
>>> Anonymous: see M 111 and 117 no 6, J 211 and EECM pp. xi–xii.

Come drink to me a4 (refrain)
I have loved the jolly tankard (verse)
>>> C xvi 114
>>> See A xvi p. viii.

Come tread the paths a1 + 4 viols
>   A xv 165 no 47 (annotation; subtitle *Guichardo*)
>   C xv 89
>   MB xxii 3 no 3
>   See A p. ix.

Conditor alme (keyboard)
>   EECM vi 76 no 39
>   Anonymous: see M 111 and 117 no 1, J 211 and EECM pp. xi–xii.

Coranto Lady Riche (keyboard)
>   FVB ii 414 no 265
>   Anonymous. Attributed to Byrd by Dart on p. 16 of *William Byrd:
>   fifteen pieces* (see T 479), in which it is no 12 on p. 11: see K
>   166–67.

Coranto (keyboard)
>   FVB ii 268 no 205 (listed in J as source for T 448)
>   Anonymous: see F p. xxiii and K 170.

Coranto (keyboard; see Alman I)

Deliver me from mine enemies a6
>   NOA
>   By Robert Parsons: see M 75.

Deus creator omnium (keyboard)
>   EECM vi 80 no 41
>   Anonymous: see M 111 and 117 no 13, J 211 and EECM
>   pp. xi–xii.

Dies illa a5
>   D ix 303
>   2nd section of *Libera me Domine de morte* by Robert Parsons: see
>   J 109.

Dum transisset a5
>   D vi 257
>   By Tallis. Attributed jointly to Tallis and Byrd in edition by H.B.
>   Collins, Birmingham: Collins, 1918.

Ecce tempus idoneum (keyboard; fragment)
> EECM vi 180 Appendix II no 1
> Anonymous: see M 111 and 117 no 21, J 211 and EECM pp. xi–xii.

Eterne rerum conditor (see *Aeterne rerum conditor*)

Ex more docti mystico (keyboard)
> EECM vi 85 no 43
> Anonymous: see M 111 and 117 no 17, J 211 and EECM pp. xi–xii.

Fantasia "a 5" (fragment)
> C xvii 119 (subtitled *Ut my re*)
> J no 3 (subtitled *Ut my re*)
> L 45 ?-part *Ut my re*
> See K 90. Possibly by Parsons.

Nine fantasias a4 (fragments)
> L A-4–5 (1 + incipits only for 2–9)
> TM plates 1–8 between 238–39 (facsimiles)

Galliard (keyboard)
> B ii 189 no 105 (incipit)
> C xix 138 no 33
> F 96 no 30 "Piece with no title"
> J no 27
> MB lv 13 no 8b *Lavecchia*
> See B 209 and K 178.

Galliard (keyboard: see Alman I, Medley, Pavan and Galliard, *Sir John Gray's galliard*)

Galliard (lute) I
> E 38 no 10
> See E 53.

Galliard (lute) II
> E 38 no 11
> See E 53.

Glory be to God a3
> PS 32
> See introduction to facsimile edition.

Glory to God (fragment)
> A xi 191 no 25
> See pp. xiii and 225.

Ground (see *The hunt's up*)

Guichardo (see *Come tread the paths*)

Haec est dies a4
> KM
> See introduction to edition and 1996MOi.
> Note: Contrary to what Warwick Edwards states in A ix p. vii fn.
> > 9, neither John Harley nor Richard Turbet "claimed for Byrd"
> > this patently spurious motet in 1996Hb.

Hey ho to the greenwood a3
> C xvi 120
> See A xvi pp. vii–viii. Also sung to *O Lord I will praise Thee.*

Holy holy holy (see Sanctus)

Hostis Herodes impie (keyboard) I
> EECM vi 89 no 44
> Anonymous: see M 111 and 117 no 11, J 211 and EECM pp. xi–xii.

Hostis Herodes impie (keyboard) II
> EECM vi 92 no 45
> Anonymous: see M 111 and 117 no 12, J 211 and EECM pp. xi–xii.

The hunt's up (keyboard)
> B i 150 no 41 II (eds 1–2 only)
> C xx 91 Grounds no 7 . . . *with ten variations*
> F 104 no 32 "Ten variations on an unnamed theme"
> J "Variations, Ten"
> See B p. xxii and K 116.

I am weary of my groaning a5
> BMSJ
> See A xvi p. vii.

I have loved the jolly tankard (see *Come drink to me*)

If trickling tears (fragment)
> A xvi 178 no 39 (incipit)

C xvi 147
See A p. ix.

In nomine a5
MB xlv 59 no 152 In nomine II
By John Baldwin: see K 26.

In nomine a6
MB xliv 141 no 72
Anonymous. Proposed for inclusion in Byrd canon by Jeremy Noble during *Early music forum* on British Broadcasting Corporation's Radio 3, 7 July 1981. In a letter to the author, Oliver Neighbour observes "all one can say is that Byrd cannot be ruled out as a claimant, but that the stylistic grounds do not warrant anything like a firm attribution" (22 July 1981).

In nomine a7
C xvii 119 (fragment)
MB xliv 148 no 74
By Robert Parsons: see K 26 and 34.

Incola ego sum (see *Retribue servo tuo*)

Irish dump (keyboard)
FVB ii 236 no 179
Anonymous: see MAS i 5 for attribution to Byrd.

It doth me good when Zephyrus reigns a4
OCS
By Thomas Whythorne. No 27 of his *Songes,* London: Daye, 1571. Attribution elsewhere to Byrd caused by misreading of p. 171 of the 2nd ed. of *The English madrigal composers* by Edmund Horace Fellowes, London: Oxford University Press, 1948.

Jerusalem a3
CC i 16 no 57
See A xvi p. vii.

Lavecchia (see Galliard (keyboard))

Let God arise a5
A xi 198 no 28 (annotation)

C xvi 141 (fragment)
MAS xiv 61 no 11
By Thomas Ford: see A.

Like as the hart (fragment)
EECM Supplementary i 28 no 225 (incipit)
MM (d) MS 34203 7v.
Anonymous in source, so M 75 is mistaken in stating that it is
attributed to Byrd in MS.

Like as the lark (keyboard)
DVB 28 no 24
Anonymous. Occasionally attributed to Byrd, as on recording of
*Historical instruments at the Victoria and Albert Museum,
London,* Musica Rara 70–1.

Lucis creator optime (keyboard)
EECM vi 99 no 48
Anonymous: see M 111 and 117 no 16, J 211 and EECM pp. xi–xii.

Manus tuae fecerunt a5
D v 137
By Robert Whyte. Attributed to Byrd in M 54.

Martin said to his man (keyboard)
FVB ii 275 no 212
Anonymous: see 1923 COOl p. 3 for attribution to Byrd.

Medley (keyboard)
B ii 189 no 111 (incipit)
C xix 112 Pavans and Galliards no 24
F 98 no 31 "Piece with no title"
J Pavans and Galliards no 36
See B 210 and K 166 and 178. See also MB lv 103 no 35.

Miserere a3–5
C xvi 78 Twenty-nine Canons on Plainsong Melodies nos 11–29
See A xvi pp. vi–vii.

Miserere nostri *Domine* a7
D vi 207
By Tallis. Attributed jointly to Byrd and Tallis in *GB–Bl* Add. MS
5054 f.1v. (index: *pace* EECM Supplementary ii 61) and to
Byrd alone in *GB–Bl* Madrigal Society MSS 710–14.

Miserere nostri Domine secundum a3
        C xvi 104 Miserere no 1
        See A xvi pp. vii–viii.

Miserere nostri Domine viventium a3
        C xvi 104 Miserere no 2
        See A xvi pp. vii–viii.

Monsieur's alman (broken consort a6)
        MCL 137 no 15
        Anonymous: see 190.

The morris (see *The battle*)

My little sweet darling a1 + 4 viols
        A xv 165 no 48 (annotation)
        C xv 105 *My sweet little darling*
        MB xxii 44 no 25
        See A p. ix; also *O heavenly God,* below.

My Lord of Oxenford's masque (broken consort a6)
        MCL 134 no 14
        Anonymous: see 190.

My sweet little darling (see *My little sweet darling*)

Non nobis Domine a2–4
        C xvi 106
        Extracted from motet by Wilder: see 2003Hw. See also A xvi
        pp. viii–ix.

O Absalom a3
        CCC 103
        By Henry Lawes: see A xvi p. vii.

O give thanks a6
O that men would therefore praise
        JM ii 123 no 13
        By John Mundy. Both sections listed separately in M 74 and 75.

O heavenly God a1 + 4 viols
        A xv 165 no 49 (annotation)
        C xv 28
        MB xxii 39 no 22

By Nicholas(?) Strogers: see A p. ix. Presumably Fellowes confused the present piece with *My little sweet darling* when, in J 163, he referred to an unspecified and otherwise unknown source which attributed the latter to Strogers.

O hold your hands a4
> CC ii 45 no 156
> See A xvi p. vii. Entitled *On a game of crib* in *GB–Bl* Add. MS 29386.

O Lord I will praise thee (see *Hey ho to the greenwood*)

O Lord turn not away a4 (fragment)
> VV 104 (excerpts)
> EECM Supplementary i 34 no 311 (incipit)
> MM (a) MS Mus. f.17–19 52/23/52
> See A xi p. xiii n. 31.

O lux beata trinitas a3–4, 6–7
> C xvi 68 Twenty-nine Canons on Plainsong Melodies nos 1–5
> See A xvi pp. vi–vii.

O mistress mine (broken consort a6)
> MCL 148 no 19
> See A. Lytton Sills' *The Italian influence in English poetry from Chaucer to Southwell* (London: Allen & Unwin, 1955, pp. 250–51).

O mortal man a5
> EECM Supplementary i 34 no 318 (incipit)
> MM (b) MS Mus. 439 f.9
> Attributed to Byrd in VV 149 and 354, but not in either MS source cited on 149.

O that men would therefore praise (see *O give thanks*)

O trifling toys (fragment)
> A xvi 180 no 43 (incipit)
> C xvi 149
> See A p. ix.

On a game of crib (see *O hold your hands*)

Out of the deep a5
> A xi 192 no 26
> See p. xiii.

Pavan and Galliard (keyboard)
> B ii 188 no 99b and c (incipits)
> C xix 87 no 18 (Galliard only)
> J no 28 (Galliard only: see n. 1)
> FVB ii 228 no 175 (Galliard only)
> See B 209 and K 178, also Pavan III, below.

Pavan and Galliard (keyboard: see Medley)

Pavan (keyboard) I
> B ii 188 no 102 (incipit)
> F 134 Appendix 11
> J Pieces with Alternative Ascriptions *Pavan F fa ut*
> FVB ii 209 no 169
> By Morley: see B 209 and K 178–79.

Pavan (keyboard) II

> E 32 no 8 (arrangement by Francis Cutting for lute)
> FVB ii 173 no 153
> By Morley: see B 209 (textual commentary on no 102), E 52 and
> K 179.

Pavan (keyboard) III
> B ii 188 no 99a (incipit)
> C xix 86 no 18
> J no 28
> FVB ii 226 no 174
> Arrangement of piece by Holborne: see B 209 and K 178.

Pavan (keyboard) IV
> MB lv 50 no 15
> See pp. xix and 179. Now thought to be by Ferdinando Richard-
> son (verbal communication from editor of MB).

Pavan (keyboard) V
> MB lv 52 no 16

See pp. xix and 179. Now thought to be by Ferdinando Richard-son (verbal communication from editor of MB).

Pavan (keyboard: see Alman (keyboard) II)

Penelope was ever praised a5
Not Cupid with his wanton wings (2nd section)
        C xvi 46
        By Alfonso Ferrabosco I: see A xvi p. v.

Per naturam a3–4
        C xvi 73 Twenty-nine Canons on Plainsong Melodies nos 6–10
        See A xvi pp. vi–vii.

Piece with no title (see Alman II, Medley)

Pietas omnium virtutum a3
        C xvi 105
        See A xvi pp. vii–viii.

Piper's galliard (keyboard)
        B ii 188 no 103 (incipit)
        C xix 157 no 40 *Pyper's galliard* . . .
        J *If my complaints (or Pyper's gal[liard])*
        See B 209 and K 165

Piper's pavan (keyboard)
        FVB ii 238 no 182
        By Peerson. See MAS i 5 for attribution to Byrd. Another setting
        in *The Byrd organ book,* edited by M.H. Glynn, London:
        Reeves, 1923, p. 6, no 6; anonymous in source: see J 214.

Preces Deo fundamus (fragment)
        A xvi 180 no 44 (incipit)
        C xvi 150
        By another William Byrd: see 1998Hn, pp. 477–78.

Prelude (keyboard)
        B ii 188 no 96 (incipit)
        C xviii 2 no 3
        J no 2
        By Tomkins: see B 208.

Prelude (keyboard: see Touch)

Primo dierum omnium (keyboard)
> EECM vi 103 no 50
> Anonymous: see M 111 and 117 no 14, J 211 and EECM pp. xi–xii.

Quia illic a4
> D ix 312 Appendix
> Part of Victoria's *Super flumina* a8: see J 107.

Retribue servo tuo a5
Incola ego sum (2nd section)
> D ix 241 *Incola ego sum* only
> By Robert Parsons: see J 109.

Robin Hood (keyboard)
> MB v 139 no 63
> Anonymous. Possibly by Tomkins, but see p. 202.

Salvator mundi (keyboard)
> EECM vi 112 no 55
> Anonymous: see M 111 and 117 no 5, J 211 and EECM pp. xi–xii.

Salve regina a4
> CCL
> Anonymous: see 1984Km p. 162.

Sancte Dei pretiose (keyboard)
> EECM vi 115 no 56
> Anonymous: see M 111 and 117 no 8, J 211 and EECM pp. xi–xii.

Sanctus (fragment)
> MM (e) Ely Cathedral MS 28 28
> Anonymous. Fair copy of setting by John Ferrabosco on same
> page of MS; both settings anotated "[th]ird."

Save me O God a5
> A xi 75 no 9
> C xi 57 pt I no 9
> D ii 282
> By Richard(?) Coste: see 1998Tc.

Service (see Sanctus, *Short Service, Short Service I*)

Short Service
   (a) Kyrie a5
     C x 80 *Short Service* no 5 setting 2
     D ii 81
     By Nathaniel Giles: see A xa p. x.
   (b) Creed a4
     D ii 82
     By Farrant: see A xa p. x.
   (c) Sanctus a5
     A xa 162 no 9 (fragment)
     C x 95
     D ii 89 (fragment)
     See A 183.

Short Service I
   WI
   By William Inglott: see introduction to edition.

Sir John Gray's galliard (keyboard)
   B ii 188 no 104 (incipit)
   C xix 134 no 31
   J no 15
   FVB ii 258 no 191
   See B 209 and K 178.

The soldiers' dance (see *The battle*)

The soldiers' delight (see *The battle*)

Summi largitor praemii (keyboard)
   EECM vi 118 no 57
   Anonymous: see M 111 and 117 no 19, J 211 and EECM pp. xi–xii.

Ten variations (see *The hunt's up*)

Touch (keyboard)
   B ii 188 no 97 (incipit) *Prelude*
   F 130 Appendix 9
   J Pieces with Alternative Ascriptions
   Two voluntaries by Orlando Gibbons: see B 208 and K 222.

Toy (see Alman II)

Ut my re (see Fantasia "a 5")

Variations, Ten (see *The hunt's up*)

Veni redemptor (keyboard)
      EECM vi 122 no 59
      Anonymous: see M 111 and 117 no 4, J 211 and EECM pp. xi–xii.

Verbum supernum (keyboard)
      EECM vi 130 no 62
      Anonymous: see M 111 and 117 no 2, J 211 and EECM pp. xi–xii.

Voluntary (see Touch)

Vox clamans (see *Vox clara*)

Vox clara (keyboard)
      EECM vi 135 no 65
      Anonymous: see M 111 and 117 no 3, J 211 and EECM
        pp. xi–xii.

Watkin's ale (keyboard)
      B ii 195 no 119 (incipit)
      FVB ii 236 no 180
      MB lv 118 no 40
      Anonymous: see K 166–67 and MAS i 5.

With fragrant flowers (text)
      EMV 642 no 20
      See 1981KNp p. 50 nn. 48 and 47.

INDEX TO TITLES

As Caesar wept	T 339
As I beheld	T 235
As I went to Walsingham	T 529
Ascendit Deus	T 144 T 146
Aspice Domine de sede	T 29
Aspice Domine quia facta	T 7
Assumpta est Maria	T 78 T 79
Attend mine humble prayer	T 257
Attollite portas	T 8
Audi benigne conditor	Apocrypha
Audi filia	T 77
Audivi vocem	T 167
Ave Maria	T 69 T 75 T 127
Ave maris stella	T 111
Ave regina	T 101 T 168
Ave verum corpus	T 92
Avertantur retrorsum	T 182
Awake mine eyes	T 296
Awake sad heart	T 340
The bagpipe and the drone	T 439f
The barley break	T 438
Barofostus' dream	Apocrypha
The battle	T 439 Apocrypha
Be not wroth very sore (contrafactum of 2nd section)	T 30
Be unto me	T 314
Beata coeli nuncio	T 108
Beata es	T 65
Beata mater	T 108
Beata virgo	T 127
Beata viscera	T 66
Beati mundo corde	T 87
Behold how good	T 280 T 368
Behold I bring you glad tidings (contrafactum)	T 30
Behold now praise the Lord (contrafactum)	T 10
Behold O God the sad and heavy case	T 210
Behold O God with thy all prosp'ring eye	T A5
The bells	T 440
Benedicta et venerabilis	T 62
Benedictio et claritas	T 31
Benedictus (see Mass, Service)	
Benedixisti Domine	T 67
Benigne fac	T 169
Bina caelestis (2 settings)	Apocrypha

Civitas sancti tui	T 30
Clarifica me pater	T 444–46
Cogitavit Dominus	T 171
Cognoverunt discipuli	T 134
Come drink to me	Apocrypha
Come help O God	T 316
Come jolly swains	T 297
Come let us rejoice	T 299
Come pretty babe	T 341
Come to me grief	T 249
Come tread the paths	Apocrypha
Come woeful Orpheus	T 302
Compel the hawk	T 273
Conditor alme	Apocrypha
Confirma hoc	T 152
Confitemini Domino	T 165
Constant Penelope	T 238
Constitues eos	T 157
Content is rich	T 342
Contumelias et terrores	T 39
Coranto	T 447–50 Apocrypha
Coranto Lady Riche	Apocrypha
Credo (see Mass)	
Creed (see Service)	
Crowned with flowers I saw fair Amaryllis	T 304
Crowned with flowers and lilies	T 354
Cui luna	T 108
Cunctis diebus	T 53
Da mihi auxilium	T 13
Da tuis fidelibus	T 154
De lamentatione Jeremiae	T 171
Decantabat populus	T 172
Dedit fragilibus	T 179
Defecit in dolore	T 19
Defixae sunt	T 171
Delight	T 498
Delight is dead	T 355
Deliver me from mine enemies	Apocrypha
Deo gratias	T 107
Deo patri sit gloria	T 9
Depart ye furies	T 369
Descendit de coelis	T 48
Deus creator omnium	Apocrypha

Eripe me	T 174
Eructavit cor meum	T 61
Et dicant semper	T 182
Et exivit per auream	T 48
Et Iesum benedictum	T 38
Et non intres	T 40
Eterne rerum conditor	Apocrypha
Even as in seas	T 343
Even from the depth	T 225
Ex more docti mystico	Apocrypha
Exalt thyself O Lord	T 200
Exsultent et laetentur	T 182
Exsurgat Deus	T 149
Exsurge Domine	T 46
Extol the greatness	T 205
Exultate Deo	T 88
Exultate iusti	T 84
Exultent et laetentur	T 182
Fac cum servo tuo	T 37
Facti sumus opprobrium	T 25
Factus est repente	T 153
Fair Britain isle	T 359
Fancy (see Fantasia)	
Fant	T 488
Fantasia	T 377–88 T 444 T 451–56 T 522–23
	T 525–28 T A10–11 Apocrypha
Farewell delight	T 457
Farewell false love	T 240
Farwell delighte	T 457
Fauxbourdon Service	T 192
Felix es	T 64
Felix namque	T 74
Fifth pavan and galliard	T 491
First French coranto	T 447
First pavan and galliard	T 487
First Preces and Psalms	T 191
First Service	T 194
The flute and the drum	T 439g
For two basses	T 386
Fortune	T 457
Fourth pavan and galliard	T 490
Fourth Service	T A4
French coranto	T 447–49

Let not our prayers (contrafactum of 3rd section)	T 32
Let not the sluggish sleep	T 294
Let not thy wrath (contrafactum)	T 30
Let others praise	T 319
Let us arise (contrafactum)	T 8
Let us be glad	T 214
Levemus corda	T 44
Libera me Domine de morte	T 18
Libera me Domine et pone	T 5
Lift up your heads	T 8 T 192e
Like as the hart	Apocrypha
Like as the lark	Apocrypha
Like Harpias vile	T 321
Lingua mea	T 72
Litany	T 103 T 193 T A3
Long Service	T 197
Look and bow down	T 372
Look down O Lord	T 315
Lord hear my prayer	T 255
Lord in thy rage	T 251
Lord in thy wrath correct me not	T 253
Lord in thy wrath reprove me not	T 224
Lord Morley	T 479
Lord to Thee I make my moan	T 330
Lord Willoughby's welcome home	T 481
Love is a fit of pleasure	T 282
Love would discharge	T 274
Lucis creator optime	Apocrypha
Lullaby	T 247
Lumen ad revelationem	T 59
Ma non si tosto	T 318
Magnificat (see Service)	
Magnificum Domini	T 35
Magnus Dominus	T 56
The maiden's song	T 482
Make ye joy to God	T 306
Malt's come down	T A12
Mane nobiscum	T 116
Manus tuae fecerunt	Apocrypha
The march before the battle	T 483
The march of footmen	T 439b
The march of horsemen	T 439c
The march to the fight	T 439h

Maria mater gratia	T 110
Martin said to his man	Apocrypha
Mass	T 1–3 T A1
The mayden's songe	T 482
Medley	T A13 Apocrypha
Medulla musicke	T 533
Memento Domine	T 23
Memento homo	T 11
Memento salutis auctor	T 110
Memor esto fili	T 175
Methought of late	T A7
Mine eyes of fervency	T 217
Miserere	T 409–10 T 445–46 T 484–85 T 533 Apocrypha
Miserere mei	T 47
Miserere mihi	T 16
Miserere nostri Domine	Apocrypha
Miserere nostri Domine secundum	Apocrypha
Miserere nostri Domine viventium	Apocrypha
Mistress Mary Brownlow	T 458 T 503
Monsieur's alman	T 431–33 Apocrypha
Monstra te esse	T 111
The morris	Apocrypha
Mount Hope	T 345
Mr William Petre	T 496
My faults O Christ	T 337
My freedom ah	T 346
My Lady Nevell's ground	T 467
My little sweet darling	Apocrypha
My Lord of Oxenford's masque	Apocrypha
My mind to me a kingdom is	T 229
My mistress had a little dog	T 361
My soul ascend	T 372
My soul oppressed	T 218
My sweet little darling	Apocrypha
My years do seek	T 344
Ne irascaris	T 30
Ne perdas cum impiis	T 174
New Service	T 197
Ninth pavan and galliard	T 495
Nobis natus nobis datus	T 95
Noctis recolitur	T 179
Non nobis Domine	Apocrypha
Non vos relinquam	T 155

Nos enim pro peccatis	T 32
Not Cupid with his wanton wings	Apocrypha
Notum fecit Dominus	T 120
Now may Israel say (contrafactum)	T 210
Nunc dimittis (see Service)	
Nunc dimittis servum tuum	T 59
Nunc scio vere	T 156
O Absalom	Apocrypha
O admirabile commercium	T 125
O clap your hands	T 191b
O dear life	T 278
O Domine adiuva me	T 21
O give thanks	Apocrypha
O gloriosa domina	T 109
O God but God	T 331
O God give ear	T 216
O God that guides	T 309
O God the proud are risen	T 202
O God which art most merciful	T 254
O God whom our offences	T 203
O happy thrice	T 373
O heavenly God	Apocrypha
O hold your hands	Apocrypha
O Lord bow down	T 332
O Lord give ear (contrafactum)	T 11
O Lord God (contrafactum)	T 42
O Lord how long	T 220
O Lord how vain	T 333
O Lord I will praise thee	Apocrypha
O Lord make thy servant Elizabeth	*T 204*
O Lord my God	T 266
O Lord rebuke me not	T 212
O Lord turn not away	Apocrypha
O Lord turn thy wrath (contrafactum)	T 30
O Lord who in thy sacred tent	T 221
O Lord within thy tabernacle	T 326
O lux beata trinitas	T 9 Apocrypha
O lux beatissima	T 154
O magnum misterium	T 126
O mistress mine	T 486 Apocrypha
O mortal man	Apocrypha
O praise our Lord	T 205
O quam gloriosum	T 31

O quam suavis	T 136
O rex gloriae	T 148
O sacrum convivium	T 94
O salutaris hostia	T 93 T 184
O sweet deceit	T 321
O that men would therefore praise	Apocrypha
O that most rare breast	T 250
O that we woeful wretches	T 334
O trifling toys	Apocrypha
O vain the toil	T 313
O worthy queen	T 354
O you that hear this voice	T 231
Oculi omnium	T 89
Of flattering speech	T 287
Of gold all burnished	T 279
Omnes gentes plaudite	T 143
Omni tempore benedic Deum	T 175
On a game of crib	Apocrypha
One other fantasi 6 voc.	T 388
Opprobrium facti sumus	T 25
Optimam partem elegit	T 80
Ora pro nobis	T 112
Orietur in diebus	T 34
Out of the deep	T 206 Apocrypha
Out of the orient crystal skies	T 335
Pange lingua	T 95
Panis angelicus	T 179
Parsons' In nomine	T 476
Pascha nostrum	T 142
Passamezzo	T 495
Passing measures	T 495
Passion according to St John	T 117
Pavan	T 389–90 T 487–512 T A14–17 Apocrypha
Pavan Bray	T 497
Pavan canon	T 493
Pavan delight	T 498
Pavan the Earl of Salisbury	T 503
Pavan fant	T 488
Pavan Johnson's dedlight	T 498
Pavan Kinborough Good	T 492
Pavan lachrymae	T 500
Pavan Mr William Petre	T 496
Pavan Ph[ilippa] Tr[egian]	T 504

Pavan Sir William Petre	T 496
Peascod time	T 474
Peccantem me quotidie	T 6
Peccavi super numerum	T 176
Penelope ever was praised	Apocrypha
Penelope that longed	T 272
Per immensa saecula	T 177
Per naturam	Apocrypha
Pescodd time	T 474
Petrus beatus	T 177
Phantasia (see Fantasia)	
Ph[ilippa] Tr[egian]	T 504
"Piece with no title"	Apocrypha
Pietas omnium virtutum	Apocrypha
Piper's galliard	T 475 Apocrypha
Piper's pavan	Apocrypha
Plainsong Service	T 192
Plorans plorabit	T 83
Post dies octo	T 116
Post partum	T 73
Posuerunt morticinia	T 25
Praise him on tube	T 205
Praise our Lord	T 310
Precamur sancte Domine	T 170 T 400 T 403–05 T 427
Preces	T 190–92
Preces Deo fundamus	Apocrypha
Prelude	T 384 T 513–17 T 520 Apocrypha
Prevent us O Lord	T 207
Primo dierum omnium	Apocrypha
Pro patribus tuis	T 157
Proceed then	T 233
Propter veritatem	T 77
Prostrate O Lord I lie	T 242
Psallite Domino	T 147
Psalm 100	T 198
Psalms	T 191–92
Puer natus est nobis	T 119
Pyper's galliard	T 475 Apocrypha
Quadran pavan and galliard	T 502
Quae lucescit	T 113
Quae te vicit	T 137
The queen's alman	T 434
Quem terra pontus	T 108

Qui passe	T 518
Quia illic	Apocrypha
Quia quem meruisti	T 112
Quia viderunt	T 59
Quid igitur faciam	T 50
Quiescat Domine	T 45
Quis ascendit	T 68
Quis est homo	T 36
Quis me statim	T 362
Quod descendit	T 96
Quod Eva tristis	T 109
Quodcunque ligaveris	T 162
Quodcunque vinclis	T 177
Quomodo cantabimus	T 186
Quoniam amaritudine	T 180
Quotiescunque manducabitis	T 91
Recordare Domine	T 45
Reges Tharsis	T 129 T 178
Regina coeli	T 112
Rejoice rejoice	T 268
Rejoice unto the Lord	T 336
Remember Lord	T 340
Respice Domine	T 29
Responses	T 190
Responsum accepit Simeon	T 60
Resurrexi	T 138
Resurrexit	T 112
Retire my soul	T 300
The retreat	T 439i
Retribue servo tuo	Apocrypha
Right blest are they	T 252
Rorate coeli	T 67
Rowland	T 481
Sacerdotes Domini	T 90
Sacris solemniis	T 179
St John Passion	T 117
Salvator mundi	T 398 T 411–12 T 519–20 Apocrypha
Salve regina	T 38 T 99 Apocrypha
Salve sancta parens	T 61
Salve sola Dei genetrix	T 104
Sancte Dei pretiose	Apocrypha
Sanctus (see also Mass, Service)	T A1
Save me O God	T 191c Apocrypha

Subsistit virgo	T 118
Sumens illud	T 111
Summi largitor praemii	Apocrypha
Surge illuminare	T 133
Susanna fair	T 244 T 258
Suscepimus Deus	T 56
Tantum ergo	T 95
Te deprecor	T 17
Te Deum (see Service)	
Te lucis	T 406 T 418–29
Te mane laudem	T 9
Teach me O Lord	T 192d
Ten variations	Apocrypha
Tenth pavan and galliard	T 496
Terra tremuit	T 141
Teth	T 171
The day delay'd	T A8
The doleful debt	T 250
The eagle's force	T 286
The fair young virgin	T 318
The gladsome sound	T 205
The greedy hawk	T 262
The Lord is only my support	T 327
The man is blest	T 329
The match that's made	T 241
The nightingale	T 259
The noble famous queen	T 353
Then for a boat	T 261
There careless thoughts	T 265
There may the solemn Stoics find	T 319
Third French coranto	T 449
Third pavan and galliard	T 489
Third Service	T 196
This day Christ was born	T 308
This Joseph's Lord	T 372
This sweet and merry month	T 293 T 320
Thou God that guid'st	T 213
Thou poets' friend	T 349
Thou Amaryllis dance	T 227
Thou I be brown	T 363
Timete Dominum	T 85
Timor et hebetudo	T 32
'Tis Joseph's herd	T 372

Tollite portas	T 68
Touch	Apocrypha
Toy	Apocrypha
Tregian's ground	T 469
Tribue Domine	T 17
Tribulatio proxima est	T 39
Tribulationes civitatum	T 32
Tristitia et anxietas	T 22
Triumph with pleasant melody	T 337
Truce for a time	T 350
The trumpets	T 439d
Truth at the first	T 351
Tu es pastor	T 161
Tu es Petrus	T 159
Tu esto nostrum gaudium	T 137
Tu regis alti	T 109
Tui sunt coeli	T 122
Turbarum voces	T 117
Turn our captivity	T 311
Twenty-nine canons on plainsong melodies	
(see Miserere, *O lux beata trinitas, Per naturam*)	
Unam petii a Domino	T 82
Unto the hills	T 284
Upon a plainsong	T 519
Upon a summer's day	T 261
Upon the same plainsong	T 520
Ut eruas nos	T 51
Ut mi re	T 522
Ut my re	Apocrypha
Ut re mi	T 523–24
Ut videam voluntatem	T 82
Variatio	T 432
Variations, Ten	Apocrypha
Veni creator spiritus	T 519–20
Veni Domine	T 20
Veni redemptor	Apocrypha
Veni sancte spiritus et emitte	T 154
Veni sancte spiritus reple	T 151
Venite (see Service)	
Venite comedite	T 132
Venite exultemus	T 164
Verbum caro	T 95
Verbum supernum	Apocrypha

Verse	T 525
Verse Service	T 195
Versicles	T 190
Vespere autem sabbathi	T 113
Victimae paschali	T 140
Victoria	T 461
Vide Domine afflictionem	T 24
Vide Domine quoniam tribulor	T 180
Viderunt omnes	T 120 T 123
Vidimus stellam	T 130
Vigilate	T 27
Virga Iesse floruit	T 75
Virgo Dei genetrix	T 63
Virgo singularis	T 111
Viri Galilaei	T 143
Visita quaesumus	T 98
Vitam praesta	T 111
Volte (see Lavolta)	
Voluntary	T 526–28 Apocrypha
Vox clamans	Apocrypha
Vox clara	Apocrypha
Vultum tuum	T 71 T 77
Walsingham	T 529
Watkin's ale	Apocrypha
Wedded to will is witless	T 305
Weeping full sore	T 271
What is life	T 298
What pleasure have great princes	T 234 T 322
What steps of strife	T 352
What unacquainted cheerful voice	T 337
What vaileth it to rule	T 323
What wights are these	T 374
When first by force	T 276
When I was otherwise	T 275
When Israel came out of Egypt	T 192b
When younglings first	T 260
Where fancy fond	T 230
Where the blind	T 364
Whereat an ant	T 288
While Phoebus us'd to dwell	T 353
While that a cruel fire	T 375
While that the sun	T 267
The whistling carman	T 442

2

Byrd Literature: The Survey Continued, 1987–2004, with a Complete Checklist from 1826

If the latter half of the twentieth century in general witnessed an acceleration in the advance of Byrd appreciation and scholarship, the period since the publication of the first edition of this book in 1987 has witnessed an eruption. That first edition contains an introductory survey of Byrd criticism up to 1986 (pp. 135–45), itself based on the fuller account in my thesis "A hundred years of Byrd criticism, 1883–1982: an annotated bibliography and critical review of writings about William Byrd" (M.Litt., University of Aberdeen, 1983), pages 83–257. Since then, there have been significant factual findings, as well as a broadening of the scope and an increase in the quantity of topics under consideration.

It is a paradox that, the further we move away from Byrd's lifetime, the more we learn about it. In 1897Sw, Squire first published Byrd's will, from the wording of which it was deduced that Byrd was born in 1543 or possibly late 1542. Exactly a hundred years later in 1997Hw, John Harley announced the discovery of a document that indicated that Byrd was born in 1540 or possibly late 1539. This meant all relevant reference books have had to be revised, but it also means Byrd's music was composed by someone three years older than previously thought. This does not matter much for the mature works, but is significant in respect of those pieces of juvenilia regarded as dubious or spurious, which can now be seen to be more credibly authentic.

Harley's monograph and succession of subsequent biographical articles—most significantly 1998Hn, 2000Hw and 2002Hby—have rendered redundant most such writings that preceded them, but other writers also have made available some new discoveries. Kerman continued his fine series of insights into Byrd's Roman Catholicism in 2000Km, while Christopher Harrison's article about Byrd's relationship with the Paget family of Staffordshire (1991Hw) was the major breakthrough concerning Byrd's recusancy between 1987Tw and 1997Hw. John Bossy, in 2002Bw, developed the good work set in train by Harrison. A different aspect of Byrd's recusancy with the focus on Middlesex is covered by David Mateer in 1997Mw. William Bankes ventured into Byrd and the law (2004Bw), whereas three other authors continued the tradition of informative general articles about Byrd: David Skinner wore his scholarship lightly in 2001Sb, Bayan Northcott ushered Byrd back to the world of daily newspapers in a spread ideal for the interested initiate (1993Nc), and Douglas Bolingbroke provided the account of Roman Catholicism in England during Byrd's lifetime (1999BOe), which should be consulted by everyone.

In their seminal monographs 1978Nc and 1981Km about the instrumental and Latin music, respectively, Neighbour and Kerman were both concerned, appropriately, with tracing the origins of Byrd's style and technique, as was Monson, so far the most significant writer about the Anglican music, in 1979Tp. So comprehensively did they succeed that relatively little has subsequently been written on the subject. There was some reference to it in a few of the essays in 1992B: Peter le Huray invoked Parsons and the obscure Thomas Knight in 1992Ls; Craig Monson, Tallis in 1992Mt; David Wulstan, Tallis again and the elder Ferrabosco in 1992Wb; and Owen Rees spread his net widely in 1992Re. These articles were succeeded by Wulstan's companion piece 1996Wb, and the brief 1997Tho, but the most substantial study has been 1997Twi in which RT confirmed the status of Sheppard among Byrd's influences. Subsequently, the subject received consideration from Lionel Pike in 2004Pb with more reference to Parsons, whereas in 2004HUMw David Humphreys focused on Wilder, previously given a passing mention in 1993Ww.

Now that it was becoming clearer which composers had influenced Byrd and patterns for future research had been established, part of the agenda for 1992B was to move on to consider Byrd's influence on his contemporaries and successors. Three essays addressed this question. In 1992BEb John Bennett looked at Mico, in 1992Ib John Irving compared Byrd's instrumental music with that of Tomkins, and in 1992Mt again Monson followed an Anglican continuum onward to Morley. Elsewhere Irving also introduced Thomas Holmes into Byrd literature (1992Iw). Stephen Jones and RT (1993Ju) and RT (1993Tmy) concentrated on two further aspects of the influence of Byrd on Tomkins. The advent of 1995A led to further such studies: 1995Ss by the distinguished Philips scholar David J. Smith; 1999BUc, in which David Buckley introduced William Child into Byrd literature; more from Irving on Tomkins in 1999Iw; and another glance at Weelkes in 1995Tbyr, a supplement to 1988Th.

Since the first edition of this *Guide*, little has been written about Byrd and foreign musicians, but Pieter Dirksen has contributed a paper on Sweelinck (2001Db), which is the opposite in substance from the cursoriness alleged in its self-effacing subtitle. RT infiltrated Clemens non Papa into 1988Th, with further information in 1989Tb.

Contrariwise, much has been written about Byrd and posterity: the musical world after 1623. The topic elicited minimal attention before 1988Pb, wherein RT isolated Byrd from within John Patton's data regarding the music sung in British cathedrals during 1986. Adhering to Byrd's music within the Anglican ethos, 1991FUw and 1992Tb followed. The latter, plus 1992Th, were the first fruits of a series of papers that were triggered by RT's research for 1993Tf and that culminated in 2002Ts. Byrd's tenure of the organistship at Lincoln Cathedral provided the source for two chapters in 1993Tw which considered his legacy within that city and beyond, whereas two other chapters summarized his legacy to posterity in general terms. The celebrations relating to what was thought to be the 450th anniversary of his birth in 1993 were reviewed in 1995Tb. Thanks to the recent emergence of 1995A, an article written by Robert Thompson (1996Tw) finally appeared connecting Byrd with Purcell. Sterndale Bennett entered Byrd literature in 1997Tw, while Holst made a partially unflattering reappearance in 1997Th. In the first article (and the only one to carry a separate title) in what became a regular series entitled "Meanings" in 1995A (for the full list, see Chapter 5), the great contemporary Scottish composer James MacMillan wrote illuminatingly in 1998Mb about the impact on him, early in his life, of the Mass for Four Voices. Illumination of another sort glowed from 2000Pb, in which Graham Parlett's cogent rumination upon the impact of the Mass for Five Voices on Bax expanded into a definitive consideration of Bax's relationship with early music. Broadly bibliographical studies of Byrd and posterity include, in addition to the nót unflattering part of 1997Th (see previous), 1995Hb, 2000Tbyr, and 2002Tt: the first charted the progress of Byrd's church music in a prestigious and durable radio programme, the second introduced a geographical element through provincial imprints, and the third brought James Oswald, albeit tenuously, into Byrd literature.

Moving from the abstraction of influence to the reality of the music itself, the first concern should be to confirm the Byrd canon: to scrutinize the authenticity or otherwise of works attributed to him, ejecting or barring the way to manifest impostors, and admitting acceptable candidates. John Morehen had begun to exploit computer analysis (1984Mt) and, in 1992MOb, announced a methodology for testing the attributions of Byrd's (relatively few) unpublished motets. This was put to use subsequently in 1996MOi to test *Haec est dies*. This spurious motet had just been published (KM) with an introduction by John Harley and RT in 1996Hb. (Edited by Brian Clark, this was the first time it had appeared in print, despite its having been known in certain quarters for a long time.) Meanwhile in something of a reaction against the methods of Oliver Neighbour and of Alan Brown in his editing of B, David Schulenberg proposed an overhaul of the criteria for admitting unpublished keyboard works (the vast majority) into the Byrd canon; even the first edition of the present book (1987Tw) earned a dismissive scowl in passing (1993Sk). Notwithstanding, Neighbour produced 1992Ns. Then in 2001KEb, Kerman devoted over three pages to "Authenticity": here, taking the sort of serious interest in recordings that is eschewed by all but a few British scholars but which comes naturally to Americans, he reassessed some conclusions that he reached in 1981Km. RT embraced to the Anglican canon the previously doubted T 206 (1995Tp) but in 1998Tc ignored the entreaty in the title of the spurious *Save me O God.* In 2003Th he suggested a different William Byrd as the possible composer of another Anglican spuriosity *Glory be to God.* The mystery of that most adhesive spurious round *Non nobis Domine,* ejected by Brett as long ago as 1972BRd, was finally solved by David Humphreys in 2003Hw. Pieter Dirksen put forward an addition to the keyboard canon in 2001Db.

The increased professionalization of musicology had, for those with a commitment to Byrd, reached its first apotheosis, heralded by 1966At, in the two monographs by Neighbour and Kerman, 1978Nc and 1981Km, respectively, volumes three and one in the series *The music of William Byrd.* Volume two, "The songs, Services and anthems of William Byrd," was to have been written by Philip Brett after he completed his general editorship of A. Although he lived to see the editing of the final two volumes completed, he died in 2002 before he could begin work on this monograph. (2003Np is an obituary in which Neighbour concentrates on the extent of Brett's work on Byrd.) The result has been that whereas the monographs on the consort and keyboard music (1978Nc) and on the Latin music (1981Km) sooner or later generated further articles on all these topics, published work on the songs has been sporadic, and that on the Anglican music took time to develop. Besides his articles before 1978Nc, Neighbour had subsequently added 1992Ns. Kerman had recycled 1963Ko and 1966Kb from among the articles he wrote before 1981Km, and had gone on to add 2000Km and 2001KEb. These topics in general, and sometimes these two monographs in particular, also generated articles by other authors.

Turning first to the keyboard music, the next significant contribution to research after 1978Nc (itself reissued in a paperback edition, 1984Nc) was Robert Pacey's discovery of a new source reported in 1985Pb. It took an additional seven years for more articles about the keyboard music to appear. This suggests that potential authors had been inhibited by the magnitude of Neighbour's opus. Such a state of affairs ended in 1992B which included, besides Neighbour's own 1992Ns, chapters by Desmond Hunter and Hilary Gaskin, 1992Hm and 1992Gb, in which they delved into evidence provided within

My Ladye Nevells Booke. In the same volume, John Irving also referred to the keyboard music in his broad study 1992Ib.

In addition to Oliver Neighbour, the other substantial contributor to our knowledge of Byrd's keyboard music since the era of Fellowes has been Alan Brown, with his complete edition B and his related articles already mentioned in 1987Tw. Most of his subsequent research has gone into refining successive editions of B, but he returned to the fray with 1993BRw, as did Davitt Moroney in 1993MOb after his review article 1987Mt, in half of which he had thought and pondered about 1978Nc. After this, and Schulenberg's *frisson* concerning authenticity (1993Sk) already mentioned, Percy Grainger in 1994Gg was of no more than historical interest. Desmond Hunter introduced some thoughts on tempo in 1995HUs and, also already mentioned, Smith and Dirksen compared the keyboard music with that of Philips and Sweelinck, respectively, in 1995Ss and 2001Db. Meanwhile, in 1998Hb Harley offered another response to Neighbour's monograph 1978Nc. Moroney's monographic notes to his complete recording are featured by RT in 2000Tby, and the recording itself is the focus of Northcott's review article 1999Nf. Illustrating the continuing vitality of Byrd research, in 2004Gc Christopher Goodwin suggested a source for the words to T 482, for which no text had hitherto been identified, and in 2005Hm, Harley revealed the identity of the elusive dedicatee of My Ladye Nevells Booke.

Byrd's surviving corpus of consort music is very small beside the keyboard music. This is complemented in the quantity of writing devoted to it. The tone of finality in Neighbour's account, the first part of 1978Nc, seeming to depict Byrd's consort music as the end of an era virtually without successors, again appeared to inhibit further comment. Indeed 1985Twr, in which RT listed and commented upon writings on the subject, was a response to this perceived finality and to the subsequent lack of articles. Not for the only time, the silence was effectively broken in 1992B. John Bennett's article 1992BEb focused on the influence of Byrd on Richard Mico, but in questioning the perceived finality in Neighbour's account, he reopened for discussion the entire subject of Byrd's consort music. Also in 1992B, John Irving touched on it in 1992Ib, mentioned earlier, as was 1992Iw, querying Byrd's alleged influence on Holmes. Anthony Rowland-Jones followed with some independent thoughts in 1993Rw. A flurry of interest in possible consort origins of some of Byrd's keyboard pavans and galliards began with 1994Tu by RT. Richard Rastall and David Smith developed this in 1997Rw and 1999Sb, and Ian Payne offered some proposals in 2000PAf which Smith had already considered and dismissed. A further paper by Rastall, 1997Rwi, was a reaction against another opinion expressed by Neighbour about T 387 and 388 in 1978Nc, and with the appearance of articles by Lionel Pike (2004Pb) on echo fantasias and David Pinto (2004PIb) on Alfonso Ferrabosco II, the boundaries of research on Byrd's consort music had been redrawn both fore and aft.

By the time Neighbour wrote 1978Nc, the complete edition of the consort music, A xvii, had long been published. When Kerman published 1981Km, the relevant volumes of A were still being edited by Philip Brett, Alan Brown, and Warwick Edwards. This was probably why there was a greater continuity in the output of writings about Byrd's Latin music. At regular intervals, the anecdotal but gratifying 1982Ol was followed by 1984Mt (already mentioned in the context of canon and authenticity) and 1986Sw, plus that half of 1987Mt that thinks and ponders about 1981Km. After a gap, John Irving produced a pair of penetrating articles, 1990Ip focusing on the *Gradualia* and 1991Iw on the masses. The Latin music was proportionately represented in 1992B; all four chapters have been mentioned: 1992Ls, 1992Re, and 1992Wb concerning influences on Byrd and 1992MOb concerning authentication of unpublished motets. There followed more articles about different aspects of the Latin music. 1996Hb and 1996MOi (authenticity), 1996TUm and 1996Wb (influences given or received) have already been mentioned, but three studies, which may broadly be described as bibliographical, appeared in which Teruhiko Nasu and John Milsom considered aspects of the publications of *Gradualia* and the 1575 *Cantiones*, respectively (1995Np, 1996MIt), and David Mateer discussed an important manuscript source (1996Mw). Then in 1997MOb Craig Monson continued and expanded the work of Kerman and others in looking at Byrd's nonliturgical Latin compositions and seeking reasons for the texts that he selected to set. There followed a short hiatus until Andrew Carwood's broad but informed overview 2001Ci, and Arne Keller's announcement in 2001Ks about another newly rediscovered source. In two studies of *Gradualia,* Kerry McCarthy looked at liturgical implications (2002Mm and 2004Mno), whereas in 2004Mn she announced an important discovery concerning the text of T 17. Byrd's Roman Catholic liturgical music also was featured by Robert Hugill in 2004HUw, the only item in either the checklist or the annotated bibliography to have its origins in an e-journal. Meanwhile, in 2003Tu, RT exposed his roots in music librarianship, and in 2004Tm he drew attention to arguably the most neglected of Byrd publications.

The premature death of Philip Brett deprived Byrd literature of his intended monograph on the Anglican music and the songs. Nevertheless, the Anglican music has come to enjoy consistent attention. Craig Monson had written three articles—1979Mp, 1981Mt, and 1982Ma—to complement his editions A xa, xb, and xi, although the researches of Andrew Johnstone published in VI.JOa (see Chapter 3) have rendered 1981Mt redundant and called into question aspects of accompaniment and pitch in Monson's edition of T 195 in A xa. Yet again there was a critical hiatus, as there had been, in a different circumstance, after the publications of 1978Nc and 1981Km, until RT produced 1988Th, previously invoked with reference to Byrd's influence on his contemporaries, and 1990Tg, on the uniqueness of T 197. The last article necessitated a postscript (1992Tg) and provoked a cogent response from Lionel Pike, 1992Pg. Again 1992B brought an author back to a familiar field, this time Craig Monson writing about the Short Service style (1992Mt, mentioned above regarding influences). In 1993Pb, Peter Phillips looked at Byrd's vocal ranges particularly in his Anglican music. Like so many other writings about pitch, transposition, and accompaniment in early Anglican church music, Phillips's article has been undermined by Andrew Johnstone in VI.JOa (mentioned earlier), who has challenged the assumptions on which many such articles were built. RT compared two anthems by Byrd and Tomkins in 1993Tmy, and returned to the status of T 197 in 1995Tby and, in part, of 1994Tb (page 101, item 6). A completely different aspect of T 197—the influence of Sheppard—was RT's approach in 1997Twi, whereas 1995Tbyr was his postscript to 1988Th. Peter James wrote the definitive account, in 1998Je, of his rediscovery of T 200, and followed this in 2001Js with a reappraisal of Byrd's verse compositions. David Buckley compared two anthems by Byrd and William Child in 1999BUc, and in 1999Iw, John Irving followed up the significance of 1993Ju in respect of T 197. RT brought to light an arrangement of T 194(c) from the eighteenth century when Byrd's reputation was at its nadir (2000Tj), whereas the obscure T 192(a) featured in 2004Tj, and the familiar T 208 in 2004Tja. John Harley continued his ruminations about the composer with some pointed questions about his choice of texts for some of his anthems (2002Hb). See Chapter 6 for RT's apostacy concerning T 197.

Relative to the size of the corpus, Byrd's songs are the most neglected of his compositions. Like the Anglican music, they have suffered from the lack of a dedicated, or even partially dedicated, monograph, nor are these two sections of Byrd's output the subjects of complete recordings. Yet again 1992B stimulated Byrd literature: by including 1992Kw, Joseph Kerman's influential analysis of T 300, it broke a silence of more than decade over Byrd's songs. In 1992Tm, RT was commissioned to look at aspects of the solo songs, and 1993Bp, which Philip Brett at an early stage considered offering to *Byrd studies,* was substantially given over to a study of performance aspects of Byrd's songs in the Paston manuscripts. There was a shorter hiatus until 1999SMf, Jeremy Smith's bibliographical study of the 1588 collection, and this was related to 1999BRs, which he wrote with Brett. Another such was Morehen's 2001Mt on the 1611 collection. Alan Charlton and John Harley viewed T 372 from different perspectives in 2003Cl and 2004Hl. In 2003MIb, John Milsom wrote about T 278. In 2003Sw, Mike Smith wrote about T 357. His 2004Sb was a more general study, pondering Byrd's attitude to some possible undercurrents from popular culture in his settings of certain texts, whereas Oliver Neighbour also cast his net widely in 2003Nb, returning to the question of influences, among other matters, this time in the partsongs.

Before leaving the literature about Byrd's compositions, it remains to mention that 1995A published 2003Mw by Stewart McCoy, the first and only article devoted to contemporary lute arrangements of Byrd's music.

Not every article about Byrd needs citing in this introduction. Some were deliberately slight, some have been superseded or become outdated, and some, it has to be said, are not good. It will have been noticed that writings on general topics tend to have been specific to the categories of Byrd's compositions: for instance, Desmond Hunter's studies of performance practice, 1992Hm and 1995HUs, are mentioned among other literature about the keyboard music. The same is true of topics such as analysis and bibliography, and indeed most of these topics appear within the monographs devoted to Byrd.

In addition, there is a gratifying number of miscellaneous articles. They can range over all or just a part of Byrd's life and music, and they do not chime in with the themes, agendas, and topics mentioned more numerously so far. To take an example close to home, 1987Tw, the first edition of the present volume, was an avowedly bibliographical approach to Byrd but included two items of source material: 1987Rw is an edition of E.H.L. Reeve's comprehensive contemporary account of the 1923 tercentenary about which it contains unique material, and 1987Tf is (still) the only edition of the full text of the Queen's letters patent to Tallis and Byrd for printing music.

The interrelation of music and literature at the cultural level is all too seldom broached, regrettably because the researchers of the one have little empathy with, and insufficient knowledge of, the other. (The same tends to be true of music and history.) Such articles that have been published, showing the required empathy with music and the other discipline, tend to whet the appetite for more. Katharine Duncan-Jones attempted to clarify the nature of Byrd's relationship with Sidney (1990Dm) and in 1994Tb, RT introduced an article from 1974 (I.Cm) revealing that Byrd had been a friend of the family of George Herbert. Other work on the connection with Sidney followed from H.R. Woudhysen (VII.Wm) and the greatest triumph in this literary sphere occurred when the long-sought link between Byrd and Shakespeare was established by Finnis and Martin in V.Fa. (All three of these references may be found in Chapter 3.) There was also a momentous development in twentieth-century literature. In 1992 Peter Ackroyd published his novel *English music*. A perceptive characterization of Byrd dominates one chapter, excerpts from which were subsequently "serialized" (XII.Ae; again, see Chapter 3).

Discography is a discipline neglected in some (mainly British) quarters, but it has been embraced increasingly to the advantage of Tudor composers. Byrd has benefitted from the attentions of Michael Greenhalgh. Thanks to 1992Gb (another groundbreaking contribution to 1992B), 1996Gb, and Chapter 4 *infra*, all commercial recordings of Byrd's music are comprehensively logged. Brian Robins deserves an honourable mention for 2000Rb and for his contribution to 2001Sb. RT was requested to provide 1993Tm, which he supplemented with 1994Tm and updated in 2002Tr. John Milsom achieved for Byrd one of his then rare appearances in the journal *Early music* with 1993Mb, as did Joseph Kerman in 2001KEb, a review article.

That there is only one article in the checklist that is not in English should be food for thought. Kevin Bazzana's subtle assessment of Byrd's music (1987Bc) deserves to be known as widely as the best articles in English.

Philip Brett wrote an article and a pamphlet about being general editor of A (1980Be, 1985Be). A was also the subject of part of 2001KEb by Joseph Kerman, mentioned above. C became the subject of an article for the first time when RT wrote 1995Tf, in which the introductions to Byrd literature of F.W. Dwelly and particularly Francis Neilson were long overdue. Subsequently it emerged that Dwelly's papers had been destroyed, but an otherwise neglected article by Neilson was rediscovered six decades later in a journal unrelated to music (1943Nw).

In 1993, then thought to be the 450th anniversary of his birth, there were exhibitions featuring Byrd at the British Library and the University of London Library. Ruth Darton compiled a catalogue for the latter (1993Df) and wrote a subsequent article (1994Df). In 1997Hi John Harley described a tour of Byrd sites in London, as if moving between related exhibits in a great and timeless museum.

1. A COMPLETE CHECKLIST OF BYRD CRITICISM FROM 1826

This checklist notes chronologically all known monographs and articles about Byrd. It comprises published monographs, essays, and lectures as well as articles, papers, and abstracts that appear in periodicals, festschriften, and conference proceedings. In their titles, items contain either Byrd's name or the name of a work by him alone, or are wholly about him. Items marked * were overlooked before the publication of the first edition and are therefore included within the checklist for the first time. Those items that do not fulfill the criteria but that make a contribution to Byrd criticism are included in Chapter 3, for which a proportion of the items in the checklist has been selected: see the Author Index.

1826Bm   Burney, Charles. "Memoir of William Birde. (From Dr. Burney's history of music)." *Harmonicon* 4 (1826): 155–57.

1826Wp   Wesley, Samuel. [Proposal to publish, by subscription, SW's transcriptions of antiphons by William Byrd in the Fitzwilliam collection.] 1826.
Note: No copies are known to survive: see Kassler, Michael and Olleson, Philip, *Samuel Wesley (1766–1837): a source book* (Aldershot: Ashgate, 2001), p. 705. *

1860Rp   Rimbault, Edward F. *The pianoforte, its origins, progress, and construction; with some account of instruments of the same class which preceded it; viz. the clavichord, the virginal, the spinet, the harpsichord, etc. to which is added a selection of interesting specimens of music composed for keyed-stringed instruments, by Blitheman, Byrd, Bull, Frescobaldi, Dumont, Chambonnieres, Lully, Purcell, Muffat, Couperin. Kuhnau, Scarlatti, Seb. Bach, Mattheson, Handel, C.P. Emanuel Bach, etc.* London: Cocks, 1860.*

1879Bw [Barrett, William Alexander.] "William Byrde." *Monthly musical record* 9 (1879): 37.
Note: Reprinted from E. Pauer's edition of *Popular pieces* by William Byrde [*sic*], London: Augener, 1879, p. 1. Article forms part of series "Biographies of old English composers. (Reprinted from E. Pauer's collection of old English composers for the virginals and harpsichord.)."

1883Sf Squire, W. Barclay. "A father of music." *Musical review* 1 (1883): 299–300, 317–18, 331–32.

1885Gw Grover, Geo. F. "William Bird." *Musical opinion* 8 (1885): 588.
Note: No XI in the series "Old English musicians."

1886Ao [Anonymous.] "Our music pages." *Monthly musical record* 16 (1886): 129.
Note: Introduction to T 442 which is printed on pp. 131–34.

1887Sl Squire, W. Barclay. "A lost mass by Byrd." *Athenaeum* 3113 i (1887): 841–42.

1889Cf Coleman, Caryl. "A forgotten Catholic: William Byrd, composer and musician." *Catholic world* 49 (1889): 235–39.

1891Ww Whymper, Fred. "William Byrd." *Early English musical magazine* (1891): 76–77.

1897Sw [Squire, William Barclay.] "The will of William Byrd." *Musician* 2 (1897): 77–78.
Note: Anonymous. Author from 1920Bw, p. 18. Part of "Historical notes."

1899Tn Terry, R. "A note on the writing of musical history." *Chord* 1 (1899): 56–58.
Note: Correct attribution of T 117.

1900Rw Runciman, John F. "William Byrde's D minor mass." *Dome* 6 (1900): 157–62.

1900Sw S[quire], W.B. "William Byrd." *Pilot* 1 (1900): 107–09.

1900Tt Terry, Richard. "Tallys, Byrde, and some popular fictions." *Downside review* 19 (1900): 75–81.

1901Be Becker, Oscar. *Die englischen Madrigalisten William Byrd, Thomas Morley und John Dowland.* Leipzig: Seidel, 1901.

1901Rw Runciman, John F. "William Byrde, his mass." In *Old scores and new readings . . . discussions on music and certain musicians.* 2nd ed. London: Unicorn, 1901, pp. 9–16.
Note: Not in 1st ed., 1899; pp. 14–16 repeat pp. 160–62 of 1900Rw.

1910As Arkwright, G.E.P. "The sharpened 'leading-notes' in a cadence." *Musical antiquary* 1 (1910): 126–27.
Note: Refers to T 245. Title of article given elsewhere as "Note on Byrd's 'Psalmes.'"

1914Aw Anderton, H. Orsmond. "William Byrd." *Musical opinion* 37 (1914): 383–84.
Note: Forms basis of Chapter IX "William Byrd" in his *Early English music,* London: Musical Opinion, 1920, pp. 127–36.

1920Bw Bridge, Frederick. "William Byrd, 1542 or 3–1623." In *Twelve good musicians from John Bull to Henry Purcell.* London: Kegan Paul; New York: Dutton, 1920, pp. 11–20.
Note: Chapter II. One of a series of lectures to the University Course, London, 1919–20.

1920Hs Hull, A. Eaglefield. "Some thoughts on modal counterpoint." *Musical opinion* 45 (1920): 144–45, 233–34.
Note: Second part devoted to Byrd. Continues in 1921Hp.

1921Hb Hull, A. Eaglefield. "Byrd's polyphony: modal counterpoint and the canto dato." *Musical opinion* 45 (1921): 693–94.
Note: Continues from 1921Hp. Concludes "more of Byrd later" but no further articles.

1921Hp Hull, A. Eaglefield. "The polyphony of William Byrd: a continuation of the modal counterpoint enquiry." *Musical opinion* 45 (1921): 422–23.
Note: Continues from 1920Hs. Continues in 1921Hb.

1921Tr Terry, R.R. "The resurrection of William Byrd." *Music student* 13 (1921): 429–30.
Note: Article I. Continues in 1923 Tw.

1922Cc   Colles, H.C. "Christmas music. A hint from William Byrd. Carols now and then." *Times* (23 December 1922): 6.
Note: Reprinted in slightly revised form as "A hint from William Byrd" in *Essays and lectures.* London: Oxford University Press, 1945, pp. 128–30.

1922Gs   Grew, Sydney. "Some aspects of William Byrd." *Musical times* 63 (1922): 698–702.

1922Wb   Warner, Sylvia Townsend. "Byrd tercentenary festival, July 1923 [William Byrd, b. 1543, d. 1623]." *British music bulletin* 4 (1922): 153–54.

1923Ab   [Anonymous.] "The Byrd tercentenary." *Musical times* 64 (1923): 545–47.

1923Au   [Anonymous.] "Unus Byrdus." *Tablet* (7 July 1923): 6–7.

1923Aw   [Anonymous.] "William Byrd's house." *Essex chronicle* (6 July 1923): 5.

1923Awi   [Anonymous.] "William Byrd's third centenary." *Living age* 318 (1923): 286.

1923Bt   Bunt, Cyril G.E. "The tercentenary of Byrd." *Graphic* 107 (1923): 980.

1923Cw   [Colles, H.C.] "William Byrd. Centenary celebrations. Their use and abuse." *Times* (30 June 1923): 10.
Note: "By our music critic."

1923COb   Collins, H.B. "Byrd's Latin church music, for practical use in the Roman liturgy." *Music & letters* 4 (1923): 254–60.

1923COOb   Cooper, Gerald. "My Ladye Nevell's booke." *Chesterian* 5 (1923): 236–39.
Note: Section IV of "The Byrd tercentenary (1542–1623)." See also 1923Fb, 1923FUb and 1923Sb.

1923COOl   [Cooper, Gerald.] *List of the music of William Byrd (born 1543–died 1623) obtainable in modern editions, drawn up by the Byrd Tercentenary Committee.* London: Oxford University Press, 1923.
Note: Compiled by Gerald Cooper, according to Reeve in 1987Rw, who also lists the members of the Committee.

1923Dt   Dent, Edward J. "The tercentenary of William Byrd." *Nation and the Athenaeum* 33 (1923): 496, 498.

1923Ew   Eggar, Katharine E. "William Byrd and his times." *Music teacher* 2 (1923): 441–43, 448.

1923Fb   Fellowes, Edmund H. "Byrd's secular vocal music." *Chesterian* 5 (1923): 234–36.
Note: Section III of "The Byrd tercentenary (1542–1623)." See also 1923COOb, 1923FUb and 1923Sb.

1923Fby   Fellowes, E.H. "Byrd's re-discovery. British Music Society congress." *Times* (5 July 1923): 12.
Note: Account of lecture "The music of the Elizabethan period" given previous day in the Aeolian Hall, Bond Street, London.

1923Fw   Fellowes, Edmund H. *William Byrd: a short account of his life and work.* Oxford: Clarendon, 1923. M.
Note: Second edition 1928Fw. Superceded by 1936Fw.

1923Fwi   Fellowes, E.H. "William Byrd 1543–1623." *Music & letters* 4 (1923): 144–48.

1923FUb   Fuller-Maitland, J.A. "Byrd and emotional expression." *Chesterian* 5 (1923): 232–34.
Note: Section II of "The Byrd tercentenary (1542–1623)." See also 1923COOb, 1923Fb and 1923Sb. Author's surname *recte* Fuller Maitland, without hyphen.

1923Gb   Gardner, George. "Byrde and the music of his period: its fitness for church use." *Musical opinion* 47 (1923): 954–55.
Note: The substance of an address given in Hereford Cathedral at the Byrde [*sic*] Centenary on 1 July 1923.

1923Hb   [Hadow, Henry.] "The British Music Society." *Musical times* 64 (1923): 571.
Note: Contains summary of lecture "William Byrd" delivered 2 July, 1923.

1923Ht   Hadow, W.H. "Tercentenary of William Byrd." *New music review and church music review* 22 (1923): 196. *

1923Hw   Hadow, W. Henry. "William Byrd, 1623–1923." *Proceedings of the British Academy* 10 (1921–1923): 395–413.
Note: Delivered 27 April 1923. Twice reprinted:

William Byrd, 1623–1923. British Academy. Annual lecture on aspects of art (including music), Henriette Hertz Trust. London: Oxford University Press, 1923. "William Byrd, 1623–1923" in *Collected essays*. London: Oxford University Press, 1928; reprint ed., Freeport: Books for Libraries, 1968, pp. 41–44.

1923HOt   Holst, Gustav. "The tercentenary of Byrd and Weelkes." *Proceedings of the Musical Society* 49 (1923): 29–37.
Note: Delivered 9 January 1923. Reprinted, abridged and twice summarized:
The tercentenary of Byrd and Weelkes. Leeds: Whitehead and Miller, 1923.
"Byrd and Weelkes. Mr. Gustav Holst on the tercentenary." *Musical news and herald* 64 (1923): 66–67.
Note: Signed J.G.
"Mr. Holst on English music. New factor in technique." *Times* (10 January 1923): 8.
"Byrd and Weelkes." *Musical times* 64 (1923): 199. *

1923HUk   Hull, A. Eaglefield. "The keyboard music of William Byrd." *Musical opinion* 47 (1923): 943–45.

1923HUm   Hull, A. Eaglefield. "Mr. William Byrd (born, 1543; died, 1623)." *Monthly musical record* 53 (1923): 194.
Note: T 442 was music supplement, pp. 207–10.

1923HUmr   Hull, A. Eaglefield. "Mr. Wylliam Byrd" (died July 5, 1623)." *Outlook* 52 (1923): 12–13.
Note: July 5 *recte* 4.

1923Rw   Reeve, E.H.L. "William Byrd, 1543–1623." *Essex review* 32 (1923): 159–70.
Note: 1934Kw is a "footnote" to this article.

1923Sb   Squire, Wm. Barclay. "William Byrd." *Chesterian* 5 (1923): 229–31.
Note: Section I of "The Byrd tercentenary (1542–1623)." See also 1923COOb, 1923Fb and 1923FUb.

1923Tw   Terry, Richard. "William Byrd." *Music teacher* 2 (1923): 613–14, 763–64.
Note: Part II, subtitled "The masses." Continued from 1921 Tr. Concludes "to be continued" but no further articles in this series.

1923Twi   Terry, R.R. "William Byrd (1543–1623)." *Queen* (5 July 1923 supplement): 8.

1923Ws Wesley, Samuel. "Samuel Wesley on Byrd." *Musical times* 64 (1923): 567.

Note: Letter to J.P. Street, 25 May 1830, with introduction.

1923WHw Whitfield, J.L. "William Byrd." *Brentwood diocesan magazine* 2 (1922–23): 121–25.

1923WOw Wortham, H.E. "William Byrd. Tercentenary homage." *Morning post* (4 July 1923): 4.
Note: Reprinted with shortened title: "William Byrd," in *A musical odyssey.* London: Methuen, 1924, pp. 130–31.

1924Bw Butterworth, Walter. "William Byrd." *Manchester Literary Club papers* 50 (1924): 82–94.

1924Fn Flood, Grattan. "A note on Byrd's 'Great Service.'" *Music bulletin* 6 (1924): 372.
Note: Signed G.F. *

1924Wm Warman, Guy. "The memory of William Byrd. Famous Elizabethan composer. Tablet unveiled in Stondon Church. Bishop on the value of good music." *Essex weekly news* (14 March 1924): 5.
Note: Includes text of Bishop Warman's address "God, my Maker, Who giveth songs in the night" (*Job* XXXV, 10).

1925Pb Porte, John F. "Byrd and Elgar." *Chesterian* 7 (1925): 13–16.

1926Bs Borren, Charles van den, "Some notes on 'My Ladye Nevells booke.'" *Musical times* 67 (1926): 1075–76.

1926Fw Flood, W.H. Grattan. "William Byrd." *Musical times* 67 (1926): 994–95.
Note: No XXII in series "New light on late Tudor composers."

1927Hw Howes, Frank. "William Byrd." *Music bulletin* 9 (1927): 149–51.

1928Fw Fellowes, Edmund H. *William Byrd: a short account of his life and work.* 2nd ed. Oxford: Clarendon, 1928.
Note: Reset and corrected version of 1923Fw with additional appendix. Superceded by 1936Fw.

1928Hw Howes, Frank. *William Byrd.* London: Kegan Paul, Trench, Trubner, 1928.
Note: Popular edition [i.e., reissue] 1933Hw. New edition [i.e., reissue] 1978Hw.

1928Jt   Jones, G. Kirkham. "Tudor music–William Byrd." *School music review*
37 (1928): 110–14.

1929Dw   Dent, Edward J. "William Byrd and the madrigal." In *Festschrift fur
Johannes Wolf zu seinem sechzigsten Geburtstage,* edited by Walter Lott et al.
Musikwissenschaftliche Beitrage. Berlin: Breslauer, 1929; reprint ed.,
Hildesheim: Olms, 1978, pp. 24–30.

1929Em   Eggar, Katharine. "'Mr. Bird's Battell.'" *Musical times* 70 (1929):
46–48, 53.

1930Ae   Andrews, Hilda. "Elizabethan keyboard music: My Ladye Nevells
booke, 1591." *Musical quarterly* 15 (1930): 59–71.

1933Hw   Howes, Frank. *William Byrd.* Popular ed. Masters of music. London:
Kegan Paul, Trench, Trubner, 1933.
Note: Reissue of 1928Hw. *

1933Mw   [Manning, W. Westley.] "William Byrd. A newly discovered holo-
graph." *Times* (12 January 1933): 10.
Note: "From a correspondent": author from 1948Fw, p. 40.

1934Fw   Fellowes, E.H. "William Byrd (1543–1623)." In *The heritage of
music,* edited by Hubert J. Foss. Second series. London: Oxford University Press,
1934; reprint ed., Essay index reprint series. New York: Arno, 1971, pp. 1–19.

1934Kw   Knights, E. Spurgeon. "William Byrd and Stondon Massey. A great
musician and his life in Essex." *Essex review* 43 (1934): 31–35.
Note: "Footnote" to 1923Rw.

1935Tw   Terry, Richard Runciman. "William Byrd, born 1543, died 4 July
1623." In *Lives of the great composers,* edited by A.L. Bacharach. London:
Gollancz, 1935, pp. 39–57.
Note: Reissue, vol.1: *From Byrd to Mozart and Haydn. The classics.* Pelican
books, 90. Harmondsworth: Penguin, 1942; reissues, West Drayton: Penguin,
1943 and 1947; *The music masters, including "Lives of the great composers."*
Vol.1: *From the sixteenth century to the time of Beethoven.* Dublin: Fridberg,
1948, pp. 79–93; *The music masters.* Vol.1: *From the sixteenth century to the time
of Beethoven.* Pelican books, A383. Harmondsworth: Penguin, 1957, pp. 85–99.

1936Br   Byrd, William. *Reasons briefely set downe by th'auctor, to perswade
every one to learne to sing.* Oxford: Venables, 1936.
Note: Single sheet with hand-colored illustration. *

1936Fw   Fellowes, Edmund H. *William Byrd*. London: Oxford University Press, 1936.
Note: Second edition 1948Fw.

1937Ew   Elvin, Laurence and Slater, Gordon. "William Byrd." *Lincolnshire magazine* 3 (1937): 160–65.
Note: Section I "His life" pp. 160–62 by Elvin. Section II "His music" pp. 163–65 by Slater. Article forms part of series "Lincolnshire worthies."

1937Fg   [Fellowes, Edmund H.] "A great composer. William Byrd's place in music. Cramb Lectures in Glasgow." *Glasgow herald* (17 December 1937): 14.
Note: Summarizes sixth of ten Cramb Lectures, University of Glasgow, 1937–38, delivered 16 December 1937.

1937Ls   Lee, E. Markham. "The student-interpreter. Old English harpsichord pieces: Arne, Dupuis, Hayes and Byrd." *Musical opinion* 60 (1937): 407–08. *

1937Mb   Maine, Basil. "Byrd's music for voices." *Choir* 28 (1937): 147–48.
Note: Based largely on excerpts from 1937Mw.

1937Mw   Maine, Basil. "William Byrd." In *The glory of English music*. London: Wilmer, 1937, pp. 22–38.
Note: Revision of one of a series of lectures, University of London, 1936.

1938Ho   Henderson, A.M. "Old English keyboard music (Byrd to Arne)." *Proceedings of the Musical Association* 64 (1938): 85–95.
Note: Delivered 29 March 1938.

1940Tk   Tuttle, Stephen D. "The keyboard music of Tallis and Byrd." *Bulletin of the American Musicological Society* 4 (1940): 31–32.
Note: Abstract of paper read before New England Chapter, 21 January 1938.

1941Wb   Whittaker, W. Gillies. "Byrd's Great Service." *Musical quarterly* 27 (1941): 474–90.

1942Fw   Fellowes, E.H. "William Byrd: 1542–1623." *Listener* 28 (1942): 637.
Note: Introduction to six programs of Byrd's music to be broadcast 17, 19, 23, and 26 November and 1 and 3 December 1942.

1942Wb   Whittaker, W. Gillies. "Byrd's and Bull's 'Walsingham' variations." *Music review* 3 (1942): 270–79.

1943Ce   Colles, H.C. *Edmund H. Fellowes, author and musicologist: about the author, by Dr. H.C. Colles, tributes to the author, his books and editions of music–with special reference to the quater-centenary of William Byrd 1543–1623*. London: Oxford University Press, 1943. *

1943Kw   King, A. Hyatt. "William Byrd (1543–1623)." *Apollo* 38 (1943): 77–78.

1943Lw   [Lowery, H.] "William Byrd, 1543–1623." *Journal of the South-West Essex Technical College and School of Art* 1 (1943): 125–29.
Note: Substance of address given 8 April 1943 by College Principal.

1943Nw   Neilson, Francis. "William Byrd (1542-43–1623): 'father of musicke.'"*American journal of economics and sociology* 2 (1943): 274–77.
Note: Reprinted in *The roots of our learning: eleven essays*. New York: Robert Schalkenbach Foundation, 1946, pp. 197–204, with minor alterations, principally to layout. *

1943Ww   Westrup, J.A. "William Byrd (1543–1623)." *Music & letters* 24 (1943): 125–30.

1943WIw   Willan, Healey. "William Byrd: choral work." *Canadian review of music and art* 2 (August/September 1943): 8–9. (III.Ww) *

1944Fb   Fellowes, E.H. "Byrd and the mass." *Listener* 32 (1944): 53.
Note: Introduction to broadcast 19 July 1944.

1946Bd   Beswick, Delbert M. "The dominant seventh chord in the works of William Byrd (1542–1623)." *Proceedings of the Music Teachers' National Association* 40 (1946): 156–66.

1948Bp   Byrd, William. *The pleasure of singing*. New York: Coq d'or, 1948.
Note: Broadside. *

1948Fw   Fellowes, Edmund H. *William Byrd*. 2nd ed. London: Oxford University Press, 1948.
Note: First edition 1936Fw. Reprinted 1953, 1963, 1967 and 1974.

1949Fm   Fellowes, Edmund H. "My Ladye Nevells booke." *Music & letters* 30 (1949): 1–7.

1950Db   Dart, Thurston. "A background to Byrd's chamber music." *Listener* 43 (1950): 264.
Note: Introduction to two recitals 15 and 16 February 1950.

1951Cd   Cox, David. "'Dear Mr William Byrd. . . . '" *Music* 2 (1951): 121–27.

1951Fw   Fellowes, E.H. "William Byrd." In *Eight concerts of music by English composers, 1300–1750,* edited by Ian MacPhail. Festival of Britain 1951: London season of the arts. London: Arts Council of Great Britain, 1951, pp. 44–48.
Note: Essay with program of sixth concert, Wigmore Hall, London, 13 June 1951.

1952Pb   Palmer, William. "Byrd's alleluias." *Music & letters* 33 (1952): 322–28.

1952Pw   Palmer, William. "Word-painting and suggestion in Byrd: an essay in tribute to the late Edmund H. Fellowes." *Music review* 13 (1952): 169–80.

1953Pb   Palmer, William. "Byrd and amen." *Music & letters* 34 (1953): 140–43.

1954Sl   Shaw, Watkins. "List of 54 Latin works by William Byrd available in separate form." In *From Tallis to Tomkins: a survey of church music, c. 1550-c. 1650.* Church Music Society occasional papers, 22. London: Oxford University Press, 1954, pp. 15–17.
Note: Appendix.

1955As   Attwell, Geoffrey. "Stondon's master of music." *Essex countryside* 4 (1955): 59.

1955Ew   Emmison, F.G. "William Byrd and the Essex Justices." *Essex review* 64 (1955): 186–87.

1955Gn   Gardner, John. "A new solution of Byrd's 'Non nobis.'" *Musical times* 96 (1955): 155.

1957Bw   Brown, David. "William Byrd's 1588 volume." *Music & letters* 38 (1957): 371–77.

1957Ww   Wright, N. Fowler. "William Byrd–the musical recusant." *Catholic choirmaster* 43 (1957): 153–54, 177.

1958Pw   Pickersgill, Ronald S. "William Byrd and Harlington." *Middlesex quarterly and London County review* 6 (1958): 372.

1959Za   Zimmerman, Franklin B. "Advanced tonal design in the part-songs of William Byrd." In *Bericht uber den siebenten Internationalen Musikwissenschaftlichen Kongress Koln 1958,* edited by Gerald Abraham et al. Kassel: Barenreiter, 1959, pp. 322–26.

1960Bb Boalch, Donald. "Byrd's mass for five voices." *Chesterian* 35 (1960): 53–56.

1960Ds Dart, Thurston and Brett, Philip. "Songs by William Byrd in manuscripts at Harvard." *Harvard library bulletin* 14 (1960): 343–65.

1961Kb Kerman, Joseph. "Byrd's motets: chronology and canon." *Journal of the American Musicological Society* 14 (1961): 359–82.

1961St Shaw, Watkins. "A textual problem in Byrd: a purely accidental matter." *Musical times* 102 (1961): 230–32.
Note: Response in 1961Wb.

1961Wb Westrup, J. A. "Bach, the Bible, and Byrd." *Musical times* 102 (1961): 288–89.
Note: No.6 in series "Personal view." Response to 1961St.

1962At Andrews, H. K. "Transposition of Byrd's vocal polyphony." *Music & letters* 43 (1962): 25–37.

1962Mw Milsome. J. R. "William Byrd: the great Elizabethan musician of Stondon Place." *Essex countryside* 10 (1962): 306.

1963Ap Andrews, H. K. "Printed sources of William Byrd's 'Psalmes, sonets and songs.'" *Music & letters* 44 (1963): 5–20.

1963Jl Jackman, James L. "Liturgical aspects of Byrd's *Gradualia*." *Musical quarterly* 49 (1963): 17–37.

1963Ko Kerman, Joseph. "On William Byrd's *Emendemus in melius*." *Musical quarterly* 49 (1963): 431–49.
Reprinted in *Chormusik und Analyse: Beitrage zur Formanalyse und Interpretation mehrstimmiger Vokalmusik,* edited by Heinrich Poos. Mainz: Schott, 1983, Bd 1, pp. 155–69; Bd 2, pp. 65–68.
Reprinted with revisions in *Hearing the motet: essays on the motet of the Middle Ages and Renaissance,* edited by Dolores Pesce. New York: Oxford University Press, 1997, pp. 329–47.

1964Ap Andrews, H. K. "The printed part-books of Byrd's vocal music: the relationship of bibliography and musical scholarship." *Library* 19 (1964): 1–10.
Note: Read before the Bibliographical Society, 18 February 1964.

1965Ow   O'Leary, J. G. "William Byrd and his family at Stondon Massey." *Essex recusant* 7 (1965): 18–23.

1966At   Andrews, H. K. *The technique of Byrd's vocal polyphony.* London: Oxford University Press, 1966.
Note: New edition [i.e., reissue] 1980At.

1966Cp   Clulow, Peter. "Publication dates for Byrd's Latin masses." *Music & letters* 47 (1966): 1–9.

1966Fs   Franks, Alfred. "'The Stondon Shakespeare of music.'" *Essex country-side* 14 (1966): 504–05.

1966Kb   Kerman, Joseph. "Byrd, Tallis, and the art of imitation." In *Aspects of medieval and Renaissance music: a birthday offering to Gustave Reese,* edited by Jan LaRue. New York: Norton, 1966; London: Dent, 1967; reprint ed., Festschrift series, 2. New York: Pendragon, 1978, pp. 519–37.
Reprinted with revisions in *Write all these down: essays on music.* Berkeley: University of California Press, 1994, pp. 90–105.

1966Nb   Northcote, Sydney. *Byrd to Britten: a survey of English song.* London: Baker, 1966.

1967Aw   [Anonymous.] "William Byrd." *Hillingdon mirror* (17 October 1967): 16–17.
Note: Forms part of series "Famous people of the borough."

1967Nn   Neighbour, Oliver. "New consort music by Byrd." *Musical times* 108 (1967): 506–08.

1967Sw   Shaw, Watkins. "William Byrd of Lincoln." *Musical & letters* 48 (1967): 52–59.

1968Aw   Arnold, Denis. "William Byrd: an outsider in the high Renaisance." *Listener* 80 (1968): 121–22.
Note: Introduction to Promenade concert containing four of Byrd's motets broadcast 30 July 1968.

1968Gm   Gray, Walter. "Motivic structure in the polyphony of William Byrd." *Music review* 29 (1968): 223–33.

1968Sm   Sharp, Geoffrey. "Master of music—and of compromise: William Byrd." *Church music* 2 (1968): 4–6.

1969Bm   Brown, Alan. "'My Lady Nevell's book' as a source of Byrd's keyboard music." *Proceedings of the Royal Musical Association* 95 (1968–69): 29–39.
Note: Delivered 7 January 1969.

1969Gs   Gray, Walter. "Some aspects of word treatment in the music of William Byrd." *Musical quarterly* 55 (1969): 45–64.

1970Ab   Abravanel, Claude and Hirschowitz, Betty. *The Bible in English music: W. Byrd–H. Purcell.* Americans for a Music Library in Israel. Studies in music bibliography, 1. Haifa: Haifa Music Museum, 1970.
Note: "The Bible in the works of William Byrd," by Claude Abravanel, pp. 7–12.

1970Gi   Gossiper. "It's music all the way—from William Byrd to Neville Marriner." *Lincolnshire echo* (29 September 1970): 4.

1970Hp   Hudson, Frederick. "The performance of William Byrd's church music. I. Music acceptable in the Anglican Church." *American choral review* 12 (1970): 147–59.
Note: Part II 1972HUp.

1970Rw   Robertson, Alec. "William Byrd and the Gradualia." *Church music* 3 (1970): 9–11.

1970Sh   [Squire, William Barclay.] "Historians record this Lincs. son 'father of musicke.'" *Lincolnshire echo* (18 September 1970): 8.
Note: Squire's entry about Byrd from, most recently, *Encyclopaedia Britannica,* 14th ed., 1929, with short introduction.

1971Lg   Lam, Basil. "The greatest English composer." *Listener* 85 (1971): 25.
Note: Introduction to broadcast of T 197, 12 January 1971.

1971Mt   Milsome, Elissa. "The troubled life of William Byrd, great Essex musician." *Essex countryside* 19 (April 1971): 46–47.

1971Nn   Neighbour, Oliver. "New keyboard music by Byrd." *Musical times* 112 (1971): 657–59.

1971NIi   Niessink, Richard."An introduction to a fantasia by William Byrd." *Clavier* 10 (1971): 29–31.
Note: Article forms part of series "Music of the Renaissance." Text of T 452 pp. 21–28.

1971Sw   [Sherwood, P.T.] "William Byrd and Harlington." *Journal of the Hayes and Harlington Local History Society* 4 (1971): 5.
Note: Anonymous: author's name from correspondence.

1971Wc   Worrall, E.C. and Briggs, Nancy. "The church courts in action against William Byrd." *Essex recusant* 13 (1971): 88–89.

1972Bb   Bernard, M. "'Byrd's association with the Catholics.'" *Essex recusant* 14 (1972): 63–65.

1972BRd   Brett, Philip. "Did Byrd write 'Non nobis, Domine'?" *Musical times* 113 (1972): 855–57.
Note: Extracted from A xvi pp. vi-ix with short introduction and a few additions.

1972BRw   Brett, Philip. "Word-setting in the songs of Byrd." *Proceedings of the Royal Musical Association* 98 (1971–72): 47–64.
Note: Delivered 16 February 1972.

1972Dw   Davidson, Alan. "William Byrd's brother: a query." *Essex recusant* 14 (1972): 66–70.

1972Hb   Holst, Imogen. *Byrd.* The great composers. London: Faber; New York: Praeger, 1972.

1972HUp   Hudson, Frederick. "The performance of William Byrd's church music. II. Music for the Catholic rites." *American choral review* 14 (1972): 3–13.
Note: Part I 1970Hp.

1973Bw   Buck, P. C. et al. "William Byrd." In *Short biographical notes and description of manuscript sources for the Tudor English church music series, Kalmus volumes 6649–6728.* New York: Kalmus, 1973, pp. 5–14.
Note: Originally published in D ii pp. xi–xx.

1973Ff   Fenlon, Iain. "Father of British music." *Music and musicians* 22 (September 1973): 42–44.

1973Hb   Henderson, Robert. "Byrd's place in English music." *Daily telegraph* (14 July 1973): 9.

1973Kw   Kerman, Joseph. "William Byrd, 1543–1623." *Musical times* 114 (1973): 687–90.

1973Lm   Lam, Basil. "Master of grief." *Listener* 89 (1973): 874.

Note: Introduction to a program commemorating the 350th anniversary of William Byrd's death, broadcast on 3 July 1973.

1973Mw   Milsome, Elissa. "William Byrd, great Essex musician." *Essex countryside* 21 (October 1973): 33.

1974Bk   Brown, Alan. "Keyboard music by Byrd 'upon a plainsong.'" *Organ yearbook* 5 (1974): 30–39.

1974Sb   Sharp, Geoffrey B. *Byrd & Victoria.* Novello short biographies. Borough Green: Novello, 1974.

1975Ko   Kerman, Joseph. "Old and new in Byrd's Cantiones sacrae." In *Essays on opera and English music in honour of Sir Jack Westrup,* edited by F. W. Sternfeld et al. Oxford: Blackwell, 1975, pp. 25–43.

1975Mb   Monson, Craig. "Byrd and the 1575 Cantiones sacrae." *Musical times* 116 (1975): 1089, 1091; 117 (1976): 65–67.

1975Rb   Roberts, Anthony. "Byrd's other conceite." *Musical times* 116 (1975): 423–27.

1976Aw   [Anonymous.] "William Byrd: musician." *Essex recusant* 18 (1976): 90.

1977Km   Koopman, Ton. "'My Ladye Nevell's booke' and old fingering." *English harpsichord magazine* 2 (1977): 5–10.

1978Hw   Howes, Frank. *William Byrd.* New ed. Westport: Greenwood, 1978. Note: Reissue of 1928Hw.

1978HYt   Hynson, Richard. "The two choral styles of William Byrd." *Choral journal* 19 (December 1978): 20–22.

1978Nc   Neighbour, Oliver. *The consort and keyboard music of William Byrd.* The music of William Byrd, 3. London: Faber; Berkeley: University of California Press, 1978. Note: Paperback edition 1984Nc.

1979Hb   Henderson, Robert. "Byrd and the English Church." *Daily telegraph* (3 February 1979): 11.

1979Kb   Kerman, Joseph. "Byrd's settings of the ordinary of the mass." *Journal of the American Musicological Society* 32 (1979): 408–39.
Note: Body of article excerpted from Chapter 4 of 1981Km.

1979Kw   Kerman, Joseph. "William Byrd and the Catholics." *New York review of books* 26 (17 May 1979): 32–36.
Note: Version of Annual Faculty Research Lecture, University of California at Berkeley, 1978.
Reprinted with revisions as "William Byrd and English Catholicism" in *Write all these down.* Berkeley: University of California Press, 1994, pp. 77–89.

1979Mp   Monson, Craig. "The Preces, Psalms and Litanies of Byrd and Tallis: another 'virtuous contention in love.'" *Music review* 40 (1979): 257–71.

1979MOe   Morin, Elisabeth. *Essai de stylistique comparee. (Les variations de William Byrd et John Tomkins sur "John come kiss me now.")* Semiologie et analyse musicales. Montreal: Les Presses de l'Universite de Montreal, 1979.

1980At   Andrews, H.K. *The technique of Byrd's vocal polyphony.* New ed. Westport: Greenwood, 1980.
Note: Reissue of 1966At.

1980Be   Brett, Philip. "Editing Byrd." *Musical times* 121 (1980): 492–95, 557–59.

1980Rc   Russell, Lucy Hallman. "A comparison of the 'Walsingham' variations by Byrd and Bull." In *Bericht uber den Internationalen Musikwissenschaftlichen Kongress, Berlin 1974,* edited by Hellmut Kuhn and Peter Nitsche. Kassel: Barenreiter, 1980, pp. 277–79.

1981Bh   Brett, Philip. "Homage to Taverner in Byrd's masses." *Early music* 9 (1981): 169–76.
Note: Expanded version of A iv pp. vi-ix.

1981Km   Kerman, Joseph. *The masses and motets of William Byrd.* The music of William Byrd, 1. London: Faber; Berkeley: University of California Press, 1981.
Note: Chapter 4 substantially excerpted in 1979Kb.

1981KNp   Knight, Ellen E. "The praise of musicke: John Case, Thomas Watson, and William Byrd." *Current musicology* 30 (1981): 37–51.

1981Mt   Monson, Craig. "Through a glass darkly: Byrd's verse service as reflected in manuscript sources." *Musical quarterly* 67 (1981): 64–81.

1981St   Sargent, Brian. "Two Byrd anthems." *Music teacher* 60 (March 1981): 13, 15.
Note: Forms part of series "Set works for 'O' level."

1982Ds   Dolmetsch, Nathalie. "Shakespeare and dancing . . . the essential pavan for which music by William Byrd is reproduced . . ." *Dancing times* 72 (1982): 584–85.

1982Ma   Monson, Craig. "Authenticity and chronology in Byrd's church anthems." *Journal of the American Musicological Society* 35 (1982): 280–305.

1982Ol   Olsson, Milton *and* Nelson, Charles. "A Latin high mass in Upper Michigan." *Sacred music* 109 (December 1982): 11–14.

1983Tb   Turbet, Richard. "Byrd on record." *Brio* 20 (1983): 41–45.

1983Ti   Turbet, Richard. " The influence of Byrd and his contemporaries on twentieth century British music." *British Music Society newsletter* 19 (1983): 14–15.

1983Tt   Turbet, Richard. "Tallis and Byrd." *Musical opinion* 106 (1983): 301.

1984Bm   Bartlett, Clifford. "Musicology and the performer." *Early music news* 76 (1984): 14–15.

1984Gw   Gould, Glenn. "William Byrd and Orlando Gibbons." In *The Glen Gould reader,* edited by Tim Page. New York: Knopf, 1984; London: Faber, 1987, pp. 11–13. *

1984Kw   Kerman, Joseph. "William Byrd." In Reese, Gustave et al. *The new Grove high Renaissance masters.* The new Grove composer biography series. London: Macmillan; New York: Norton, 1984, pp. 229–88.
Note: Revised version of entry in *The new Grove dictionary of music and musicians.* London: Macmillan, 1980.

1984Mt   Morehen, John. "The Tallis/Byrd 'Cantiones sacrae' (1575): an appraisal of current methodology in computer-assisted analysis." In *Informatique et musique: session musicologique de l'International Computer Music Conference, Paris, 1984,* edited by Helene Charnasse. Publications Elmeratto. Ivry sur Seine: Eratto, 1984, pp. 59–76. *

1984Nc   Neighbour, Oliver. *The consort and keyboard music of William Byrd.* London: Faber, 1984.
Note: Paperback edition of 1978Nc.

1984Oc   Owens, Jessie Ann. "Charles Butler: a key to the music of William Byrd." In *Abstracts of papers read at the fiftieth annual meeting of the American Musicological Society meeting jointly with the Society for Music Theory,* edited by Anne Dhu Shapiro and Peter Breslauer. Philadelphia: American Musicological Society, 1984, pp. 40–41. *

1984Tc   Turbet, William [*recte* Richard]. "Composer Byrd among the world's greatest." *Essex countryside* 32 (November 1984): 50–51.

1985Be   Brett, Philip. *Editing Renaissance music: The Byrd edition.* Chicago: Renaissance English Text Society, 1985. *

1985Pb   Pacey, Robert. "Byrd's keyboard music: a Lincolnshire source." *Music & letters* 66 (1985): 123–26.

1985Tb   Turbet, Richard. "Byrd's recusancy reconsidered." *Music & letters* 66 (1985): 51–52.

1985To   Turbet, Richard. "Organ music by William Byrd (1542/3–1623)." *BIOS journal* 9 (1985): 20–27.
Note: See also letter, 10 (1986): 132.

1985Tw   Turbet, Richard. "William Byrd." *Aberdeen University review* 51 (1985): 219–25.
Note: An abridged version of a paper "William Byrd: what he composed and why" given to Aberdeen University Renaissance Seminar 26 April 1983.

1985Twr   Turbet, Richard. "Writings about Byrd's consort music: a bibliographical note." *Consort* 41 (1985): 74–75.

1985Ww   Woodward, Daphne. "William Byrd, 1543–1623." In *Essex composers,* edited by Daphne Woodward. Chelmsford: Essex Libraries, 1985, pp. 10–16.

1986Ht   Harris, David. "Two Elizabethan lute masterpieces by John Dowland (1563–1626) & William Byrd (1543–1623)." *Guitarra* 12.68 (1986): 4–9. *

1986Sw   Sargent, Brian. "William Byrd: mass for five voices." *Music teacher* 65 (April 1986): 19. *

1986Tb   Turbet, Richard. "Byrd, Birmingham and Elgar." *British Music Society newsletter* 31 (1986): 1.
Note: Revised version 1989Tb.

1986Ti   Turbet, Richard. "I am weary of my groaning: a hitherto unpublished round attributed to Morley or Byrd." *British Music Society journal* 8 (1986): 10–11.
Note: See also 9 (1987): inside front cover.

1986Tl   Turbet, Richard. "Lincoln, Lincolnshire and William Byrd." *Society for Lincolnshire History and Archaeology newsletter* 50 (1986): 3–4.

1987Bc   Bazzana, Kevin. "La conciliation dans la musique de William Byrd." *Sonances* 6 (juillet 1987): 24–28. (II.Bc)

1987Mt   Moroney, Davitt. "'Thinking and pondering' about Byrd . . . on two recent books." *Musical times* 128 (1987): 18–20.

1987Rw   Reeve, Edward Henry Lisle. "The William Byrd tercentenary," in 1987Tw, pp. 303–16. (XII.Rw)

1987Tf   Turbet, Richard, ed. "The full original text of the Queen's Majesty's Letters Patent to Thomas Tallis and William Byrd for the printing of music," in 1987Tw, pp. 325–27. (XI.Tf)

1987Tw   Turbet, Richard. *William Byrd: a guide to research.* Garland composer resource manuals, 7; Garland reference library of the humanities, 759. New York: Garland, 1987.
Note: First edition of present volume.

1987Ww   Winch, Nicholas. "William Byrd." *Pastoral Music newsletter* (June/July 1987): 3–5.

1987WOa   Wood, Anthony. "Anthony Wood's notes on Byrd," in 1987Tw, pp. 329–33. (I.WOa)

1988Br   [Beechey, Gwilym.] "Reasons briefly set down . . . 1588." *Consort* 44 (1988): 2–7.

1988Pb   Patton, John and Turbet, Richard. "Byrd in British cathedrals, 1986." *Musical opinion* 111 (1988): 52–59. (XII.PAb)

1988Th   Turbet, Richard. "Homage to Byrd in Tudor verse Services." *Musical times* 129 (1988): 485–90. (VI.Th)

1989Bw   [Beechey, Gwilym.] "William Byrd 1589." *Consort* 45 (1989): 1–3.

1989Hw   Howard, Michael. "William Byrd: an account of his life and work." In Day, Timothy. *A discography of Tudor church music.* London: British Library, 1989, p. 313.
Note: Abstract of talk, with note of source.

1989Tb   Turbet, Richard. "Byrd, Birmingham and Elgar." *Elgar Society journal* 6 (1989): 7–8.
Note: Revised version of 1986Tb.

1989Tby   Turbet, Richard. "Byrd and Clemens non Papa." *Musical times* 130 (1989): 129. (V.Tb)
Note: Letter amplifying point made in 1988Th.

1989Tw   Turbet, Richard. "William Byrd: Lincoln Cathedral's greatest musician." *Lincolnshire life* 29 (October 1989): 63.

1990Bm   Banks, Janet. "Mr Byrd's musical feast." *Radio times* (23 December 1989–5 January 1990): 128.

1990Dm   Duncan-Jones, Katherine. "'Melancholie times': musical recollections of Sidney by William Byrd and Thomas Watson." In *The well enchanting skill: music, poetry, and drama in the culture of the Renaissance: essays in honour of F.W. Sternfeld,* edited by John Caldwell, Edward Olleson and Susan Wollenberg. Oxford: Clarendon, 1990, pp. 171–80. (VII.DUm)

1990Ip   Irving, John. "Penetrating the preface to *Gradualia*." *Music review* 51 (1990): 157–66. (V.Ip)

1990Tb   Turbet, Richard. "A Byrd miscellany." *Fontes artis musicae* 37 (1990): 299–302. (VI.Tby)

1990Tc   Turbet, Richard. "Continuing Byrd." *Musical times* 131 (1990): 544. (V.Tc)

1990Tg   Turbet, Richard. "The Great Service: Byrd, Tomkins and their contemporaries and the meaning of 'great.'" *Musical times* 131 (1990): 275–77. (VI.Tg)

1990Tw   Turbet, Richard. "William Byrd and the English musical renaissance." *British Music Society newsletter* 45 (1990): 123–24. (XII.TUw)

1991Fp   Fawkes, Richard. "Protest songs: were there coded messages in Byrd's sacred works?" *Classical music* (23 March 1991): 33.

1991FUw   Fulton, Kenneth and McCord, Dawn H. "William Byrd's music and its use within the Anglican rite." *American organist* 25 (January 1991): 62–69.

1991Hw   Harrison, Christopher. "William Byrd and the Pagets of Beaudesert: a musical connection." *Staffordshire studies* 3 (1990–91): 51–63. (I.HAw)

1991Iw   Irving, John. "Words and music combined: some questions of text-music integration in Byrd's masses." *Music review* 52 (1991): 267–78. (V.Iw)

1991Nb   Norris, David Owen. "Byrd's alman." *Keyboard classics* 11.5 (1991): 40–41.

1992B   Brown, Alan and Turbet, Richard, eds. *Byrd studies*. Cambridge: Cambridge University Press, 1992. (II.BROb)
Note: Contains essays by le Huray, Rees, Morehen, Wulstan, Monson, Kerman, Bennett, Irving, Gaskin, Hunter, Neighbour, and Greenhalgh: see below. Reissue 1999B.

1992BEb   Bennett, John. "Byrd and Jacobean consort music: a look at Richard Mico." In 1992B, pp. 129–40. (IX.Bb)

1992Gb   Gaskin, Hilary. "Baldwin and the Nevell hand." In 1992B, pp. 159–73. (X.Gb)

1992GRb   Greenhalgh, Michael. "A Byrd discography." In 1992B, pp. 202–64. (XI.Gb)
Note: Supplements in 1996Gb and Chapter 4.

1992Hm   Hunter, Desmond. "My Ladye Nevells booke and the art of gracing." In 1992B, pp. 174–92. (X.HUm)

1992Ib   Irving, John. "Byrd and Tomkins: the instrumental music." In 1992B, pp. 141–58. (VIII.Ib)

1992Iw   Irving, John. "William Byrd and the three-part ayres of Thomas Holmes." *Brio* 29 (1992): 71–77. (IX.Iw)

1992Kw   Kerman, Joseph. "'Write all these down': notes on a Byrd song." In 1992B, pp. 112–28. (VII.Kw)
Reprinted with revisions in *Write all these down* [see 1966Kb], pp. 106–24.

1992Ls   le Huray, Peter. "Some thoughts about cantus firmus composition; and a plea for Byrd's Christus resurgens." In 1992B, pp. 1–23. (V.Ls)

1992Mt   Monson, Craig. "'Throughout all generations': intimations of influence in the short Service styles of Tallis, Byrd and Morley." In 1992B, pp. 83–111. (VI.Mt)

1992MOb   Morehen, John. "Byrd's manuscript motets: a new perspective." In 1992B, pp. 51–62. (V.MORb)

1992Ns   Neighbour, Oliver. "Some anonymous pieces considered in relation to Byrd." In 1992B, pp. 193–201. (X.Ns)

1992Pg   Pike, Lionel. "The Great Service: some observations on Byrd and Tomkins." *Musical times* 133 (1992): 421–22. (VI.Pg)

1992Re   Rees, Owen. "The English background to Byrd's motets: textual and stylistic models for Infelix ego." In 1992B, pp. 24–50. (V.Re)

1992Sw   Stern, David. "William Byrd: Mass for Five Voices." In *Music before 1600,* edited by Mark Everist. Models of musical analysis. Oxford: Blackwell, 1992, pp. 208–24. (V.STw)

1992Tb   Turbet, Richard. "Byrd throughout all generations." *Cathedral music* 35 (1992): 19–24. (XII.TUbyrdth)

1992Tg   Turbet, Richard. "The Great Service: a postscript." *Musical times* 133 (1992): 206. (VI.Tgr)

1992Th   Turbet, Richard, "Horsley's 1842 edition of Byrd and its infamous introduction." *British music* 14 (1992): 36–46. (V.Th)

1992Tm   Turbet, Richard. "'Melodious Birde': the solo songs of William Byrd." In *Aspects of British song,* edited by Brian Blyth Daubney. Upminster: British Music Society, 1992, pp. 10–14. (VII.TUm)

1992Wb   Wulstan, David. "Birdus tantum natus decorare magistrum." In 1992B, pp.63–82. (IV.Wb)

1993Bp   Brett, Philip. "Pitch and transformation in the Paston manuscripts." In *Sundry sorts of music books: essays on the British Library collections, presented to O.W. Neighbour on his 70th birthday,* edited by Chris Banks, Arthur Searle and Malcolm Turner, London: British Library, 1993, pp. 89–118. (III.Bp)
Note: Originally considered for submission to *Byrd studies* (1992B).

1993BRw Brown, Alan. "'The woods so wild': notes on a Byrd text." In *Sundry sorts of music books* [see 1993Bp], pp. 54–66. (X.BRwo)

1993Df Darton, Ruth. *"A father of musick": an exhibition to mark the 450th anniversary of the birth of William Byrd 1543–1623*. London: University of London Library, 1993.
Note: Exhibition catalogue.

1993Ju Jones, Stephen and Turbet, Richard. "Unknown ground." *Musical times* 134 (1993): 615–16. (VI.JONu)

1993Lo Lindley, Simon. "Of Byrd, bargains and banter." *Church music quarterly* 123 (July 1993): 16–17.

1993Mb Milsom, John. "Byrd on record: an anniversary survey." *Early music* 21 (1993): 446–50. (See "A note on recommended recordings" in Chapter 4, *infra.*)

1993Mc Milsom, John. "Composer of the month: William Byrd, 1543–1623." *BBC music magazine* 2 (November 1993): 47–50.

1993MOb Moroney, Davitt. "'Bounds and compasses': the range of Byrd's keyboards. In *Sundry sorts of music books* [see 1993Bp], pp. 67–88. (X.Mb)

1993Nc Northcott, Bayan. "A Catholic outlaw in his own country." *Independent* (3 April 1993): 31. (I.Nc)

1993Pb Phillips, Peter. "Byrd's nest." *Musical times* 134 (1993): 628–31.

1993PRc Procter, Michael. "Composer of the year: William Byrd 1543–1623." *Early music yearbook* 1 (1993): xi.

1993Rw Rowland-Jones, Anthony. "William Byrd, for the 450th anniversary of his birth: some thoughts on a familiar three-part consort." *Recorder magazine* 13 (1993): 52–54. (IX.ROw)

1993Sk Schulenberg, David L. "The keyboard works of William Byrd: some questions of attribution, chronology, and style." *Musica disciplina* 47 (1993): 99–121. (X.Sk)

1993Tf Turbet, Richard. "The fall and rise of William Byrd 1623–1901." In *Sundry sorts of music books* [see 1993Bp], pp. 119–28. (XII.TUf)

1993Tm   Turbet, Richard. "Mr Byrd will never die." *International Association of Music Libraries, Archives and Documentation Centres United Kingdom Branch newsletter* 25 (1993): 16–18.
Note: "Mr Byrd: corrigendum and addendum," 26 (1994): 8.

1993Tmy   Turbet, Richard. "'My ancient and much reverenced master': two anthems by Byrd and Tomkins." *Choir & organ* 1 (November 1993): 15–18. (VI.Tm)

1993Tw   Turbet, Richard. *William Byrd, 1543–1623: Lincoln's greatest musician.* Lincoln: Honywood, 1993. (II.Tw)
Note: Second edition 1999Tw.

1993Ww   Westover, Catherine. "William Byrd and his time." *Viola da Gamba Society of Great Britain newsletter* 82 (1993): 6–9. (II.Ww)

1994Df   Darton, Ruth. "'A father of musick': an exhibition on William Byrd." *FULLview* 12 (1994): 4–5.
Note: Report on 1993Df.

1994Gg   Grainger, Percy. "Grainger lectures on Byrd." *British Music Society news* 62 (1994): 39.
Note: Transcription of short talk on Pearl CD, GEMM 9013.

1994Tb   Turbet, Richard. "Byrd at 450." *Brio* 31 (1994): 96–102. (XII.TUbyr)

1994Tm   Turbet, Richard. "Mr Byrd will never die–part 2." *International Association of Music Libraries, Archives and Documentation Centres United Kingdom Branch newsletter* 27 (1994): 37.
Note: Discographical supplement to 1993Tm.

1994Tt   Turbet, Richard. *Tudor music: a research and information guide, with an appendix updating William Byrd: a guide to research.* Music research and information guides, 18; Garland reference library of the humanities, 1122. New York: Garland, 1994. (XI.Ttu)

1994Tu   Turbet, Richard. "A unique Byrd arrangement." *Early Music Forum of Scotland newsletter* 6 (1994): [15–16]. (IX.Tu)

1995A   *Annual Byrd newsletter.* Nos 1–10. Wyton: King's Music, 1995–2004. (I.A)

1995Hb   Holdsworth, Donald. "Broadcast Choral Evensong: survey of Byrd's music performed." *Annual Byrd newsletter* 1 (1995): 6.

1995HUs   Hunter, Desmond. "Some preliminary thoughts on tempo in virginalist music by Byrd." *Annual Byrd newsletter* 1 (1995): 5–6. (X.HUs)

1995Np   Nasu, Teruhiko. "The publication of Byrd's *Gradualia* reconsidered." *Brio* 32 (1995): 109–20. (V.Np)

1995Ss   Smith, David. "Some stylistic correspondences between the keyboard music of Byrd and Philips: an introductory note." *Annual Byrd newsletter* 1 (1995): 7–8. (X.SMs)

1995Tb   Turbet, Richard. "Byrd 450: a review of events." *Early Music Forum of Scotland newsletter* 9 (1995): 4–6. (XII.TUb)

1995Tby   Turbet, Richard. "Byrd and Tomkins: the Great Service revisited." *Leading notes* 9 (1995): 10–11. (VI.Tb)

1995Tbyr   Turbet, Richard. "Byrd, Weelkes and verse Services." *Annual Byrd newsletter* 1 (1995): 5. (VI.Tbyr)

1995Tf   Turbet, Richard. "Francis Neilson, F.W. Dwelly and the first complete edition of Byrd." *Bulletin of the John Rylands University Library of Manchester* 77 (Summer 1995): 53–58. (XII.TUfr)

1995Tp   Turbet, Richard. "Postscript." *Annual Byrd newsletter* 1 (1995): 4. (VI.Tp)

1996Dm   Dixon, Jon. "Multum in parvo IV." *Musical times* 137 (1996): 32–36.

1996Gb   Greenhalgh, Michael. "A Byrd discography supplement." *Brio* 33 (1996): 19–54. (XI.Gby)

1996Hb   Harley, John and Turbet, Richard. "Byrd: *Haec est dies.*" *Early music review* 21 (1996): 16. (V.Hb)

1996Mw   Mateer, David. "William Byrd, John Petre and Oxford, Bodleian MS Mus. Sch. E. 423." *Royal Musical Association research chronicle* 29 (1996): 21–46. (XI.Mw)

1996MIt   Milsom, John. "Tallis, Byrd and the "incorrected copy": some cautionary notes for editors of early music printed from movable type." *Music & letters* 77 (1996): 348–67. (V.MIt)

1996MOi   Morehen, John. "Is 'Byrd's' *Haec* a fake?" *Early music review* 24 (1996): 8–9. (V.MORi)

1996Tw   Thompson, Robert. "William Byrd and the late 17th century." *Annual Byrd newsletter* 2 (1996): 10–12. (XII.Tw)

1996TUb   Turbet, Richard. "Byrd's music at Lincoln: a supplementary note." *Annual Byrd newsletter* 2 (1996): 9. (XII.TUbyrd)

1996TUc   Turbet, Richard. "The Carnegie Trust and Byrd's music in the 1920s." *Annual Byrd newsletter* 2 (1996): 9. (XII.TUc)

1996TUm   Turbet, Richard. "A model from Byrd." *Choir & organ* 4 (July 1996): 13–15. (V.Tmo)

1996Wb   Wulstan, David. "Byrd, Tallis and Ferrabosco." In *English choral practice, 1400–1650,* edited by John Morehen. Cambridge: Cambridge University Press, 1996, pp. 109–42. (IV.Wby)

1997Be   Banks, Paul and Turbet, Richard. "Early printed source of Byrd at the Britten-Pears Library." *Annual Byrd newsletter* 3 (1997): 7. (V.Be)

1997Hi   Harley, John. "In search of Byrd's London." *Annual Byrd newsletter* 3 (1997): 9–10. (I.Hi)

1997Hw   Harley, John. *William Byrd, Gentleman of the Chapel Royal.* Aldershot: Scolar, 1997. (I.Hwi)
Amended reprint and paperback edition, 1999Hw.

1997Kb   Kemp, Lindsay. "Byrd 'the beautiful.'" *Gramophone* 75 (September 1997): 22.

1997Mw   Mateer, David. "William Byrd's Middlesex recusancy." *Music & letters* 78 (1997): 1–14. (I.Mw)

1997MOb   Monson, Craig. "Byrd, the Catholics, and the motet: the hearing reopened." In *Hearing the motet: essays on the motet in the Middle Ages and Renaissance,* edited by Dolores Pesce. New York: Oxford University Press, 1997, pp. 348–74. (V.MOb)

1997Oh   Ota, Diane O. and Turbet, Richard. "Heathen poets." *Annual Byrd newsletter* 3 (1997): 7. (VII.Oh)

1997Rw   Rastall, Richard. "William Byrd: Fifth Pavan reconstructed for viols." *Annual Byrd newsletter* 3 (1997): 11. (IX.Rw)

1997Rwi   Rastall, Richard. "William Byrd's string fantasia 6/g1." In *Liber amicorum John Steele: a musicological tribute,* edited by Warren Drake. Festschrift series, 16. Stuyvesant: Pendragon, 1997, pp. 139–70. (IX.Rwi)

1997Su   Staines, Joe. "Uncaging Byrd." *Classic CD* 91 (November 1997): 80–81.

1997Tb   Turbet, Richard. "Byrd & Ivor Gurney." *Annual Byrd newsletter* 3 (1997): 7. (XII.TUby)

1997Th   Turbet, Richard. "Holst's editions of Byrd." *International Association of Music Libraries, Archives and Documentation Centres United Kingdom Branch newsletter* 33 (1997): 7–8. (XI.Tho)

1997Tho   Turbet, Richard. "Homage to Fayrfax." *Annual Byrd newsletter* 3 (1997): 6–7. (III.Th)

1997Tp   Turbet, Richard. "Pauer's edition of Byrd." *Annual Byrd newsletter* 3 (1997): 6. (X.Tp)

1997Tw   Turbet, Richard. "W. Sterndale Bennett — Fugue on Byrd's *Bow Thine ear.*" *Annual Byrd newsletter* 3 (1997): 12. (XII.TUws)

1997Twi   Turbet, Richard. "Wings of faith: Richard Turbet uncovers a close relationship between Services by William Byrd and John Sheppard." *Musical times* 138 (December 1997): 5–10. (VI.Tw)

1998Hb   Harley, John. "Byrd's semidetached keyboard fantasia." *Annual Byrd newsletter* 4 (1998): 10. (X.Hby)

1998Hn   Harley, John. "New light on William Byrd." *Music & letters* 79 (1998): 475–88. (I.Hn)

1998Je   James, Peter. "*Exalt Thyself, O God:* the rediscovery of Byrd's festive anthem." *Annual Byrd newsletter* 4 (1998): 9–10. (VI.Je)

1998Mb   MacMillan, James. "Byrd's Mass for Four Voices." *Annual Byrd newsletter* 4 (1998): 5.

1998Tb Turbet, Richard. "Byrd tercentenary keyboard anthologies: an appendix to Routh." *Annual Byrd newsletter* 4 (1998): 10–11. (X.Tb)

1998Tby Turbet, Richard. "Byrds at Brightwell." *Annual Byrd newsletter* 4 (1998): 5. (I.Tb)

1998Tc Turbet, Richard. "Coste not Byrd." *Annual Byrd newsletter* 4 (1998): 4. (VI.Tc)

1998Tm Turbet, Richard. "More early printed editions attributed to Byrd." *Brio* 35 (1998): 105. (XI.TUm)

1998W *William Byrd Festival.* US–Portland, OR, 1998–. (XII.W)
Note: Annual program.

1999B Brown, Alan and Turbet, Richard, eds. *Byrd studies.* Cambridge: Cambridge University Press, 1999. (II.BROb)
Note: Reissue of 1992B, transferred to digital printing.

1999BOe Bolingbroke, Douglas. "English Catholics in the time of Byrd." *Annual Byrd newsletter* 5 (1999): 4–5. (I.BOe)

1999BRc Brett, Philip and Smith, Jeremy. "Computer collation of divergent early prints in The Byrd edition." *Computing in musicology* 12 (1999–2000): 251–60. (XI.Bc)

1999BUc Buckley, David. "A comparison of William Child's *Sing we merrily* with William Byrd's *Sing joyfully.*" *Annual Byrd newsletter* 5 (1999): 8–9. (VI.BUc)

1999Hw Harley, John. *William Byrd, Gentleman of the Chapel Royal.* Aldershot: Scolar, 1997 rev. 1999. (I.Hwi)
Note: Amended reprint and paperback edition of 1997Hw.

1999Iw Irving, John. "William Byrd and Thomas Tomkins's Offertory: (re-) evaluating text and context." *Annual Byrd newsletter* 5 (1999): 10–12. (VI.Iw)

1999Kb Kemp, Lindsay. "A Byrd in the can." *Gramophone* 77 (October 1999): 18–19.

1999Mt May, Katharine. "Top flight." *Early music today* (October/November 1999): 18–19.

1999Nf   Northcott, Bayan. "The first genius of the keyboard." *Independent* (1 October 1999): 19. (X.NOf)

1999Sb   Smith, David J. "Byrd reconstructed: in search of consort models for keyboard dances by Byrd." *Annual Byrd newsletter* 5 (1999): 6–8. (VIII.Sb)

1999SMf   Smith, Jeremy L. "From "rights to copy" to the "bibliographic ego": a new look at the last early edition of Byrd's 'Psalmes, sonets and songs.'" *Music & letters* 80 (1999): 511–30. (VII.Sf)

1999Tw   Turbet, Richard. *William Byrd, 1540–1623: Lincoln's greatest musician.* Rev. ed. Lincoln: Honeywood, 1999. (II.Tw)
Note: Second edition of 1993Tw.

2000Hb   Harley, John. "Byrd the farmer." *Annual Byrd newsletter* 6 (2000): 6. (I.Hb)

2000Hw   Harley, John. "William Byrd and his social circle." *Early music performer* 7 (2000): 4–9. (I.Hw)

2000HOh   Howells, Herbert. "Herbert Howells' notes on Byrd." *Annual Byrd newsletter* 6 (2000): 7–8.

2000Km   Kerman, Joseph. "Music and politics: the case of William Byrd (1540–1623)." *Proceedings of the American Philosophical Association* 144 (2000): 275–87. (V.KEm)

2000Pb   Parlett, Graham. "Byrd and Bax." *Annual Byrd newsletter* 6 (2000): 8–11. (XII.Pb)

2000PAf   Payne, Ian. "'The first that ever he made': Byrd's First Pavan and Galliard, and techniques of transcription and reconstruction in the 'lost' consort dances." *Chelys* 28 (2000): 28–58.

2000Rb   Robins, Brian. "The Byrd sanctuary." *Gramophone early music* 1.4 (2000): 12–14.

2000Tb   Turbet, Richard. "Byrd tercentenary dinner." *Annual Byrd newsletter* 6 (2000): 6. (XII.TUbyrdt)

2000Tby   Turbet, Richard. "Byrd sleevenotes." *Annual Byrd newsletter* 6 (2000): 12. (XI.Tb)

2000Tbyr   Turbet, Richard. "Byrd's music in provincial imprints from 1770 to the present, with special reference to H.B. Collins." In *Branches of literature and music: proceedings of the thirteenth Seminar on the History of the Provincial Book Trade held in Bristol, 11–13 July 1995,* edited by M.T. Richardson. Bristol: University of Bristol Library, 2000, pp. 64–74. (XI.Tby)

2000Tj   Turbet, Richard. "Jubilate for Mr Bird's Service." *Annual Byrd newsletter* 6 (2000): 12. (XII.TUj)

2001Bb   Bartlett, Clifford. "Byrd, Bach, Handel & the press." *Early music review* 69 (2001): 24–25.

2001Ci   Carwood, Andrew. "An inimitable inheritance." *Choir & organ* 9.1 (2001): 46–49. (IV.Ci)

2001Db   Dirksen, Pieter. "Byrd and Sweelinck: some cursory notes." *Annual Byrd newsletter* 7 (2001): 11–20. (X.Db)

2001Js   James, Peter. "The significance of Byrd's verse compositions: a reappraisal." *Annual Byrd newsletter* 7 (2001): 7–10. (VI.Js)

2001Ks   Keller, Arne. "Some observations on R134 of the Herlufsholm Collection, with proposed identifications of owners and compilers: a new source for Byrd's *In resurrectione.*" *Annual Byrd newsletter* 7 (2001): 10–11. (V.Ks)

2001KEb   Kerman, Joseph. "The Byrd Edition—in print and on disc." *Early music* 29 (2001): 109–18. (XI.Kb)

2001Mt   Morehen, John. "Thomas Snodham, and the printing of William Byrd's *Psalmes, songs, and sonnets* (1611)." *Transactions of the Cambridge Bibliographical Society* 12 (2001): 91–131. (XI.Mt)

2001Sb   Skinner, David. "Byrd." *Goldberg* 14 (2001): 22–33.

2001Th   Turbet, Richard. "H.B. Collins's editions of Byrd: a supplementary note." *Annual Byrd newsletter* 7 (2001): 6. (XI.Th)

2002Bw   Bossy, John. "William Byrd investigated, 1583–84." *Annual Byrd newsletter* 8 (2002): 5–7. (I.BOSw)

2002Hb   Harley, John. "Byrd's 'Catholic' anthems." *Annual Byrd newsletter* 8 (2002): 8–9. (VI.Hb)

2002Hby   Harley, John. "Byrd's friends the Ropers." *Annual Byrd newsletter* 8 (2002): 9–10. (I.Hby)

2002Mm   McCarthy, Kerry. "Music for all seasons: the Byrd *Gradualia* revisited." *Sacred music* 129 (2002): 5–12. (V.MCm)

2002To   Turbet, Richard. "Ordinary Byrd: masses and preces." *Annual Byrd newsletter* 8 (2002): 4–5. (IV.To)

2002Tr   Turbet, Richard. "Recommended recordings of music by Byrd." *International Association of Music Libraries, Archives and Documentation Centres United Kingdom Branch newsletter* 42 (2002): 10–11.

2002Ts   Turbet, Richard. "Stopped by the outbreak of war: the Byrd Festival of 1914." *Brio* 39 (Spring/Summer 2002): 24–25. (XII.TUs)

2002Tt   Turbet, Richard. "Two early printed attributions to Byrd in the Wighton Collection, Dundee." *Annual Byrd newsletter* 8 (2002): 10–13. (XI.TUt)

2003Cl   Charlton, Alan. "*Look and bow down:* a 21st century compositional response." *Annual Byrd newsletter* 9 (2003): 13–19. (XII.Cl)

2003Hw   Humphreys, David. "Wilder's hand?" *Musical times* 144 (Summer 2003): 4. (VII.HUw)

2003Mw   McCoy, Stewart. "William Byrd's *Lullaby:* an example of contemporary intabulation." *Annual Byrd newsletter* 9 (2003): 10–13. (VII.Mw)

2003MIb   Milsom, John. "Byrd, Sidney, and the art of melting." *Early music* 31 (2003): 437–48. (VII.MIb)

2003Nb   Neighbour, Oliver. "Byrd's treatment of verse in his partsongs." *Early music* 31 (2003): 413–22. (VII.Nb)

2003Np   Neighbour, Oliver. "Philip Brett, 1937–2002." *Annual Byrd newsletter* 9 (2003): 20. (XII.Np)
Note: Reprinted as "In memoriam Philip Brett, 1937–2002: a great friend of the William Byrd Festival, to whom this year's Festival is dedicated," in *William Byrd Festival, August 18–31, 2003,* pp. 2–3, Portland, OR, U.S.A.

2003Ow   Olleson, Philip. "'William Byrde's excellent antiphone': Samuel Wesley's projected edition of selections from *Gradualia.*" *Annual Byrd newsletter* 9 (2003): 7–9. (XII.Ow)
Note: *Recte* "antiphones."

2003Sw   Smith, Mike. "'Whom Music's lore delighteth': words-and-music in Byrd's *Ye sacred Muses.*" *Early music* 31 (2003): 425–35. (VII.SMw)

2003Th   Turbet, Richard. "A hymn attributed to Byrd." *Annual Byrd newsletter* 9 (2003): 5. (VI.Thy)

2003Tu   Turbet, Richard. "The unique first edition of Byrd's *Gradualia* in York Minster Library," in *Music librarianship in the United Kingdom: fifty years of the United Kingdom Branch of the International Association of Music Libraries, Archives and Documentation Centres,* ed. Richard Turbet. Aldershot: Ashgate, 2003, pp. 137–40. (V.Tu)

2003Wc   Weaver, Geoff. "Choral masterclass: *Sing joyfully* by William Byrd." *Church music quarterly* 161 (2003): 36–37. (VI.Wc)

2004Bw   Bankes, William. "William Byrd and the Statute of Uses: some thoughts on land tenure during his lifetime." *Annual Byrd newsletter* 10 (2004): 15–16. (I.Bw)

2004Gc   Goodwin, Christopher. "A candidate lyric for Byrd's *The maidens songe.*" *Annual Byrd newsletter* 10 (2004): 19–26. (X.GOc)
Note: See also Turbet, Richard. "More on a Byrd source" [letter], *Early music review* 100 (2004): 24.

2004Ha   Harley, John. "Alice and Hester Cole, nees Byrd." *Annual Byrd newsletter* 10 (2004): 6–7. (I.Ha)

2004Hl   Harley, John. "Look and bow down." *Annual Byrd newsletter* 10 (2004): 4–6. (VII.Hl)

2004HUw   Hugill, Robert. "What sound? Robert Hugill asks some questions about the music of William Byrd." *Music & vision* (1 January 2004): <http://www.mvdaily.com/articles/2004/01/Byrd1.htm> (V.HUw)

2004HUMw   Humphreys, David. "Wilder and Byrd: Wilder's *Aspice Domine a6*." *Annual Byrd newsletter* 10 (2004): 26–28. (V.HUMw)

2004Mb   McCarthy, Kerry. "Byrd's English music: conference: *The English-texted music of William Byrd*, University of Leeds, 11 September 2004." *Early music* 32 (2004): 640-41. (Chapter 6)

2004Mn   McCarthy, Kerry. "Byrd, Augustine, and *Tribue, Domine*." *Early music* 32 (2004): 569-76. (V.MCn)

2004Mno   McCarthy, Kerry. "'Notes as a garland': the chronology and narrative of Byrd's *Gradualia*." *Early music history* 23 (2004): 49–84. (V.MCno)

2004Pb   Pike, Lionel. "Byrd's 'echo' fantasias?" *Annual Byrd newsletter* 10 (2004): 7–10. (IX.Pb)

2004PIb   Pinto, David. "Byrd and Ferrabosco, a generation on." *Annual Byrd newsletter* 10 (2004): 10–14. (IX.PIb)

2004Sb   Smith, Mike. "Bawdry, balladry, Byrd." *Annual Byrd newsletter* 10 (2004): 16–19. (VII.SMb)

2004Te   Turbet, Richard. "Early printed editions of Byrd: an addendum and a checklist of articles." *Annual Byrd newsletter* 10 (2004): 16. (XI.Te)

2004Tj   Turbet, Richard. "J. Guggenheim as music publisher: Tallis and Byrd restored." *Brio* 41 (Spring/Summer 2004): 49–52. (VI.Tj)

2004Tjo   Turbet, Richard. "Joyful singing: Byrd's music at a royal christening." *Musical times* 145 (Spring 2004): 85–86. (VI.Tjo)

2004Tm   Turbet, Richard. "Macfarren's organ parts for Byrd's Latin music." *Annual Byrd newsletter* 10 (2004): 16. (V.Tm)

2005Hm   Harley, John. "'My Ladye Nevell' revealed." *Music & letters* 86 (2005): 1–15. (X.Hm)

3

Classified Annotated Bibliography

I

BIOGRAPHY AND FAMILY HISTORY

I.A   *Annual Byrd newsletter.* Nos 1–10. Wyton: King's Music, 1995–2004.

The first and only periodical devoted to an early English composer. Each issue contains an annotated list of all new writings about Byrd, forthcoming research, significant new recordings (reviewed if copies submitted), miscellaneous news, and a few short scholarly papers. Published as supplements to the June issues of *Early music review.* See Chapter 5; see also Chapter 6 concerning reissue.

I.Ac   Ashbee, Andrew and Harley, John, eds. *The cheque books of the Chapel Royal, with additional material from the manuscripts of William Lovegrove and Marmaduke Alford.* 2v. Aldershot: Ashgate, 2000.

All the references to Byrd occur in the "Old cheque book" (see index to volume one, p. 363). Sets Byrd in the context of the Chapel Royal's activities during the reigns of Elizabeth I and James I.

I.Ar   Ashbee, Andrew. *Records of English court music.* 9v. Snodland: Ashbee, 1986–91; Aldershot: Scolar, 1992–96.

Volumes IV (covering 1603–25) and VI (1558–1603) contain many indexed items for Byrd concerning matters not discussed elsewhere. Note, for instance, the account for mourning livery for the funeral of Queen Anne, wife of King James, on 13 May 1619 (not 1618 as stated elsewhere), when Byrd was seventy-nine.

I.Bw   Bankes, William. "William Byrd and the Statute of Uses: some thoughts on land tenure during his lifetime." *Annual Byrd newsletter* 10 (2004): 15–16.

Describes how Byrd benefitted from the law.

I.BOe   Bolingbroke, Douglas. "English Catholics in the time of Byrd." *Annual Byrd newsletter* 5 (1999): 4–5.

Unravels the complexities of whether Byrd spent his life in perpetual fear of persecution as a member of a Catholic group. This article is essential reading for an understanding of the religious environment in which Byrd lived and functioned.

I.BOSw   Bossy, John. "William Byrd investigated, 1583–84." *Annual Byrd newsletter* 8 (2002): 5–7.

Reveals how seriously Byrd was under suspicion as a collaborator in the treasonable conspiracy known as the Throckmorton Plot. Includes first published transcription of letter to Charles Paget from W:B, thought to be Byrd and probably part of the original dossier against him.

I.BOWEm Bowers, Roger. "Music and worship to 1640," in *A history of Lincoln Minster,* ed. Dorothy Owen. Cambridge: Cambridge University Press, 1994, pp. 47–76.

Pages 65–68 cover Byrd's career in Lincoln. Valuable for setting Byrd's career in the context of the history of the music in Lincoln Minster (or Cathedral), and for placing the music within the history of the Cathedral itself.

I.Cm   Charles, Amy M. "Mrs. Herbert's kitchin booke." *English literary renaissance* 4 (1974): 164–73.

Notes Byrd among the guests for dinner in 1601 at the house of Magdalen Herbert, mother of, *inter alia,* the future poet George Herbert.

I.CLv   Clayton, Janet. "A visit to Old Thorndon Hall." *Annual Byrd newsletter* 4 (1998): 11–12.

Archaeological observations on a home of the Petre family where Byrd had a chamber. The house was demolished, but the site is visible. See plates 1 and 2. See also I.WAo.

I.Dg   Dawson, Giles E. "A gentleman's purse." *Yale review* 39 (1949–50): 631–46.

Anecdotal review of the account book of William Petre. dedicatee of T 496. The composer is mentioned only twice in the article.

I.Fa   Finnis, John and Martin, Patrick. "Another turn for the turtle: Shakespeare's intercession for love's martyr." *Times literary supplement* (18 April 2003): 12–14.

In attempting to interpret (successfully) the poem by Shakespeare which has been given the title "The phoenix and the turtle" the authors suggest that "The bird of loudest lay" refers to Byrd as composer of T 25. In so doing they make a case for a hitherto elusive link between Byrd and Shakespeare, which in this instance would run via Byrd's patron Worcester and Shakespeare's patron Southampton who are known to have been well acquainted. See also Gerald Kilroy's letter, May 2003, page 17.

I.Ha   Harley, John. "Alice and Hester Cole, nees Byrd." *Annual Byrd newsletter* 10 (2004): 6–7.

More information about members of Byrd's immediate family.

I.Hb   Harley, John. "Byrd the farmer." *Annual Byrd newsletter* 6 (2000): 6.

Newly discovered document relating to property maintenance.

I.Hby   Harley, John. "Byrd's friends the Ropers." *Annual Byrd newsletter* 8 (2002): 9–10.

Further investigations into Byrd's influential social connexions.

I.Hi   Harley, John. "In search of Byrd's London." *Annual Byrd newsletter*
            3 (1997): 9–10.

            A walk round Byrd sites in the cities of London and Westminster.

I.Hj   Harley, John. "The Judd memorial." *Annual Byrd newsletter* 6
            (2000): 7.

            Suggests Judd family may have been part of Byrd's social circle, and
            ponders whether Byrd knew of the painting in question and if its
            imagery and inscriptions formed part of his mental equipment.

I.Hn   Harley, John. "New light on William Byrd." *Music & letters* 79
            (1998): 475–88.

            Supplements information in 1997Hw, some of it summarized on
            p. xvi of the the amended reprint and paperback edition of I.Hwi.

I.Hs   Harley, John. "Symond Byrd's inventory." *Annual Byrd newsletter* 4
            (1998): 6–7.

            Transcribes inventory drawn up after the death in 1578 or 1579 of
            the elder of William's brothers, listing the contents of his house in
            Brightwell, Berkshire (now Oxfordshire). See also two corrigenda
            among "Miscellany," *Annual Byrd newsletter* 5 (1999): 3.

I.Hw   Harley, John. "William Byrd and his social circle." *Early music per-
            former* 7 (2000): 4–9.

            Further biographical information supplementing I.Hn and I.Hwi.

I.Hwi   Harley, John. *William Byrd, Gentleman of the Chapel Royal.* Alder-
            shot: Scolar, 1997; amended repr. and paperback ed., 1999.

                1: London and Westminster 1540–1562

                2: Lincoln 1563–1572

                3: Clerkenwell and Westminster 1572–c.1576

                4: Harlington 1577–1594

                5: Stondon Massey 1594–1623

6: Sources and chronology of Byrd's music

7: Earliest vocal music

8: Instrumental music with cantus firmi

9: Early music for the Anglican church

10: Early instrumental works without cantus firmi

11: The first "sacred songs"

12: Motets of the middle period

13: Motets: style and development

14: Instrumental works of the middle period

15: Secular songs of the middle period

16: Anglican music of the middle period

17: Masses

18: Gradualia

19: Later vocal and instrumental music

Postscript

Appendix A: The Byrd family

Appendix B: Byrd's children

Appendix C: Wills

Appendix D: Byrd's handwriting

Appendix E: William Byrd and St Paul's

Appendix F: Byrd's portrait

Appendix G: My Ladye Nevells booke

Appendix H: Catalogue of Byrd's works

On its original publication in 1997, this monograph prompted all relevant works of reference to be revised. Such is the significance of the author's biographical discoveries, it is no longer necessary to refer to any other writings specifically about Byrd's life, apart from those by Harrison, Kerman, Mateer, and Shaw (on Lincoln) listed below. The most notable of these discoveries was that Byrd was born somewhat earlier than had been thought, but the book contains much more besides that concerning himself and his family. For this reason, its first five chapters are the most important to have been written about his life.

Not many new monographs about a composer can have produced so much new biographical information. Chapter 1 fairly teems with it. We are introduced to Byrd's family from its known origins in fourteenth-century Essex, with increasing detail up to his brothers and sisters. Harley then follows this with his revelation about the year of Byrd's birth and confirms his place of birth beyond all reasonable doubt as London, even whittling this down to two possible parishes. He goes on to discuss the careers of William's elder brothers Symond and John at St Paul's Cathedral, a topic which had recently become the focus of some gallant though misdirected scholarship which, thanks to Harley, narrowly avoided getting into print. Moving on to informed speculation about William's own early training, he devotes the rest of the chapter to more information about Byrd's siblings.

Chapter 2 supplements the information in Shaw's seminal article about the composer in Lincoln (see the list of recommended articles at the end of this section) with more biographical material. The title of Chapter 3 confronts the possibility that Byrd lived in these two places, offering more substantial evidence for the latter, which Harley supports with the fruits of further biographical research. This was also a time when Byrd's interest in property began to make a stir, and when the queen awarded Tallis and him their famous patent for printing music and lined music paper.

There has always been irrefuteable evidence that Byrd fetched up in Harlington by 1577. It was here that the recusancy of the composer and his family comes to the fore, and in Chapter 4 Harley focuses on this while retaining his sights on the other activities of the family in business, property, patronage, and employment: in William's case, the Chapel Royal.

Byrd spent the last thirty years of his long life with members of his family at the village of Stondon Massey in rural Essex. Chapter 5 is the last of this sequence of astonishing chapters, and besides attempting to elucidate Byrd's legal affairs and transactions in property, Harley continues to deliver biographical discoveries, such as the identity of Byrd's putative second "wife" and more about his family, patrons, recusancy, and relationship with the Chapel Royal.

Uniquely in a single review of Byrd's musical corpus, it is studied chronologically. The concise but informative titles of the fourteen chapters make it clear to the reader precisely what is under discussion and where it fits into the broader picture. The objective and analytical narrative judiciously makes use of the researches of other writers about Byrd where this is appropriate (scrupulously acknowledged), announcing the fruits of the author's own researches where these provide new insights or supercede previous writings.

The minute Chapter 6 on sources and chronology prepares the way for the succeeding thirteen chapters on Byrd's music itself. Chapters 7 to 11 deal with Byrd's earliest music in the various genres in which he composed. Using copious illustrations, Harley seeks to discover the origins and inspiration for Byrd's work in each of these spheres, and to describe how his work develops and matures until he becomes his own man. Chapters 12 to 17 unemotionally describe the fruitful and tumultuous middle period in which the mature and confident Byrd is setting theologically contentious texts while also singlehandedly creating modern keyboard technique and sensibility with his series of pavans and variations. The two final chapters confront the *Gradualia* and the late instrumental music in which Byrd's thoughts and technique are distilled, leading Harley in his Postscript to ponder soberly what gives this music such preeminence. The appendices elucidate, expand, and illustrate much of what has gone before, adding to our knowledge of Byrd and his world. In a subsequent article X.Hm, Harley added significantly to the information in Appendix G. This monograph is consciously a successor to, and replacement for, the deservedly famous study by Fellowes, 1948Fw.

See also I.Hn, I.Hw, and "John Byrd: a correction," *Annual Byrd newsletter* 7 (2001): 6.

I.HAw   Harrison, Christopher. "William Byrd and the Pagets of Beaudesert: a musical connection." *Staffordshire studies* 3 (1990–91): 51–63.

Investigates whether Byrd was dangerously linked to Catholic conspirators through his friendship with the Paget family. In pursuance
of this, the author reproduces all or part of eight hitherto unpublished
letters from the early Paget correspondence, 1573–81. Of these, one
is from Byrd himself, offering further evidence of his movements
after leaving Lincoln in 1572; five mention him; and one mentions
music. The author concludes that Byrd was possibly more closely
connected with active Catholic conspiracy than had previously been
thought, but further evidence is necessary. For the letters alone this is
a most important article in Byrd biography.

I.Mw   Mateer, David. "William Byrd's Middlesex recusancy." *Music & letters* 78 (1997): 1–14.

            Full account of the legal documentation concerning the recusancy of
            Byrd and his family when resident in Harlington. Concludes that
            they were not punished as heavily as they might have been, and
            points out possible musical implications of Byrd's actions.

I.MCd   McVeigh, S.A.J. *Drayton of the Pagets.* West Drayton: West Drayton
            & District Local History Society, 1970.

            Useful background about a part of Byrd's social circle.

I.Nc   Northcott, Bayan. "A Catholic outlaw in his own country." *Independent* (3 April 1993): 31.

            "Celebrates the still-mysterious genius of William Byrd."

I.Pi   Peacham, Henry. "Impresa's. To Maister William Bird, the glory of
            our nation for musique. Epigram 97." In *Thalias banquet: furnished
            with an hundred and odde dishes of newly devised epigrammes,
            whereunto (beside many worthy friends) are invited all that love in
            offensive mirth, and the Muses.* London: Constable, 1620, sig. [C5]v.

            According to the *The shorter Oxford English dictionary,* an impresa
            is "The sentence accompanying an emblem; hence, a motto, maxim,
            proverb." In the title of Peacham's book, the words *in offensive*
            should form one word.

I.PUo   Purser, John. "On the trail of the spies." *Scotlands* 5 (1998): 23–44.

Suggests that Byrd and William Kinloch may have been in contact as Roman Catholic spies, noting passages in common in their keyboard music and drawing on other musical and biographical material.

I.Ss   Shaw, Watkins. *The succession of organists of the Chapel Royal and the cathedrals of England and Wales from c.1538, also of the organists of the collegiate churches of Westminster and Windsor, certain academic choral foundations, and the cathedrals of Armagh and Dublin.* Oxford studies in British church music. Oxford: Clarendon, 1991.

Important for having established the date when Robert Parsons died (two years later than thought previously) and when Byrd left Lincoln to succeed him, almost immediately rather than after a hiatus of two years, in the Chapel Royal. Valuable for placing Byrd in the broadest possible context of his fellow organists.

I.SMg   Smith, Alan. "The Gentlemen and Children of the Chapel Royal of Elizabeth I: an annotated register." *Royal Musical Association research chronicle* 5 (1965): 13–46.

Provides circumstantial evidence that Byrd may have been a countertenor.

I.Tb   Turbet, Richard. "Byrds at Brightwell." *Annual Byrd newsletter* 4 (1998): 5.

Provides biographical details concerning close members of Byrd's family in the parish records of this Berkshire (from 1974 Oxfordshire) village.

I.Wt   Wadmore, J.F. "Thomas Smythe, of Westenhanger, commonly called Customer Smythe." *Archaeologia Cantiana* 17 (1874): 193–208.

Biography of the master of Symond Byrd, the elder of William's brothers. Contains reference to John, his other (also older) brother.

I.WAo   Ward, Jennifer C. and Marshall, Kenneth. *Old Thorndon Hall.* Essex Record Office publications, 61. Chelmsford: Essex County Council, 1972.

Description of Petre family residence, no longer standing, where Byrd is known to have stayed. See plates 1 and 2. See also I.CLv.

I.WOa   Wood, Anthony. "Anthony Wood's notes on William Byrd," in Tur-
            bet, Richard. *William Byrd: a guide to research*. Garland composer
            resource manuals, 7; Garland reference library of the humanities,
            759. New York: Garland, 1987, pp. 329–33.

            Transcription, with introduction and editorial notes, of earliest
            attempt at a biography of Byrd. The editor draws attention to differ-
            ing opinions as to the dates of Wood's writings.

            Recommended items from the first edition:

            9: Reeve, E.H.L. *Stondon Massey, Essex*. Colchester: Wiles, 1900.

            20: Shaw, Watkins. "William Byrd of Lincoln." *Music & letters* 48
                (1967): 52–59.

            25: Johnson, Ian. "Shaking off the dust — walks in recusant Essex,
                no.1." *Essex recusant* 29 (1978): 19–24.

            26: Kerman, Joseph. "William Byrd and the Catholics." *New York
                review of books* 26 (17 May 1979): 32–36; reprinted with
                updated endnotes as "William Byrd and English Catholicism," in
                Write all these down: essays on music. Berkeley: University of
                California Press, 1994, pp. 77–89.

II

BYRD'S MUSIC IN GENERAL

II.Ar   Atlas, Alan W. *Renaissance music: music in western Europe,
            1400–1600*. The Norton introduction to music history. New York:
            Norton, 1998.

            Contains a section devoted to Byrd within the second of two substan-
            tial chapters on Tudor music. Written before the publication of I.Hwi
            so some facts about Byrd are out of date, but shows awareness of his
            status and position in contemporary music. Good bibliographies.

II.Bc   Bazzana, Kevin. "La conciliation dans la musique de William Byrd."
            Sonances 6 (juillet 1987): 24–28.

"Comme tous les grands compositeurs, Byrd a culmine, invente et anticipe." Suggests that Byrd assimilated the full range of contemporary compositional techniques so effectively that he was able to reconcile the musical and social extremities of his own day in a manner that has transcended time and place.

II.BRm Bray, Roger, ed. *Music in Britain: the sixteenth century.* The Blackwell history of music in Britain, 3. Oxford: Blackwell, 1995.

Contains numerous references to Byrd throughout. (In John Morehen's discussion of T 197 on page 344, the reference to Morley's *Best* (or *First*) *Service* being in "some York Minster manuscripts" should refer to *GB-Drc* MS E 11a.)

II.BROb Brown, Alan and Turbet, Richard, eds. *Byrd studies.* Cambridge: Cambridge University Press, 1992; reissued 1999.

Consists of twelve essays covering all the genres of Byrd's output. The writers offer between them a wide variety of approaches to the music. Some of the conclusions are controversial or revisionist. As a celebration of what was then thought to be the 450th anniversary of his birth, the essays consolidate Byrd research to that time, and indicate future directions. See IV.Wb, V.Ls, V.MORb, V.Re, VI.Mt, VII.Kw, VIII.Ib, IX.Bb, X.Gb, X.HUm, X.Ns and XI.Gb. Related correspondence in *GB-Au* MS 3469.

II.Co Caldwell, John. *The Oxford history of English music.* Vol. 1: *From the beginnings to c.1715.* Oxford: Clarendon, 1991.

Supercedes all previous histories of English music. Chapters 4–8 deal comprehensively with all aspects of the Tudor period, and it is valuable to be able to appreciate, from surrounding chapters, the continuum within which Tudor music evolved, and what it in turn became. Illustrations are good, the bibliography less so. Caldwell's judgments are judicious throughout. He endeavours to mention as many significant musicians as possible without allowing his narrative to degenerate into a mere list. All aspects of Byrd's music are discussed cogently.

II.COl Cooke, Deryck. *The language of music.* London: Oxford University Press, 1959.

Suggests that certain musical outlines possess specific expressive resonances. Many examples are taken from Byrd's music: see the index.

II.Ho   Harley, John. *Orlando Gibbons and the Gibbons family of musicians.* Aldershot: Ashgate, 1999.

Contains many references to Byrd, such as the discovery that Gibbons's *Second Preces* are based on T 191(a).

II.Mm   Mellers, Wilfrid. *Music and society: England and the European tradition.* 2nd ed. London: Dobson, 1950.

Attempts to describe the evolution of English musical styles in relation to the European tradition, and to relate this evolution to the social and philosophical concepts that went to produce it. There are many references to Byrd in Chapters III–V and also in some later chapters. Moreover there are some, not indexed, in Chapter II (pp. 56 and 62–64) and additional references, again not indexed, in Chapter III (pp. 65–67, 71–73, and 77).

II.MUa   Murray, Sterling E. *Anthologies of music: an annotated index.* Detroit studies in music bibliography, 55. Detroit: Information Co-ordinators, 1987.

Provides access to the contents of many modern historical anthologies of musical examples. Byrd has twenty-three entries.

II.Oc   Owens, Jessie Ann. "Concepts of pitch in English music and theory, c. 1560–1640." In *Tonal structures in early music,* ed. Cristle Collins Judd. New York: Garland, 1998, pp. 183–246.

Develops ideas first propounded in 1984Oc, in which she suggests that Byrd did not think along traditionally modal lines, but used four principal scale types.

II.Tw   Turbet, Richard. *William Byrd, 1540–1623: Lincoln's greatest musician.* Rev. ed. Lincoln: Honywood, 1999.

Introduction

Life at Lincoln

Life after Lincoln

Works: the Lincoln period and before

The legacy of Lincoln

The legacy of Byrd: until the 19th century

The legacy of Byrd: the 20th century

Byrd's music at Lincoln from the 17th century

Focuses on the life and music of Byrd when he was at Lincoln, 1563–72. The principal events of his life before and during his sojourn here are surveyed in the first chapter, then the remainder of his career and life in the second. The third chapter estimates what Byrd brought to Lincoln from wherever he was musically educated, possibly the Chapel Royal, and assesses how that assisted him to develop as a composer when at Lincoln; the influence of Sheppard is featured. Similarly the following chapter suggests what he carried forward from his development in Lincoln. The fall and subsequent rise in his reputation to date are discussed in the next two chapters. Finally there is a complete list of music by Byrd in Lincoln Cathedral manuscripts in the eighteenth and nineteenth centuries, and music by Byrd in service lists from selected years 1893–1992, covering all the cathedral organists from that century. Many illustrations unique to Byrdian literature are included.

II.Ww   Westover, Catherine. "William Byrd and his time." *Viola da Gamba Society of Great Britain newsletter* 82 (1993): 6–9.

Headed "Report of the June Meeting," summarizes the four papers "celebrating the 450th anniversary of Byrd's birth." Alex Walsham spoke on "Musicians in Elizabethan and Jacobean England," concentrating on aspects of Byrd's Roman Catholicism, notably his donations to missions abroad. Stewart McCoy's topic was the "Paston lute sources," a study of performance problems, using Byrd's songs to illustrate the various possible scorings implied by the sources. John Milsom's paper "Philip van Wilder's consort music" was only "tangentially" related to Byrd, but noted a clear example of Byrd's familiarity with Wilder's music. (Milsom noted another — Wilder's *Une nonnain* bars 36–40 and Byrd's motets T 50 bars 108–13 and T 54 bars 19–23 — in a subsequent version of this paper at the 21st Annual Conference on Medieval and Renaissance Music, Bangor, 1993.)

Finally, in "William Byrd's consort music," Oliver Neighbour pondered the instrumentation of Byrd's corpus.

Recommended items from the first edition:

23: Henderson, Robert. "Byrd's place in English music." *Daily telegraph* (14 July 1973): 9.

35: Wulstan, David. *Tudor music.* London: Dent, 1985; Iowa City: University of Iowa Press, 1986.

III

BYRD'S VOCAL MUSIC IN GENERAL

III.Bp   Brett, Philip. "Pitch and transposition in the Paston manuscripts," in *Sundry sorts of music books: essays on the British Library collections, presented to O.W. Neighbour on his 70th birthday,* ed. Chris Banks, Arthur Searle and Malcolm Turner. London: British Library, 1993, pp. 89–118.

Exhaustive investigation, which concludes that as regards pitch and transposition, this particular collection of manuscripts is *sui generis.* Brett provides an introductory account of Paston and his relationship with Byrd, plus three appendices, comprehensively listing and commenting upon the pieces by Byrd from the collection. Virtually the entire repertory under consideration is by Byrd. Indeed, the author originally considered offering this research to *Byrd studies* (II.BROb).

III.Mb   Mellers, Wilfrid. "Byrd as Roman-Anglican, Elizabethan-Jacobean, double man: his *Mass* in five voices (1588) and his psalm-sonet, 'Lullaby, my swete litel baby' (first version for solo voice and viols [1588], second version for *a cappella* voices [1607])," in *Celestial music: some masterpieces of European religious music.* Woodbridge: Boydell, 2002, pp. 42–49.

Provocative ideas amid hopelessly outdated scholarship (e.g., first and last dates in title above).

III.Th   Turbet, Richard. "Homage to Fayrfax." *Annual Byrd newsletter* 3 (1997): 6–7.

Suggests that Byrd adopted a particular theme from Fayrfax, which seemed to hold personal significance for him, and discusses its use by Tomkins in his Funeral Sentences.

III.Ww   Willan, Healey. "William Byrd: choral work." *Canadian review of music and art* 2 (August/September 1943): 8–9.

Emphasizes the value of hearing Byrd's choral music, not just studying it on the printed page.

Recommended items from the first edition:

10: Grew, Sidney. "Some aspects of William Byrd." *Musical times* 63 (1922): 698–702.

43: Beswick, Delbert M. "The dominant seventh chord in the works of William Byrd (1542–1623)." *Proceedings of the Music Teachers' National Association* 40 (1946): 156–66.

62: Andrews, H. K "The printed part-books of Byrd's vocal music: the relationship of bibliography and musical scholarship." *Music & letters* 19 (1964): 1–10; repr. as *The printed part-books of Byrd's vocal music.* London: Bibliographical Society, 1968.

64: Andrews, H. K. *The technique of Byrd's vocal polyphony.* London: Oxford University Press, 1966; reprint ed., Westport: Greenwood, 1980.

67: Kerman, Joseph. "Byrd, Tallis, and the art of imitation," in *Aspects of medieval and Renaissance music: a birthday offering to Gustave Reese,* ed. Jan LaRue. New York: Norton, 1966; London: Dent, 1967; reprint ed., Festschrift series, 2. New York: Pendragon, 1978, pp. 519–37; repr. with updated endnotes in *Write all these down: essays on music.* Berkeley: University of California Press, 1994, pp. 90–105.

88: Lam, Basil. "Master of grief." *Listener* 89 (1973): 874.

94: Hynson, Richard. "The two choral styles of William Byrd." *Choral journal* (December 1978): 20–22.

IV

SACRED VOCAL MUSIC

IV.Ci   Carwood, Andrew. "An inimitable inheritance." *Choir & organ* 9.1
            (2001): 46–49.

            Reflects on Byrd's sacred music with particular reference to the
            Gradualia, which the author was in the middle of recording as con-
            ductor of The Cardinall's Musick. He pays particular attention to
            pitch, and the ramifications for transposition and scoring, which
            impinge on eventual performance. Referring to the fact that transpo-
            sition always by the same interval makes works such as T 1, T 196,
            and the *Gradualia* often unsingable, he concludes there is no room
            for dogmatic theory that emphasizes alleged historical accuracy over
            the practicalities of performance, yet there is always room for the dil-
            igent, understanding, and sensitive application of historical aware-
            ness that will be convincing.

IV.Pp   Payne, Ian. *The provision and practice of sacred music at Cambridge
            colleges and selected cathedrals c.1547-c.1646: a comparative study
            of the archival evidence.* Outstanding dissertations in music from
            British universities. New York: Garland, 1993.

            Expands some information in I.BOm, notably concerning Byrd's
            recruitment of choristers and the circumstances of the possible per-
            formance of Byrd's Latin music in Lincoln, although the case for its
            being performed liturgically in the cathedral is not tenable. The
            author also gives the size of the choir during Byrd's organistship.
            Plate II reproduces the signatures of an early owner of a set of 1575
            partbooks, omitted from the published facsimile (see catalogue)
            although mentioned on page vii by the editor, Richard Rastall.

IV.To   Turbet, Richard. "Ordinary Byrd: masses and preces." *Annual Byrd
            newsletter* 8 (2002): 4–5.

            Poses questions as to how aspects of Byrd's compositions were per-
            formed liturgically during his lifetime.

IV.Wb   Wulstan, David. "Birdus tantum natus decorare magistrum," in *Byrd
            studies,* ed. Alan Brown and Richard Turbet. Cambridge: Cambridge
            University Press, 1992, pp. 63–82.

Partly assisted by computer analysis, describes Byrd's vocal scoring at different stages in his career, supporting the author's view that the performing level of the Latin music was closely related to that of the Anglican music. He is combative in disputing with musicologists to whose views he is opposed, and concludes his discussion of this matter in IV.Wby, which includes statistical data necessarily omitted from the present article.

IV.Wby   Wulstan, David. "Byrd, Tallis and Ferrabosco," in *English choral practice, 1400–1650,* ed. John Morehen. Cambridge: Cambridge University Press, 1996, pp. 109–42.

Exploits computer analysis to compare the extents to which Tallis and Alfonso Ferrabosco the elder influenced Byrd. Includes the statistics, compiled by John Duffill, mentioned as forthcoming in footnote 128 at the end of IV.Wb. As ever with this author there are some contentious issues. He questions the authenticity of T 166, proposing the shadowy Thomas Byrd of the Chapel Royal who was for long a convenient dumping ground for what was considered a dubious attribution among William's early motets. Harley disposes of any reasonable doubt on page 159 of I.Hwi. Timothy Symons puts a good case for Sheppard's *Second Service,* the model for T 197, being one of the composer's later works and not, *pace* Wulstan, from the Edwardine period: see his edition (Guildford: Cantus Firmus Music, 1995). It is surprising that a musicologist writing at this date could still be stating that Byrd joined the Chapel Royal in 1570 not 1572, though such solecisms still occur at the time of writing. And Wulstan is rather hard on T 206, the indexed attribution to Gibbons now discarded as a red herring: see VI.Tp. Nevertheless, he is right to query the patently spurious anthem *Save me O God:* see VI.Tc.

Recommended items from the first edition:

68: Stevens, Denis. *Tudor church music.* 2nd ed. London: Faber; New York: Norton, 1966.

70: le Huray, Peter. "The late sixteenth and early seventeenth centuries: William Byrd and his contemporaries," in *Music and the Reformation in England, 1549–1660.* London: Jenkins; New York: Oxford University Press, 1967; reprint ed., Cambridge studies in music. Cambridge: Cambridge University Press, 1978, pp. 227–73.

71: Arnold, Denis. "William Byrd: an outsider in the High Renaissance." *Listener* 80 (1968): 121–22.

74: Gray, Walter. "Motivic structure in the polyphony of William Byrd." *Musical review* 29 (1968): 223–33.

77: Gray, Walter. "Some aspects of word treatment in the music of William Byrd." *Musical quarterly* 55 (1969): 45–64.

78: Abravanel, Claude and Hirshowitz, Betty. *The Bible in English music: W. Byrd–H. Purcell.* Americans for a Music Library in Israel. Studies in music bibliography, 1. Haifa: Haifa Museum, 1970.

95: Henderson, Robert. "Byrd and the English church." *Daily telegraph* (3 February 1979): 11.

103: Sargent, Brian. "Two Byrd anthems." *Music teacher* 60 (March 1981): 13–15.

V

LATIN CHURCH MUSIC

V.Be   Banks, Paul and Turbet, Richard. "Early printed source of Byrd at the Britten-Pears Library." *Annual Byrd newsletter* 3 (1997): 7.

Notes sixteenth-century Byrd partbooks not reported to RISM (Repertoire international des sources musicales), with provenance where known and descriptions.

V.BLm   Blezzard, Judith. "Monsters and messages: the Willmott and Braikenridge manuscripts of Latin Tudor church music, 1591." *Antiquaries journal* 75 (1995): 311–38.

Discusses a pair of partbooks that are an important source for ten motets by Byrd, all but two of which were published in the first (6) and second (2) books of *Cantiones*.

V.Ch   Copeman, Harold. "How should we pronounce Latin?" *Church music quarterly* 140 (1998): 16–17.

Using T 92 as an example, explains, with reference to the most recent research, what Byrd could have expected to hear.

V.Dn   Duffin, Ross W. "New light on Jacobean taste and practice in music for voices and viols," in *Le concert des voix et des instruments a la Renaissance: actes du XXXIVe Colloque international d'etudes humanistes,* Tours, 1991, ed. Jean-Michel Vaccaro. Arts du spectacle. Paris: CNRS Editions, 1995, pp. 601–19.

Introduces the Blossom partbooks, a new source for T 30, T 25, and T 28.

V.Eb   Elders, Willem. "Byrd," in *Symbolic scores: studies in the music of the Renaissance.* Symbolica et emblemata, 5. Leiden: Brill, 1994, pp. 113–17.

Subsection of section on "Symbolic scoring in Tudor England" taking Byrd's four compositions in more than six parts and offering explanations for their scoring.

V.Fs   Flanagan, David. "Some aspects of the sixteenth-century parody mass in England." *Music review* 48 (1988): 1–11.

Notes a similarity between the openings of the Glorias of T 1 and Taverner's *Missa Mater Christi.*

V.Hb   Harley, John and Turbet, Richard. "Byrd: *Haec est dies.*" *Early music review* 21 (1996): 16.

Introduction to motet with spurious attribution to Byrd, first published in *Annual Byrd newsletter* 2 (1996): 6–7 and subsequently by King's Music (Wyton, 1996), edited by Brian Clark. Contrary to what is stated in the penultimate sentence of footnote 9 on p. vii of BE 9, neither author claims the motet for Byrd.

V.HUw   Hugill, Robert. "What sound? Robert Hugill asks some questions about the music of William Byrd." *Music & vision* (1 January 2004): <http://www.mvdaily.com/articles/2004/01/Byrd1.htm>

Cogent rumination concerning the distribution of vocal resources in performing Byrd's Roman Catholic liturgical music.

V.HUMw   Humphreys, David. "Wilder and Byrd: Wilder's *Aspice Domine a6.*"
          Annual Byrd newsletter 10 (2004): 26–28.

          Suggests that T 7 is based on the setting of *Aspice Domine quia facta*
          by Wilder also in six parts, and not on his setting in five as previ-
          ously proposed elsewhere (1981Km). The complete fragments of
          Wilder's six-part setting are published here for the first time.

V.Ip   Irving, John. "Penetrating the preface to *Gradualia.*" *Music review*
          51 (1990): 157–66.

          Considers Byrd's comments, in the preface to the first *Gradualia,*
          about inspiration, and applies them to Byrd's own compositional
          process, using T 86 as a model.

V.Iw   Irving, John. "Words and music combined: some questions of text-
          music integration in Byrd's masses." *Music review* 52 (1991):
          267–78.

          Demonstrates how Byrd illuminates the meaning of his text by set-
          ting successive related verbal phrases to musical phrases that also
          reflect a relationship to one another.

V.Ks   Keller, Arne. "Some observations on R134 of the Herlufsholm
          Collection, with proposed identifications of owners and compilers: a
          new source for Byrd's *In resurrectione.*" *Annual Byrd newsletter*
          7 (2001): 10–11.

          Draws attention to Danish manuscript containing the tenor part of
          Byrd's motet, reproduced in facsimile in *Early music review*
          71 (2001): 23.

V.KEm   Kerman, Joseph. "Music and politics: the case of William Byrd
          (1540–1623)." *Proceedings of the American Philosophical Associa-*
          tion 144 (2000): 275–87.

          Reconsiders Byrd's music in the light of the political agenda he
          shared with the Jesuits. Kerman describes the Catholic Byrd as an
          ornament not only to the court of the Protestant Queen Elizabeth, but
          also to the Jesuit enterprise to reconvert England. He surveys some
          of Byrd's polemical texts and ponders what effect they had on their
          hearers, making the point that the Jesuits would have ensured they
          were circulated where needed most. Kerman then speculates on how

Byrd got away with this, before dealing with the question of Byrd's retirement to Stondon Massey (Kerman strays in naming his eventual home and resting place as where his family originated: this, as Harley states in the passage cited by Kerman, is Ingatestone, home of his patrons the Petres) and the composition of his final Catholic project, the *Gradualia*. Kerman concludes that Byrd's political advocacy would not have been possible had he not been the composer he was, and he closes with an example of Byrd's miraculous rhetoric, T 92, which spoke to the Catholic flock of his time and speaks to us today.

V.Ls   le Huray, Peter. "Some thoughts about cantus firmus composition; and a plea for Byrd's Christus resurgens," in *Byrd studies,* ed. Alan Brown and Richard Turbet. Cambridge: Cambridge University Press, 1923, pp. 1–23.

Considers English cantus firmus composition in the sixteenth century, with special reference to T 97 from the first *Gradualia. Pace* Kerman in 1981Kw, le Huray suggests it is a relatively late work by Byrd. The essay is generously illustrated, notably with substantial extracts from the otherwise unpublished setting of *Christus resurgens* by Byrd's older contemporary Thomas Knight (or Knyght).

V.Mb   Macey, Patrick. "Byrd, *Infelix ego,*" in *Bonfire songs: Savanarola's musical legacy.* Oxford: Clarendon: 1998, pp. 287–302.

Part of a chapter on the influence of Savanarola in England, referring specifically to T 50, from Savanarola's meditation on Psalm L, which became associated with both Protestant and Catholic martyrdom.

V.MCm   McCarthy, Kerry. "Music for all seasons: the Byrd *Gradualia* revisited." *Sacred music* 129 (2002): 5–12.

Describes the background and structure of the cycle, with reflections on a series of performances of the twelve principal sets of propers.

V.MCn   McCarthy, Kerry. "Byrd, Augustine, and *Tribue, Domine.*" *Early music* 32 (2004): 569–76.

Announces the discovery of the source for the text of T 17.

V.MCno McCarthy, Kerry. "'Notes as a garland': the chronology and narrative of Byrd's *Gradualia.*" *Early music history* 23 (2004): 49–84.

Discusses the liturgical and musical organization of *Gradualia.*

V.MEm   Meier, Bernhard. *The modes of classical vocal polyphony, described according to the sources,* transl. Ellen S. Beebe. New York: Broude, 1988.

Translation of *Die Tonarten der klassischen Vokalpolyphonie* (Utrecht: Oosthoek, Scheltema & Holkema, 1974) after revisions by the author. Attempts to explain how composers went about the business of creating music within the modal system as they comprehended it in their own day. Byrd is the only British composer whose works appear in the tables of examples. Eight of his works are discussed by the author and six are included in his tables, including two not hitherto discussed. The topic of mode is controversial, but the author's comments on T 17 and T 86 are illuminating.

V.MIs   Milsom, John. "Sacred songs in the chamber," in *English choral practice, 1400–1650,* ed. John Morehen. Cambridge: Cambridge University Press, 1995, pp. 161–79.

Byrd is mentioned on all but two of this essay's pages. It surveys all Elizabethan and Jacobean sources containing Latin music, and concludes that with a few exceptions they were intended for domestic consumption, renewing his plea in 1993Mb for more authentic performances of this repertory. On pages 176–77 he notes contemporaries of Byrd known to have owned sets of the 1575 *Cantiones.*

V.MIt   Milsom, John. "Tallis, Byrd and the 'incorrected copy': some cautionary notes for editors of early music printed from movable type." *Music & letters* 77 (1996): 348–67.

Having examined all known surviving copies of the 1575 *Cantiones* (but see V.Be), warns against the likelihood of a perfect copy emerging at any stage in the printing process. Explains on p. 358 why Byrd is sometimes associated with Tallis's *Miserere nostri;* see also p. 207, addenda to p. 94, in 1994Tt.

V.MItr   Milsom, John. "Tracking Tomkins: three verse anthems retrieved." *Musical times* 142 (Summer 2001): 54–63.

During the course of reclaiming three fragmentary anonymous verse anthems for Tomkins, notes that in one of them, *O God the heathen are come,* Tomkins uses the same text as Byrd in T 25 and borrows musical material from Byrd's motet.

V.MOb   Monson, Craig. "Byrd, the Catholics, and the motet: the hearing reopened," in *Hearing the motet: essays on the motet of the Middle Ages and Renaissance,* ed. Dolores Pesce. New York: Oxford University Press, 1997, pp. 348–74.

Consults contemporary clandestine Roman Catholic writings to expand our knowledge of the background to Byrd's choice of texts for his nonliturgical Latin music. A trickle of such literature during the 1570s became a sizeable stream after the execution of Edmund Campion in 1581 (see T 248): 225 volumes were printed between then and the execution of the Jesuit Henry Garnet in 1606. Monson demonstrates how Byrd "heard" the polemics of the Jesuit tracts, and particularly the extent to which their political vocabulary permeated his chosen texts and, via them, his music. Monson develops the preceding work of Kerman (1981Kw) and Brett (prefaces to A 5–7) on this topic, and the breadth of his findings is revelatory concerning Byrd's adherence to Jesuit thinking.

V.MORb   Morehen, John. "Byrd's manuscript motets: a new perspective," in *Byrd studies,* ed. Alan Brown and Richard Turbet. Cambridge: Cambridge University Press, pp. 51–62.

Describes a computer-assisted project to test the authenticity of eleven motets whose attributions to Byrd are questionable. A listing on p. 61 provides a useful guide to which motets Byrd is more or less likely to have composed, though footnote 28 on p. 62 concedes that the apparent inauthenticity of T 166 is, for a reason easily explained, misleading; indeed, it is now generally accepted as authentic: see p. 159 of I.Hwi.

V.MORi   Morehen, John. "Is 'Byrd's' *Haec* a fake?" *Early music review* 24 (1996): 8–9.

Using computer procedures described in V.MORb, rejects attribution to Byrd of *Haec est dies:* see V.Hb.

V.Np   Nasu, Teruhiko. "The publication of Byrd's *Gradualia* reconsidered." *Brio* 32 (1995): 109–20.

Produces evidence suggesting that Richard Bancroft, archbishop of Canterbury, should be numbered among Byrd's patrons, and explains how Richard Redmer came to reissue both volumes of *Gradualia* in 1610. For an alternative view about the role of Bancroft, see XI.St, especially pp. 99–100 and 205, note 25.

V.Pg Paisey, David. "German book fair catalogues." *Library,* 7th ser., 4 (2003): 417–27.

Contains further information about the presence of the 1575 *Cantiones* in continental Europe during the sixteenth century; see p. 422, also 426.

V.Re Rees, Owen. "The English background to Byrd's motets: textual and stylistic models for Infelix ego," in *Byrd studies,* ed. Alan Brown and Richard Turbet. Cambridge: Cambridge University Press, pp. 24–50.

Querying received wisdom, argues that the English psalm motet was not so much a response to continental developments as a reflection of the content of Primers in use in English religious institutions. Turning to T 50, he argues that Kerman in 1981Kw had insufficiently penetrated the magnitude of Byrd's rhetorical achievement, based on his exploitation of inherited techniques, and his own originality and formidable technical skill.

V.Sn Skinner, David. "A new Elizabethan keyboard source in the archives of Arundel Castle." *Brio* 39 (Spring/Summer 2002): 18–23.

Includes fragment of unique arrangement for keyboard of T 30, reproduced on p. 23.

V.STw Stern, David. "William Byrd: Mass for Five Voices," in *Music before 1600,* ed. Mark Everist. Models of musical analysis. Oxford: Blackwell, 1992, pp. 208–24.

Schenkerian analysis of the Kyrie.

V.Tb Turbet, Richard. "Byrd and Clemens non Papa." *Musical times* 130 (1989): 129.

Letter amplifying a point made in VI.Th (*q.v.*) but which relates to Byrd's borrowing from Clemens in one of his motets.

V.Tc   Turbet, Richard. "Continuing Byrd." *Musical times* 131 (1990): 544.

Review-article that identifies the transcribers, Overend and Danby, responsible for two eighteenth-century scores of the elusive first edition of the first *Gradualia*. Identity of the former had already been suggested by Harry Colin Miller on p. 30 of *Introductory Euing lectures on music bibliography and history* (Glasgow: Bayley & Ferguson, 1914).

V.Th   Turbet, Richard. "Horsley's 1842 edition of Byrd and its infamous introduction." *British music* 14 (1992): 36–46.

In 1842 the Musical Antiquarian Society published William Horsley's edition of Byrd's first *Cantiones* with an editorial introduction by the editor, which was dismissive of Byrd's music. The article traces Horsley's progress on his edition by quoting hitherto unpublished entries from his diary, and for the first time in 150 years reproduces in full his notorious and uncomprehending introduction.

V.Tm   Turbet, Richard. "Macfarren's organ parts for Byrd's Latin music." *Annual Byrd newsletter* 10 (2004): 16.

Brief account of the accompaniments, by Alexander Macfarren and published by Chappell, provided separately for the two volumes of Byrd's music published by the Musical Antiquarian Society in 1841 and 1842.

V.Tmo   Turbet, Richard. "A model from Byrd." *Choir & organ* 4 (July 1996): 13–15.

Byrd's Welsh pupil Thomas Tomkins composed only one motet among his otherwise vast output, and the author sees a model for it in a motet by Byrd himself.

V.Tu   Turbet, Richard. "The unique first edition of Byrd's *Gradualia* in York Minster Library," in *Music librarianship in the United Kingdom: fifty years of the United Kingdom Branch of the International Association of Music Libraries, Archives and Documentation Centres,* ed. Richard Turbet. Aldershot: Ashgate, 2003, pp. 137–40.

Celebrates a bibliographical jewel that resided in its library for many years undetected and then, even when detected, unappreciated.

Recommended items from the first edition:

37: Collins, H.B. "Byrd's Latin church music, for practical use in the Roman liturgy." *Music & letters* 4 (1923): 254–60.

60: Jackman, James L. "Liturgical aspects of Byrd's *Gradualia.*" *Musical quarterly* 49 (1963): 17–37.

61: Kerman, Joseph. "On William Byrd's *Emendemus in melius.*" *Musical quarterly* 49 (1963): 431–49; rev. repr. in *Hearing the motet: essays on the motet of the Middle Ages and Renaissance,* ed. Dolores Pesce. New York: Oxford University Press, 1997, pp. 329–47. *Note*: Revisions summarized on page 346.

65: Clulow, Peter. "Publication dates for Byrd's Latin masses." *Music & letters* 47 (1966): 1–9.

87: Kerman, Joseph. "William Byrd, 1543–1623." *Musical times* 114 (1973): 687–90.

90: Kerman, Joseph. "Old and new in Byrd's Cantiones sacrae," in *Essays on opera and English music in honour of Sir Jack Westrup,* ed. F.W. Sternfeld, Nigel Fortune, and Edward Olleson. Oxford: Blackwell, 1975, pp. 25–43.

91: Monson, Craig. "Byrd and the 1575 Cantiones sacrae." *Musical times* 116 (1975): 1089, 1091; 117 (1976): 65–67.

93: Benham, Hugh. "William Byrd: a note on the 1575 Cantiones," in *Latin church music in England, c. 1460–1575.* London: Barrie & Jenkins, 1977, pp. 220–23.

97: Humphreys, David. "Philip van Wilder: a study of his work and its sources." *Soundings* 9 (1979/80): 13–36.

99: Brett, Philip. "Homage to Taverner in Byrd's masses." *Early music* 9 (1981): 169–76.

100: Kerman, Joseph. *The masses and motets of William Byrd.* The music of William Byrd, 1. London: Faber; Berkeley: University of California Press, 1981.

VI

ANGLICAN CHURCH MUSIC

VI.Bp   Bowers, Roger. "The Prayer Book and the musicians, 1549–1662." *Cathedral music* (April 2002): 36–44.

Sweeping account of the effect of the *Book of Common Prayer,* especially its rubrics, on music in English cathedrals, with cogent reference to the theological and political thinking behind successive editions and to contemporary developments, with several references to Byrd. The text of the article is a lecture read on 17 June 2001 at the parish church of St. Edward, Cambridge, delivered as one of the church's annual Prayer Book Lectures.

VI.BUc   Buckley, David. "A comparison of William Child's *Sing we merrily* with William Byrd's *Sing joyfully.*" *Annual Byrd newsletter* 5 (1999): 8–9.

Advances the probability that Child had studied Byrd's setting of the same psalm before or while composing his own. Although Child could compose in a progressive style, this anthem betrays his debt to an earlier musician.

VI.Ft   Fellowes, Edmund H. [Two letters] in *Music and friends: seven decades of letters to Adrian Boult,* ed. Jerrold Northrop Moore. London: Hamilton, 1979, pp. 77–78.

Dated 26 November and 15 December 1926, concerning T 197, to be sung by the Birmingham Festival Choral Society, conducted by Boult, on 23 January 1927. The first concerns parts still missing from the original work, the more interesting second concerns interpretation.

VI.Hb   Harley, John. "Byrd's 'Catholic' anthems." *Annual Byrd newsletter* 8 (2002): 8–9.

Raises the possibility that some of the texts Byrd selected for his anthems and sacred songs were, like those of some of his motets, covert messages of support to the beleagured Roman Catholic community in England.

VI.Iw   Irving, John. "William Byrd and Thomas Tomkins's Offertory: (re-)evaluating text and context." *Annual Byrd newsletter* 5 (1999): 10–12.

            Reconsiders Tomkins's *Offertorium* in the light of its recently discovered debt (see VI.JOu) to part of T 197.

VI.Je   James, Peter. "*Exalt Thyself, O Lord:* the rediscovery of Byrd's festive anthem." *Annual Byrd newsletter* 4 (1998): 9–10.

            Fullest and most authoritative account of the rediscovery and reconstruction of a work the previously surviving skeletal fragments of which had been ascribed to Tomkins.

VI.Js   James, Peter. "The significance of Byrd's verse compositions: a reappraisal." *Annual Byrd newsletter* 7 (2001): 7–10.

            Places T 195 and the verse anthems in the context of the origins and development of the verse idiom.

VI.JOa   Johnstone, Andrew. "'As it was in the beginning': organ and choir pitch in early Anglican church music." *Early music* 31 (2003): 506–25.

            Reports evidence from the Early English Organ Project about pitch and the nature of accompaniments, which impinges on Byrd's Anglican music, most significantly on T 195, and challenges all previous writings on these topics.

VI.JONu   Jones, Stephen and Turbet, Richard. "Unknown ground." *Musical times* 134 (1993): 615–16.

            An announcement, submitted to the journal as an article but subsequently divested of its footnotes and published as a letter, of Jones's finding, researched by RT, that Tomkins's keyboard *Offertorium* is based on a passage from T 197 and not, as previously thought, on plainsong.

VI.Mt   Monson, Craig. "'Throughout all generations': intimations of influence in the short Service styles of Tallis, Byrd and Morley," in *Byrd studies,* ed. Alan Brown and Richard Turbet. Cambridge: Cambridge University Press, 1992, pp. 83–111.

Considers Byrd's T 194 and T 196 in respect of their debt to Tallis's *Short Service* and their influence on Morley's *Short Evening* and *Second Services.* With reference to footnote 3 on p. 84, Morley's Services were published in EECM 41, separately from the anthems and other liturgical music in volume 38 mentioned in the note.

VI.MOe   Morehen, John. "The English anthem text." *Journal of the Royal Musical Association* 117 (1992): 62–85.

Comprehensive account of the range and variety of texts set by English composers for use in Divine Service in the new Church of England between the Reformation and the Restoration. The author divides them into psalm, metrical, scriptural, and unidentified texts, seasonal collects, prayers, and miscellaneous texts. He illustrates the broad distribution of anthem texts by percentages using these divisions, and tabulates contrafacta and seasonal collects set between 1549 and 1660. Byrd's anthems are therefore considered in the context of what other composers were writing at the same time.

VI.Pg   Pike, Lionel. "The Great Service: some observations on Byrd and Tomkins." *Musical times* 133 (1992): 421–22.

Disagrees with the arguments advanced in VI.Tgr and maintains that there was indeed a category of "Great Services" consisting, at the least, of T 197 and Tomkins's *Third Service.* Makes interesting analytical comparisons between the two works, suggesting that Tomkins's work was, in the musicological sense, derived from Byrd's.

VI.Tb   Turbet, Richard. "Byrd and Tomkins: the Great Service revisited." *Leading notes* 9 (1995): 10–11.

Response to VI.Pg, emphasizing the need to perceive early music as its contemporaries did. Reiterates that T 197 was the only work so titled and that scribal errors explain such headings in the Services by Tomkins and Hooper. But see Chapter 6.

VI.Tby   Turbet, Richard. "A Byrd miscellany." *Fontes artis musicae* 37 (1990): 299–302.

Contains the first complete listing of those anthems by Byrd whose texts appear in either edition of James Clifford's *Divine services and anthems,* 1663–64. Discusses problematical entries in the list of anthems by Byrd in Myles Birket Foster's *Anthems and anthem composers,* 1901. The section about Byrd's son Thomas has been superceded by the researches of Harley in I.Hwi.

VI.Tbyr   Turbet, Richard. "Byrd, Weelkes and verse Services." *Annual Byrd newsletter* 1 (1995): 5.

          Appendix to VI.Th. Suggests Weelkes's *First Service* is another homage to T 195.

VI.Tc   Turbet, Richard. "Coste not Byrd." *Annual Byrd newsletter* 4 (1998): 4.

          Presents evidence that the anthem *Save me O God,* attributed both to Byrd and to Coste (without Christian name in any attribution of any surviving work to Coste), is by Coste, subsequently identified by Roger Bowers as Richard Coste. See *Early music review* 41 (1998): 11–12 for the first published edition of Coste's only other surviving anthem (and reconstructable work) *He that hath my commandments* with the commentary in *Annual Byrd newsletter* 4 (1998): 12. See also Roger Bowers's letter in *Early music review* 42 (1998): 27; Richard Turbet's letter "Counting the Coste," *Musical times* (Autumn 2001): 3–4; and Roger Bowers, *English church polyphony: singers and sources from the 14th to the 17th century,* Aldershot: Ashgate Variorum, 1999, Commentary and corrigenda, p. 5, *re* p. 436.

VI.Tg   Turbet, Richard. "The Great Service: Byrd, Tomkins and their contemporaries, and the meaning of 'great.'" *Musical times* 131 (1990): 275–77.

          Provides contemporary Tudor definition of "great," argues that Tomkins's *Third Service* was mistitled "Great" in the source, which also contains T 197, and concludes that Fellowes invented a category of "Great Services," whereas the only work ever known correctly as the *Great Service* is Byrd's. See subsequent letter "Tidying up" on p. 527 of the same volume, and also Chapter 6.

VI.Tgr   Turbet, Richard. "The Great Service: a postscript." *Musical times* 133 (1992): 206.

          Appendix to VI.Tgr. Notes that Hooper's *Full Service* also was entitled "Great" in part of one source, and suggests that this was a mistake for T 197, which is in the same manuscript. But see Chapter 6.

VI.Th   Turbet, Richard. "Homage to Byrd in Tudor verse Services." *Musical times* 129 (1988): 485–90.

Demonstrates that several of Byrd's younger contemporaries paid musical homage to him by basing the opening phrases of their own verse Services on that of T 195. See also the subsequent letter "Byrd and Clemens non Papa," 130 (1989): 129.

VI.Thy   Turbet, Richard. "A hymn attributed to Byrd." *Annual Byrd newsletter* 9 (2003): 5.

Suggests the identity of the composer of the apocryphal *Glory be to God.*

VI.Tj   Turbet, Richard. "J. Guggenheim as music publisher: Tallis and Byrd restored." *Brio* 41 (Spring/Summer 2004): 49–52.

Inducts Jules Guggenheim into the fraternity of music publishers. His sole musical publication, 1882, features the obscure and neglected T 192(a).

VI.Tjo   Turbet, Richard. "Joyful singing: Byrd's music at a royal christening." *Musical times* 145 (Spring 2004): 85–86.

Reveals that T 208 was sung at the christening of one of James I's children.

VI.Tm   Turbet, Richard. "'My ancient and much reverenced master': two anthems by Byrd and Tomkins." *Choir & organ* 1 (November 1993): 15–18.

Illustrates how Tomkins based his setting of *O God the proud are risen* on T 202; with a postscript describing a borrowing from Byrd in Tomkins's Funeral Sentences.

VI.Tp   Turbet, Richard. "Postscript." *Annual Byrd newsletter* 1 (1995): 4.

First paragraph provides evidence that T 206, attributed both to Byrd and to Gibbons, as well as being published and recently twice recorded as by the latter, is indeed by Byrd.

VI.Tw   Turbet, Richard. "Wings of faith: Richard Turbet uncovers a close relationship between Services by William Byrd and John Sheppard." *Musical times* 138 (December 1997): 5–10.

Uncovers the extent to which Byrd drew guidance from Sheppard's *Second Service* when composing T 197.

VI.Wc   Weaver, Geoff. "Choral masterclass: *Sing joyfully* by William Byrd." *Church music quarterly* 161 (2003): 36–37.

Contains practical suggestions about performance.

Recommended items from the first edition:

41: Whittaker, W. Gillies. "Byrd's Great Service." *Musical quarterly* 27 (1941): 474–90.

80: Lam, Basil. "The greatest English composer." *Listener* 85 (1971): 25.

84: Daniel, Ralph T. and le Huray, Peter. *The sources of English church music 1549–1660*. Early English church music, supplementary vol.1. 2 pts paginated consecutively. London: Stainer and Bell, 1972.

96: Monson, Craig. "The Preces, Psalms and Litanies of Byrd and Tallis: another 'virtuous contention in love.'" *Music review* 40 (1979): 257–71.

104: Monson, Craig. "Authenticity and chronology in Byrd's church anthems." *Journal of the American Musicological Society* 35 (1982): 280–305.

VII

SECULAR VOCAL MUSIC

VII.Ds   Dahlhous, Carl. *Studies on the origin of harmonic tonality*. Princeton: Princeton University Press, 1990.

At pages 246–48, takes issue with 1959Za and maitains that Byrd's cadential practice tends to be intermediate, between modality and tonality.

VII.DOw   Doughtie, Edward. "William Byrd and the consort song," in *English Renaissance song.* Twayne's English authors series, 424. Boston, MA: Twayne, 1986, pp. 62–79.

General introduction, including close analysis of T 218 within section entitled "William Byrd" pp. 68–79.

VII.DUm   Duncan-Jones, Katherine. "'Melancholie times': musical recollections of Sidney by William Byrd and Thomas Watson," in *The well enchanting skill: music, poetry, and drama in the culture of the Renaissance: essays in honour of F.W. Sternfeld,* ed. John Caldwell, Edward Olleson, and Susan Wollenberg. Oxford: Clarendon, 1990, pp. 171–80.

Investigates the interrelationships between the three men. Byrd set Sidney's lyrics and two surviving funeral songs for Sidney of which one or both may have been the work of Watson. The texts of those lyrics he set are in some cases different from the published versions, but the author concludes, somewhat surprisingly, there is too little evidence to claim for Byrd either personal knowledge of Sidney or privileged access to his texts. Watson seems to have been closer, albeit subordinate, to Sidney. Byrd and Watson collaborated on T 319 and MB LXXIV, and she offers some speculations about the purpose of the latter, possibly a posthumous tribute to Sidney, and why Byrd made two settings of the same text addressed to the Queen, T 293 and T 320.

VII.Gf   Gelder, Gaert Jan van. "From Horwood to the greenwood: a round and its origin in rondellus." *Leading notes* 9 (1995): 5–6.

Traces the round *Hey ho to the greenwood,* spuriously attributed to Byrd, back to William Horwood's *Magnificat* in which phrases from the round are used as the contrapuntal technique of phrase-exchange *rondellus.*

VII.GRm   Greer, David. "Manuscript additions in *Parthenia* and other early English printed music in America." *Music & letters* 77 (1996): 169–81.

Discusses, describes, and where appropriate, reproduces or transcribes manuscript additions to the unique copy of *Parthenia* in the Huntington Library and to English musical publications up to 1650 in this and six other American libraries. Finds a new source for

T 247 and further evidence that *Non nobis Domine* was not composed by Byrd; see also VII.HUw.

VII.Hl   Harley, John. "Look and bow down." *Annual Byrd newsletter* 10 (2004): 4–6.

Assembles available evidence concerning where, how, and by whom this song was originally performed.

VII.HOo   Horner, Bruce. "On the study of music as material social practice." *Journal of musicology* 16 (1998): 159–97.

Final section, "Toward the study of music as material social practice," consists largely of analyses of T 234 and T 248.

VII.HUw   Humphreys, David. "Wilder's hand?" *Musical times* 144 (Summer 2003): 4.

Establishes that *Non nobis Domine,* long thought to be by Byrd, originated in a motet by Wilder.

VII.Kw   Kerman, Joseph. "'Write all these down': notes on a Byrd song," in *Byrd studies,* ed. Alan Brown and Richard Turbet. Cambridge: Cambridge University Press, 1992, pp. 112–28; repr. with extra endnote as "Write all these down: notes on a song by Byrd," in *Write all these down: essays on music.* Berkeley: University of California Press, 1994, pp. 106–24.

Close analysis of T 300, taking the reader through Byrd's compositional process, with a digression to T 248.

VII.KIp   Kilroy, Gerard. "Paper, inke and penne: the literary *memoria* of the recusant community." *Downside review* 119 (2001): 95–124.

Useful background, especially to T 248.

VII.Mw   McCoy, Stewart. "William Byrd's *Lullaby:* an example of contemporary intabulation." *Annual Byrd newsletter* 9 (2003): 10–13.

After a comprehensive introduction to the surviving contemporary intabulations for the lute of Byrd's music, analyses the technique displayed by Francis Cutting in arranging T 247.

VII.MIb   Milsom, John. "Byrd, Sidney, and the art of melting." *Early music* 31 (2003): 437–48.

Proposes that T 278 was originally composed as a consort song for high voice and four viols, for which there is, however, no surviving evidence. Ponders whether Byrd expected that just the first three stanzas of Sidney's poem would be sung, as printed in the 1589 *Songs,* or all eight; the latter has implications for performance practice. Observes and explains how Byrd creates exactly the right music to express Sidney's tortured stream of erotic consciousness.

VII.Nb   Neighbour, Oliver. "Byrd's treatment of verse in his partsongs." *Early music* 31 (2003): 413–22.

Detailed consideration of the sources, influences and originality discernable in Byrd's method of composing his partsongs. Concentrates on the works not originally written as consort songs, but notes the extent to which song form is, and is not, evident in his partsongs, with comments on many individual pieces.

VII.Oh   Ota, Diane O. and Turbet, Richard. "Heathen poets." *Annual Byrd newsletter* 3 (1997): 7.

Information about an as yet unidentified source from the early nineteenth century for T 236.

VII.Sf   Smith, Jeremy L. "From 'rights to copy' to the 'bibliographic ego': a new look at the last early edition of Byrd's 'Psalmes, sonets & songs.'" *Music & letters* 80 (1999): 511–30.

Establishes that this undated edition, previously put at *circa* 1599, was probably published during 1606 or 1607.

VII.SMb   Smith, Mike. "Bawdry, balladry, Byrd." *Annual Byrd newsletter* 10 (2004): 16–19.

Investigates how Byrd responded in his compositions to bawdy ballads.

VII.SMw   Smith, Mike. "'Whom Music's lore delighteth': words-and-music in Byrd's *Ye sacred Muses.*" *Early music* 31 (2003): 425–35.

Demonstrates how Byrd's engagement with the meaning and poetic structure of his texts produces a transcendant musical rhetoric, not only preeminently in the song in question but also throughout his corpus of consort songs.

VII.Tc   Teo, Kian-Seng. "Chromaticism in Thomas Weelkes's 1600 collection: possible models." *Musicology Australia* 13 (1990): 2–14.

Supports the attribution of T 180 to Byrd (p. 13, n. 15).

VII.Tw   Teo, Kian-Seng. "William Byrd and chromaticism," in *Chromaticism in the English madrigal.* Outstanding dissertations in music from British universities. New York: Garland, 1989, pp. 485–90.

Places Byrd in the continuum of the development and assimilation of chromaticism into the English madrigal, noting his roots in Netherlandish polyphony and possible knowledge of the Italian madrigal. Notes Byrd's judicious use of chromaticism for expressive effect and to create an overall mood, and comments on Byrd's considerable influence on Morley and the later madrigalists.

VII.TUm Turbet, Richard. "'Melodious Birde': the solo songs of William Byrd," in *Aspects of British song,* ed. Brian Blyth Daubney. Upminster: British Music Society, 1992, pp. 10–14.

Assesses Byrd's consort songs, using lesser known examples from the recorded repertory.

VII.Wm   Woudhuysen, H.R. "Musical admirers," in *Sir Philip Sidney and the circulation of manuscripts, 1558–1640.* Oxford: Clarendon, 1996, pp. 249–57.

Seeks to discover from whom Byrd received manuscript copies of Sidney's poems before their publication.

Recommended items from the first edition:

39: Dent, Edward J. "William Byrd and the madrigal," in *Festschrift fur Johannes Wolf zu seinem sechsigsten Geburtstage,* ed. Walter Lott *et al.* Muiskwissenschaftliche Beitrage. Berlin: Breslauer, 1929; reprint ed., Hildesheim: Olms, 1978, pp. 24–30.

42: Einstein, Alfred. "The Elizabethan madrigal and 'Musica transalpina.'" *Music & letters* 25 (1944): 66–77.

49: Brown, David. "William Byrd's 1588 volume." *Music & letters* 38 (1957): 371–77.

51: Zimmerman, Franklin B. "Advanced tonal design in the partsongs of William Byrd," in *Bericht uber den siebenten Internationalen Musikwissenschaftlichen Kongress Koln 1958,* ed. Gerald Abraham et al. Kassel: Barenreiter, 1959, pp. 322–26.

53: Dart, Thurston and Brett, Philip. "Songs by William Byrd in manuscripts at Harvard." *Harvard library bulletin* 14 (1960): 343–65.

56: Andrews, H.K. "Transposition of Byrd's vocal polyphony." *Music & letters* 43 (1962): 25–37.

57: Brett, Philip. "The English consort song." *Proceedings of the Royal Musical Association* 88 (1961/62): 73–88.

58: Kerman, Joseph. "The native tradition of secular song: Byrd and Gibbons," in *The Elizabethan madrigal: a comparative study.* American Musicological Society studies and documents, 4. New York: American Musicological Society; London: Oxford University Press, 1962, pp. 99–127.

59: Andrews, H. K. "Printed sources of William Byrd's 'Psalmes, sonets and songs.'" *Music & letters* 44 (1963): 5–20.

63: Brett, Philip. "Edward Paston (1550–1630): a Norfolk gentleman and his musical collection." *Transactions of the Cambridge Bibliographical Society* 4 (1964): 51–69.

66: Duckles, Vincent. "The English musical elegy of the late Renaissance," in *Aspects of medieval and Renaissance music: a birthday offering to Gustave Reese,* ed. Jan LaRue. New York: Norton, 1966; London: Dent, 1967; reprint ed., Festschrift series, 2. New York: Pendragon, 1978, pp. 134–53.

69: Fellowes, E.H. *English madrigal verse, 1588–1632,* 3rd ed., rev. and enl. Frederick W. Sternfeld and David Greer. Oxford: Clarendon, 1967.

82: Brett, Philip. "Did Byrd write 'Non nobis, Domine'?" *Musical times* 113 (1972): 855–57.

83: Brett, Philip. "Word-setting in the songs of William Byrd." *Proceedings of the Royal Musical Association* 98 (1971–72): 47–64.

92: Roberts, Anthony. "Byrd's other conceite." *Musical times* 116 (1975): 423–27.

101: Knight, Ellen E. "The praise of musicke: John Case, Thomas Watson, and William Byrd." *Current musicology* 30 (1981): 37–51.

105: Monson, Craig. *Voices and viols in England, 1600–1650: the sources and the music.* Studies in musicology, 55. Ann Arbor: UMI Research Press, 1982.

106: Hall, Alison. "William Byrd," in *E.H. Fellowes: an index to The English madrigalists and The English school of lutenist song writers.* Music Library Association index and bibliography series, 23. Boston, MA: Music Library Association, 1984, pp. 12–15.

VIII

BYRD'S INSTRUMENTAL MUSIC IN GENERAL

VIII.Ib   Irving, John. "Byrd and Tomkins: the instrumental music," in *Byrd studies,* ed. Alan Brown and Richard Turbet. Cambridge: Cambridge University Press, 1992, pp. 141–58.

Compares the full range of either composers' keyboard corpus, noting not only where Tomkins follows Byrd but also where he develops certain of Byrd's traits, and where he seems uninfluenced. Though the author mentions in a footnote Tomkins's familiarity with Byrd's fantasias in six parts, he confines his comments on the consort corpus to those in three; Tomkins composed fifteen such works, Byrd only three, and he sees little debt to Byrd among Tomkins's more voluminous output.

VIII.Sb   Smith, David J. "Byrd reconstructed: in search of consort models for keyboard dances by Byrd." *Annual Byrd newsletter* 5 (1999): 6–8.

Review article in which the author discusses the reconstructions of what may have been the original versions of several of Byrd's pavans and galliards, and reaches challenging conclusions concerning the number of works that may have originated in this way.

Recommended item from the first edition:

129: Neighbour, Oliver. *The consort and keyboard music of William Byrd.* The music of William Byrd, 3. London: Faber; Berkeley: University of California Press, 1978; paperback ed., London: Faber, 1984.

IX

CONSORT MUSIC

IX.Ah   Ashbee, Andrew. *The harmonious music of John Jenkins.* Vol.1: *The fantasias for viols.* Surbiton: Toccata, 1992.

Chapter two, "The English consort fantasia before Jenkins," contains many references to Byrd, of interest for being from the perspective of the half-century-younger Jenkins.

IX.Av   Ashbee, Andrew, Thompson, Andrew, and Wainwright, Jonathan, comps. *The viola da Gamba Society index of manuscripts containing consort music.* Vol. 1. Aldershot: Ashgate, 2001.

Many entries under Byrd, page 397. Winner of the year's C.B. Oldman Prize.

IX.Bb   Bennett, John. "Byrd and Jacobean consort music: a look at Richard Mico," in *Byrd studies,* ed. Alan Brown and Richard Turbet. Cambridge: Cambridge University Press, 1992, pp. 129–40.

Takes issue with the opinion expressed in 1978Nc that Byrd's consort music exerted a minimal influence over later composers in the genre, and considers its effect on the small but refined corpus of Byrd's younger contemporary, Richard Mico.

IX.Iw   Irving, John. "William Byrd and the three-part ayres of Thomas
               Holmes." *Brio* 29 (1992): 71–77.

               Concludes that, *pace* Ernst H. Meyer in *English chamber music from
               the Middle Ages to Purcell,* 2nd ed. (London: Lawrence and Wishart,
               1982), p. 172, Holmes's pieces owe little to comparable works by
               Byrd in terms of structure, and nothing in terms of intellectual depth.
               The article is carefully argued and well illustrated.

               Note: Holmes's pieces were subsequently published as *Pavin, almain
               and 3 ayres a3 (Tr Tr B),* ed. Patrice Connelly. Viola da Gamba Soci-
               ety of Great Britain supplementary publications, 168. York: Viola da
               Gamba Society of Great Britain, 1993.

IX.Ml   McCoy, Stewart. "Lost lute solos revealed in a Paston manuscript."
               Lute 26 (1986): 21–39.

               Includes reconstruction as a lute solo of T 378 based on a study of
               cantus contamination — inconsistent inclusion of the cantus part in
               the intabulation — in Paston lute sources.

IX.Pb   Pike, Lionel. "Byrd's 'echo' fantasias?" *Annual Byrd newsletter* 10
               (2004): 7–10.

               Looks at aspects of the structural influence of T 387 and T 388 on
               later composers, and at what might originally have influenced Byrd.

IX.PIb   Pinto, David. "Byrd and Ferrabosco, a generation on." *Annual Byrd
               newsletter* 10 (2004): 10–14.

               Investigates the interplay of influences between Byrd and the older
               and younger Ferrabosco, culminating in an assessment of the recep-
               tion of Byrd's consort music among Jacobean players.

IX.Rw   Rastall, Richard. "William Byrd: Fifth Pavan reconstructed for
               viols." *Annual Byrd newsletter* 3 (1997): 11.

               Introduction to edition of T 491 printed in *Early music review* 31
               (1997): 20–21 and subsequently revised in R.

IX.Rwi   Rastall, Richard. "William Byrd's string fantasia 6/g1," in *Liber ami-
               corum John Steele: a musicological tribute,* ed. Warren Duke.
               Festschrift series, 16. Stuyvesant: Pendragon, 1997, pp. 139–70.

Disputes received wisdom that Byrd was dissatisfied with aspects of this fantasy (T 387) and that the fellow work he published in 1611 made good some inadequacies allegedly perceived by Byrd in his "earlier" piece. Suggests that the fantasy in question may not have been the earlier of the two, and can be judged a success on its own terms.

IX.ROw   Rowland-Jones, Anthony. "William Byrd, for the 450th anniversary of his birth: some thoughts on a familiar three-part consort." *Recorder magazine* 13 (1993): 52–54.

Musical analysis of T 377 with practical thoughts on performance by recorders.

IX.Tu   Turbet, Richard. "A unique Byrd arrangement." *Early Music Forum of Scotland newsletter* 6 (1994): [15–16].

Discussion of editorial decisions taken when reconstructing the 1588 arrangement for broken consort of T 491 for publication as P and subsequent performance. See also the editorial notes to this edition, and the author's letter "Byrd reconstructed," *Early music news* 180 (1993): 16.

X

KEYBOARD MUSIC

X.Bb   Brookes, Virginia. *British keyboard music to c. 1660: sources and thematic index.* Oxford: Clarendon, 1996.

Part I lists MS and printed sources with their contents. Part II, the thematic index, is also an index to part I. Byrd is on pages 276–96 and 1332–478. After two addenda and a short apppendix, the volume concludes with "Computerized codes of musical incipits." This book covers some of the same ground as X.Hb, which lacks the listings of contents and the thematic index but notes more printed editions and has a bibliography. Despite the date of publication, the present volume does not include reference to MB LXVI.

X.BRw   Brown, Alan. "William Byrd (1539 or 1540–1623)," in *Keyboard music before 1700*, ed. Alexander Silbiger. 2nd ed. Routledge studies in musical genres. New York: Routledge, 2004, pp. 36–47.

Magisterial survey within chapter on "England," pp. 23–89. The succeeding section, "Performance practice," pp. 47–50, is based on
Byrd's music. Placing Byrd in context makes clear what little he had
on which to build his pioneering compositions for keyboard, an
achievement that seems ever more remarkable. The author includes
many fresh and perceptive observations.

X.BRwo   Brown, Alan "'The woods so wild': notes on a Byrd text," in *Sundry
           sorts of music books: essays on the British Library collections, pre-
           sented to O.W. Neighbour on his 70th birthday,* ed. Chris Banks,
           Arthur Searle, and Malcolm Turner. London: British Library, 1993,
           pp. 54–66.

           Discusses the value of sources other than the copy text in editing this
           piece and, by implication, others.

X.Db   Dirksen, Pieter. "Byrd and Sweelinck: some cursory notes." *Annual
           Byrd newsletter* 7 (2001): 11–20.

           Far-from-cursory consideration of evidence linking the two compos-
           ers. Suggests that an anonymous *Praeludium* (FVB [CXVII]) once
           ascribed to Sweelinck may be by Byrd. Discusses and transcribes the
           version of T 496 from the Duben Tablature Book, "the only source
           with a documented connection with the Sweelinck school."

X.Gb   Gaskin, Hilary. "Baldwin and the Nevell hand," in *Byrd studies,* ed.
           Alan Brown and Richard Turbet. Cambridge: Cambridge University
           Press, 1992, pp. 159–73.

           Examines the hand employed by the scribe John Baldwin in My
           Ladye Nevells Booke and discusses his copying procedures.

X.GOc   Goodwin, Christopher. "A candidate lyric for Byrd's *The maiden's
           songe.*" *Annual Byrd newsletter* 10 (2004): 19–26.

           Proposes and quotes in full the relevant lyric from *GB-Lbl* Add. MS
           15233, noting and dismissing alternatives. Discusses in great depth
           the manuscript's contents and provenance, concluding that it may
           have been owned by William Byrd's brother Symond. Further support
           for this source's association with Byrd is provided in Richard Turbet's
           letter "More on a Byrd source," in *Early music review* 100 (2004): 24,
           to which this issue of *Annual Byrd newsletter* is a supplement.

X.Hb   Harley, John. *British harpsichord music.* Aldershot: Scolar, 1992-94. Vol. 1: *Sources.* Vol. 2: *History.*

Volume 1 covers printed and manuscript sources, though access is by composer, e.g. Byrd, not by individual pieces: for this, see 125 (in list of "Recommended items from first edition" below). The first three chapters of volume 2 are "The sixteenth century before Byrd," "William Byrd," and "Byrd's successors." Appendix F is "Dates of Byrd's keyboard music." The chronological treatment is useful in placing Byrd in perspective, and it is extended to the individual chapter on Byrd, in which the author endeavours to construct a chronology for Byrd's pieces and discusses the structure of several of them by category. In Appendix F, he is able to supply or suggest broad or latest datings for about half of Byrd's works for keyboard.

X.Hby   Harley, John. "Byrd's semidetached keyboard fantasia." *Annual Byrd newsletter* 4 (1998): 10.

A note on the structure of T 456.

X.Hm   Harley, John. "'My Ladye Nevell' revealed." *Music & letters* 86 (2005): 1–15.

Identifies the dedicatee of My Ladye Nevells Book, and draws attention to a newly discovered document about Byrd himself.

X.HUm   Hunter, Desmond. "My Ladye Nevells Booke and the art of gracing," in *Byrd studies,* ed. Alan Brown and Richard Turbet. Cambridge: Cambridge University Press, 1992, pp. 174–92.

Examines the application of grace signs in H and reappraises keyboard gracing from evidence in the manuscript against the background of a more general discussion of virginalist ornamentation.

X.HUs   Hunter, Desmond. "Some preliminary thoughts on tempo in virginalist music by Byrd." *Annual Byrd newsletter* 1 (1995): 5–6.

Considering figuration, texture, and mode, makes a case for flexible tempi in the performance of fantasias and variations by Byrd.

X.KEs   Kent, Christopher. "The 16th-century English organ repertoire, reviewed in the light of the Suffolk fragments," in *Fanfare for an organ builder: essays presented to Noel Mander to celebrate the six-tieth anniversary of his commencement in business as an organ builder.* Oxford: Positif, 1996, pp. 109–16.

Although it is accepted that all the pieces in H are playable on the virginals, Kent demonstrates that five pieces from H — both fanta-sias, both complete voluntaries, and the hexachord fantasia (T 451, 453, 526, 527 and 523) — have compasses playable on the contem-porary organ manual.

X.Mb   Moroney, Davitt. "'Bounds and compasses': the range of Byrd's keyboards," in *Sundry sorts of music books: essays on the British Library collections, presented to Oliver Neighbour on his 70th birth-day,* ed. Chris Banks, Arthur Searle, and Malcolm Turner. London: British Library, 1993, pp. 67–88.

Describes the features of the three ranges of keyboard, taking tuning and retuning into account, with a view to establishing whether cer-tain pieces were written for specific instruments, at particular periods in Byrd's composing life.

X.Ns   Neighbour, Oliver. "Some anonymous keyboard pieces considered in relation to Byrd," in *Byrd studies,* ed. Alan Brown and Richard Tur-bet. Cambridge: Cambridge University Press, 1992, pp. 193–201.

Looks at pieces from the Forster and Weelkes virginal books, *GB-Lbl* R.M. 24.d.3 and Add.30485 respectively. Four of the anonymous works are now established in the Byrd canon — T 437, 475, 516 and 517. He then considers whether Byrd was responsible for some key-board arrangements of his own vocal music, and devotes his final section to one particularly example, T 31.

X.NIk   Nitz, Genoveva. *Die Klanglichkeit in der englischen Virginalmusik der 16. Jahrhunderts.* Munchner Veroffentlichungen zur Musikge-schichte, 27. Tutzing: Schneider, 1979.

Devotes four of ten chapters (III–VI) to Byrd, discussing the fanta-sias, grounds, and descriptive music, and comparing him with younger virginalists such as Bull and Gibbons.

X.NOf   Northcott, Bayan. "The first genius of the keyboard." *Independent* (1 October 1999): 19.

Review article inspired by Davitt Moroney's recording of Byrd's complete keyboard works, and emphasizing the originality, skill, and attractiveness of Byrd's music.

X.Ph   Pike, Lionel. *Hexachords in late-Reaissance music.* Aldershot: Ashgate, 1998.

The section "The basic hexachords" contains a stimulating analysis of T 524, and the section "New directions" begins with similarly revelatory anayses of T 522 and 523. New light is shed on all three compositions from the perspective of the author's study of the evolution of hexachords.

X.PIm   Pinto, David. "Marsh, Mico and attributions." *Chelys* 27 (1999): 40–58.

Notes that the third strain of pavan T 499 is quoted by Mico in the "second" (*recte* third) of his pavan no. 3 for four viols MB LXV no. 14.

X.Sk   Schulenberg, David L. "The keyboard works of William Byrd: some questions of attribution, chronology, and style." *Musica disciplina* 47 (1993): 99–121.

Raises provocative questions about Byrd's keyboard canon. Disputes the existence of a "late" keyboard style, and queries attributions based on fewer than two corroborative independent sources or on one of proven proximity to the composer.

X.SMs   Smith, David. "Some stylistic correspondences between the keyboard music of Byrd and Philips: an introductory note." *Annual Byrd newsletter* 1 (1995): 7–8.

Noting that Philips was a pupil of Byrd, identifies the former's keyboard figuration as one of the superficial details in which he is indebted to his master. Goes on to point out that Philips composed a fantasia on the same theme as one of Byrd's. Nevertheless beneath the surface detail, Philips's keyboard music was a product of the Spanish Netherlands whither he emigrated.

X.Tb   Turbet, Richard. "Byrd tercentenary keyboard anthologies: an appendix to Routh." *Annual Byrd newsletter* 4 (1998): 10–11.

Lists the contents of three anthologies of keyboard music by Byrd, published during 1923, and, quite appropriately, omitted from 125 (see list of "Recommended items from the first edition" below).

Note: The following two corrigenda are required: item 6 from *The Byrd organ book* is an anonymous item, numbered 852 in X.Bb; and item 7 is not attributed to, nor is it by, Martin Peerson, but is misattributed to Byrd in its source.

X.Tp   Turbet, Richard. "Pauer's edition of Byrd." *Annual Byrd newsletter* 3 (1997): 6.

Short paragraph containing list of contents of historically significant publication.

Recommended items from the first edition:

110: Borren, Charles van den. "Some notes on 'My Ladye Nevells booke.'" *Musical times* 67 (1926): 1075–76.

114: Tuttle, Stephen D. "The keyboard music of Tallis and Byrd." *Bulletin of the American Musicological Society* 4 (1940): 31–32.

115: Whittaker, W. Gillies. "Byrd's and Bull's 'Walsingham' variations." *Music review* 3 (1942): 270–79.

119: Brown, Alan. "'My Lady Nevell's book' as a source of Byrd's keyboard music." *Proceedings of the Royal Musical Association* 95 (1968–69): 29–39.

121: Apel, Willi. *The history of keyboard music to 1700,* transl. & rev. Hans Tischler. Bloomington: Indiana University Press, 1972.

124: Caldwell, John. *English keyboard music before the nineteenth century.* Blackwell's music series. Oxford: Blackwell, 1973; reprint ed., New York: Dover, 1985.

125: Routh, Francis. "William Byrd 1543–1623," in *Early English organ music from the Middle Ages to 1837.* Studies in church music. London: Barrie & Jenkins; New York: Barnes & Noble, 1973, pp. 67–79.

126: Brown, Alan. "Keyboard music by Byrd 'upon a plainsong.'" *Organ yearbook* 5 (1974): 30–39.

127: Brown, Alan. "Parthenia: some aspects of notation and performance." *Consort* 32 (1976): 176–82.

128: Koopman, Ton. "'My Ladye Nevell's booke' and old fingering." *English harpsichord magazine* 2 (1977): 5–10.

131: Morin, Elisabeth. *Essai de stylistique comparee. (Les variations de William Byrd et John Tomkins sur "John come kiss me now.")* Semiologie et analyse musicales. 2 vols. Montreal: Les presses de l'Universite de Montreal, 1979. French and English texts.

132: Russell, Lucy Hallman. "A comparison of the 'Walsingham' variations by Byrd and Bull," in *Bericht uber den Internationalen Musikwissenschaftlichen Kongress, Berlin 1974*, ed. Hellmut Kuhn and Peter Nitsche. Kassel: Barenreiter, 1980, pp. 277–79.

133: le Huray, Peter. "English keyboard fingering in the 16th and early 17th centuries," in *Source materials and the interpretation of music: a memorial volume to Thurston Dart*, ed. Ian Bent. London: Stainer & Bell, 1981, pp. 227–57.

136: Chaplin, Sylvia A. "English virginal music between 1560 and 1660." *Music teacher* 63 (July 1984): 8–9; (August 1984): 10–11, 29; (September 1984): 14–15, 19.

137: Cunningham, Walker. *The keyboard music of John Bull.* Studies in musicology, 71. Ann Arbor: UMI Research Press, 1984.

138: Pacey, Robert. "Byrd's keyboard music: a Lincolnshire source." *Music & letters* 66 (1985): 123–26.

140: Arneson, Arne J. and Williams, Stacie. *The harpsichord booke: being a plaine & simple index to printed colections of musick by different masters for the harpsichord, spinnet, clavichord, & virginall.* Madison: Index House, 1986.

XI

BIBLIOGRAPHICAL STUDIES

XI.Bc   Brett, Philip and Smith, Jeremy. "Computer collation of divergent early prints in The Byrd edition." *Computing in musicology* 12 (1999–2000): 251–60.

Demonstrates that within a single print run, typesetting by hand allowed small changes to be made from one copy to another.

XI.Cm   Charteris, Richard. "Manuscript additions of music by John Dowland and his contemporaries in two sixteenth-century prints." *Consort* 37 (1981): 399–401.

The additions relevant to Byrd consist of fragmentary secular vocal and instrumental pieces in the copy of the 1575 *Cantiones* at *EIRE-Dtc* B.1.32.

XI.Eb   Eccles, Mark "Bynneman's books." *Library,* 5th ser., 12 (1957): 81–92.

Inventory of books, 1583, owned by leading London printer Henry Bynneman. Includes important references to his stock of the 1575 *Cantiones.*

XI.Gb   Greenhalgh, Michael. "A Byrd discography," in *Byrd studies,* ed. Alan Brown and Richard Turbet. Cambridge: Cambridge University Press, 1992, pp. 202–64.

Lists all recordings of Byrd's original music available commercially in the United Kingdom between 1923 and 1988, effectively covering period up to and including the long playing (LP) disc. See also XI.Gby and Chapter 4.

XI.Gby   Greenhalgh, Michael. "A Byrd discography supplement." *Brio* 33 (1996): 19–54.

Updates XI.Gb from 1989 to 1994, effectively the beginning of the period when the compact disc (CD) began to dominate. Includes addenda from 1922–88. See also Chapter 4.

XI.Kb   Kerman, Joseph. "The Byrd edition—in print and on disc." *Early music* 29 (2001): 109–18.

Review-article discussing volumes 5–9 of the printed *Byrd edition* and discs 1–5 of the recorded *Byrd edition*. In the light of the latter, Kerman revises his opinions about the authenticity of some motets, but in other instances he is critical of The Cardinall's Musick for "lumbering" Byrd with what he still regards as inauthentic pieces. As to the former, he queries aspects of Edwards's reconstruction of T 182 but is complimentary about other such efforts. Having discussed the pitch preferred by The Cardinall's Musick, he closes with praise for the way Philip Brett, in his introductions to the printed *Gradualia* volumes, succeeded in imbuing each mass with "a new aesthetic and a new spiritual profile."

XI.Mw   Mateer, David. "William Byrd, John Petre and Oxford, Bodleian MS Mus. Sch. E. 423." *Royal Musical Association research chronicle* 29 (1996): 21–46.

Establishes that this "important and authoritative source for the vocal music of William Byrd" was originally owned by Byrd's patron John, Lord Petre, and that the sole surviving partbook is in the hand of Petre's chief steward John Bentley.

XI.Mt   Morehen, John. "Thomas Snodham, and the printing of William Byrd's *Psalmes, songs, and sonnets* (1611)." *Transactions of the Cambridge Bibliographical Society* 12 (2001): 91–131.

Detailed account of the procedures of Snodham, the adopted son of the late Thomas East, Byrd's favoured printer.

XI.Sh   Smith, Jeremy L. "The hidden editions of Thomas East." *Notes* 53 (1997): 1059–91.

Includes identification of five such editions of music by Byrd. See also XI.St.

XI.Sp   Smith, Jeremy. "Print culture and the Elizabethan composer." *Fontes artis musicae* 48 (2001): 156–70.

Pays particular attention to Byrd in this discussion about the new relationship between composers and consumers (and their intermediaries, patrons, and printers) during the early development of music printing.

XI.St   Smith, Jeremy L. *Thomas East and music publishing in Renaissance England.* New York: Oxford University Press, 2003.

Comprehensive biography and study of Byrd's sometime assign. There are many references to Byrd throughout the book, especially in Chapters 4 and 5: "Music publishing during Byrd's monopoly (1588–1593). Part I: Byrd's publishing agenda" and "Music printing during Byrd's monopoly (1588–1593). Part II: The benefits to East."

XI.Tb   Turbet, Richard. "Byrd sleevenotes." *Annual Byrd newsletter* 6 (2000): 12.

Summary of notes containing original material. See also "More Byrd sleevenotes," 7 (2001): 6. In the light of the continuing absence of the second volume of *The music of William Byrd,* it is worth adding that the notes accompanying *William Byrd: songs and ensemble music* (Musicaphon M 56808) written by David Pinto are both perceptive and informative, drawing attention to an otherwise neglected appearance of the ubiquitous "Goodnight" ground.

XI.Tby   Turbet, Richard. "Byrd's music in provincial imprints from 1770 to the present, with special reference to H.B. Collins," in *Branches of literature and music: proceedings of the thirteenth Seminar on the History of the Provincial Book Trade held in Bristol, 11–13 July 1995,* ed. M.T. Richardson. Bristol: University of Bristol Library, 2000, pp. 64–74.

Notes all such items, paying particular attention to the early-twentieth-century editions of Colins, some of which are shown to qualify as provincial. See also XI.Th.

Note: An inaccuracy in footnote 3 is corrected in XII.Ts.

XI.Te   Turbet, Richard. "Early printed editions of Byrd: an addendum and a checklist of articles." *Annual Byrd newsletter* 10 (2004): 16.

Brings together the literature about all known publications of Byrd's music, 1623–1901.

XI.Tf   Turbet, Richard, ed. "The full original text of the Queen's Majesty's letters patent to Thomas Tallis and William Byrd for the printing of music," in *William Byrd: a guide to research*. Garland composer resource manuals, 7; Garland reference library of the humanities, 759. New York: Garland, 1987, pp. 325–27.

The only complete published transcription of the original Elizabethan text, as distinct from "The extract and effect," which is reproduced everywhere else.

XI.Th   Turbet, Richard. "H.B. Collins's editions of Byrd: a supplementary note." *Annual Byrd newsletter* 7 (2001): 6.

Further information about the lithographer, supplementary to XI.Tby.

XI.Tho   Turbet, Richard. "Holst's editions of Byrd." *International Assocation of Music Libraries, Archives and Documentation Centres United Kingdom Branch newsletter* 33 (1997): 7–8.

Mentions Holst's misattribution of T 126 to Samuel Wesley (see also XII.Ow), his Anglican adaptation of T 2, and the problems of cataloguing his edition of the Benedictus from T 2.

XI.Tt   Turbet, Richard. "To Oliver Neighbour on his eightieth birthday." *Brio* 40 (Spring/Summer 2003): 47–48.

The Fitzwilliam Virginal Book was first published in fascicles, 1894–99. Using data supplied by Oliver Neighbour, lists each fascicle and provides date on wrapper and date of copyright deposit at British Museum.

XI.Ttu   Turbet, Richard. *Tudor music: a research and information guide with an appendix updating William Byrd: a guide to research*. Music research and information guides, 18; Garland reference library of the humanities, 1122. New York: Garland, 1994.

Many items in the main subject sequence refer to Byrd, traceable in the index. The appendix consists of ten sections the contents of which are subsumed within the present volume, except for TM.

Recommended items from the first edition:

24: Krummel, D.W. "Thomas Tallis and William Byrd (1575)," in *English music printing, 1553–1700.* Bibliographical Society publications, 1971. London: Bibliographical Society, 1975, pp. 15–17.

27: Brett, Philip. "Editing Byrd." *Musical times* 121 (1980): 492–95, 557–59.

31: Fenlon, Iain and Milsom, John. "'Ruled paper imprinted': music paper and patents in sixteenth-century England." *Journal of the American Musicological Society* 37 (1984): 139–63.

XII

BYRD SINCE THE SEVENTEENTH CENTURY

XII.Ae   Ackroyd, Peter. *English music.* London: Hamilton, 1992.

Chapter 10 of Peter Ackroyd's novel focuses on Byrd, and two excerpts were published in *Early music news* 208 (1996): 14–15 and 212 (1996): 10–11.

XII.Bh   Bolt, Rodney. *History play: the lives and afterlife of Christopher Marlowe.* London: HarperCollins, 2004.

Byrd appears in this work of fiction as a great figure known to Marlowe. Bolt creditably cites I.Hwi (1997) to confirm that William Byrd composed the incidental music to *Ricardus Tertius.* Had he but read the revised reprint he would have caught up with the discovery that it was composed by a namesake.

XII.Cl   Charlton, Alan. "*Look and bow down:* a 21st century compositional response." *Annual Byrd newsletter* 9 (2003): 13–19.

Describes the circumstances of the commission to compose a work based on the fragments of T 372 printed in A xvi, pp. 178–79, and how the task of composition was approached.

XII.Gc   Gordon, Mary. *The Children of the Chapel.* London: Masters, 1864; reprint ed., Athens, OH: Ohio University Press, 1982.

"William Byrd is one of the central figures of the novel and probably the closest thing in the work to a hero" (Introduction, reprint ed., p. xxiv). On the title page of the reprint edition, edited with an introduction by Robert E. Lougy, Algernon Charles Swinburne is added as co-author. This is, by a considerable distance, qualitatively the worst item listed within the present monograph, and a most dislikeable book, its sadistic sanctimony masquerading as moral evangelism.

XII.GRm   Griffiths, David. "The music in York Minster." *Musical times* 123 (1982): 633–37.

Contains a brief biography of Jane Stainton who, during the seventeenth century, owned the only surviving set of the first edition of Byrd's first *Gradualia,* 1605.

XII.Hb   Holdsworth, Donald "Broadcast Choral Evensong: survey of Byrd's music performed." *Annual Byrd newsletter* 1 (1995): 6.

Table showing frequency with which works by Byrd have been included in "Choral Evensong," a programme broadcast on radio by the British Broadcasting Corporation (BBC) since 1926, generally once a week from a cathedral, collegiate chapel, or royal peculiar. The survey runs to 1989.

XII.Hs   Holdsworth, Donald. *Survey of church music performed in UK cathedrals (39) & churches (34) during 1962.* Stretton-on-Fosse: Holdsworth, 1963.

The list includes 44 works by Byrd not mentioned in *Sixty years of church music* (Church Music Society occasional paper no. 24) published in 1960 with data compiled in 1958, which concentrated on pieces sung in ten or more places. See XII.TUbyrdt.

XII.Np   Neighbour, Oliver. "Philip Brett, 1937–2002." *Annual Byrd newsletter* 9 (2003): 20.

Obituary that penetrates to the heart of why Brett's Byrd scholarship has such seminal and resonating significance.

Note: Reprinted as "In memoriam Philip Brett. 1937–2002: a great friend of the William Byrd Festival, to whom this year's Festival is dedicated," in *William Byrd Festival, August 18–31, 2003,* pp. 2–3, Portland, OR, U.S.A. (see XII.W).

XII.Ob   Olleson, Philip. "Byrd, the Confitebor, and Handel's hymns," in *Samuel Wesley: the man and his music.* Woodbridge: Boydell, 2003, pp. 187–202.

Condensed account of events described in 2003Ow, within the broad context of Wesley's biography.

XII.Ow   Olleson, Philip. "'William Byrde's excellent antiphone': Samuel Wesley's projected edition of selections from *Gradualia.*" *Annual Byrd newsletter* 9 (2003): 7–9.

Comprehensive account of Wesley's abortive project of the mid-1820s.

Note: An error in transmission caused the word "antiphone" to appear in the title instead of "antiphones."

XII.Pb   Parlett, Graham. "Byrd and Bax." *Annual Byrd newsletter* 6 (2000): 8–11.

Ponders what impressed Bax about Byrd, particularly the influence of T 3 on *Mater ora filium,* and broadens the discussion to consider Bax's attitude to early music in general.

XII.PAb   Patton, John and Turbet, Richard. "Byrd in British cathedrals, 1986." *Musical opinion* 111 (1988): 52–59.

Lists all works by Byrd sung in cathedrals and comparable establishments in the British Isles during 1986. Two complementary listings indicate which choirs sang the various works, listed alphabetically, and which works were in the repertories of the listed choirs. The relevant information concerning three cathedral choirs absent from this survey is listed in XII.TUbyrdt. See also XII.PAc.

XII.PAc   Patton, John and Taylor, Steve. *A century of cathedral music, 1898–1998: a comparison with previous music surveys.* Winchester: Patton, 2000.

Includes data about performances of Byrd's music in British cathedrals during 1998. Much less detailed than XII.PAb, and inaccurate: for instance, on page 172, T 197 (the *Great Service*) had 0 performances at Eucharists in 1986, not 15, and the single performance — gratifying, if genuine — in 1998 therefore warrants a different symbol.

XII.POm   Popkin, J.M. *Musical monuments.* London: Saur, 1986.

Contains descriptions of memorials to Byrd in English churches.

XII.Rw   Reeve, Edward Henry Lisle. "The William Byrd tercentenary," in Turbet, Richard. *William Byrd: a guide to research.* Garland composer resource manuals, 7; Garland reference library of the humanities, 759. New York: Garland, 1987, pp. 303–16.

First hand descriptions of the main events of 1923 transcribed from a record kept by the Rector of Stondon Massey, where Byrd is buried, and where many of the events took place. Reeve also provides the only surviving list of the members of the impressive Byrd Tercentenary Committee. All members noted as being listed in the first edition of *New Grove* survived into the second (London: Macmillan; New York: Grove Dictionaries, 2001) except The Rev. A. Ramsbotham: see note 1 on page 313. On page 305 the name following that of Ramsbotham should be Cyril B. Rootham, not Bootham.

XII.Sp   Shay, Robert. "Purcell as collector of 'ancient' music: Fitzwilliam MS 88," in *Purcell studies,* ed. Curtis Price. Cambridge: Cambridge University Press, 1995, pp. 35–50.

Directs attention to Purcell's method of copying T 204 and T 207. See also XII.Tw.

XII.SPr   Spink, Ian. *Restoration cathedral music, 1660–1714.* Oxford studies in British church music. Oxford: Clarendon, 1993.

Contains some interesting observations concerning Blow's debt to composers such as Byrd and Gibbons. Of particular value is the inclusion of prefaces to all six volumes of Tudway's MS "Services and anthems" (1715–20), which provide an indication of albeit conservative contemporary attitudes to the music of Byrd and his contemporaries, during the period when Byrd's reputation was at its nadir.

XII.Tw   Thompson, Robert. "William Byrd and the late 17th century." *Annual Byrd newsletter* 2 (1996): 10–12.

Discusses the treatment of Byrd's music, particularly T 30 at the hands of Purcell and Henry Aldrich in post-Restoration manuscripts.

XII.TUa   Turbet, Richard. "An affair of honour: 'Tudor church music,' the ousting of Richard Terry, and a Trust vindicated." *Music & letters* 76 (1995): 593–600.

              Brings to the attention of researchers the Tudor Church Music Archive of the Carnegie United Kingdom Trust at the Scottish Record Office, Edinburgh, and reveals the conception, progress, and disintegration of the *Tudor church music* series (*vide* TCM *supra*) including the remarkable events surrounding the removal of Terry as editor-in-chief. Three of the series' ten volumes are devoted to Byrd. See also XII.TUm.

XII.TUb   Turbet, Richard. "Byrd 450: a review of events." *Early Music Forum of Scotland newsletter* 9 (1995): 4–6.

              Account of the many musical activities celebrating what was then thought to be the 450th anniversary of Byrd's birth in 1993.

XII.TUby   Turbet, Richard. "Byrd & Ivor Gurney."*Annual Byrd newsletter* 3 (1997): 7.

              Comments on Gurney's two intense poems about Byrd.

XII.TUbyr   Turbet, Richard. "Byrd at 450." *Brio* 31 (1994): 96–102.

              Adds biographical and bibliographical information that had come to light since the publication of XI.Tt. See also XII.TUf and XII.TUm.

XII.TUbyrd   Turbet, Richard. "Byrd's music at Lincoln: a supplementary note." *Annual Byrd newsletter* 2 (1996): 9.

              Looks at the fortunes of Byrd's music in two collections of anthem texts published in Lincoln during the eighteenth and nineteenth centuries. Supplements II.Tw.

XII.TUbyrdt   Turbet, Richard. "Byrd tercentenary dinner." *Annual Byrd newsletter* 6 (2000): 6.

              Identifies location, music performed and the performers, 1923.

XII.TUbyrdth Turbet, Richard. "Byrd throughout all generations." *Cathedral music* 35 (1992): 19–24.

Traces the popularity or otherwise of Byrd's sacred music in English cathedrals from the seventeenth century to 1986. Includes a supplement to XII.Pb.

XII.TUc   Turbet, Richard. "The Carnegie Trust and Byrd's music in the 1920s." *Annual Byrd newsletter* 2 (1996): 9.

Provides full information about two files devoted to Byrd in the Trust's Tudor Church Music Archive (see XII.TUa).

XII.TUf   Turbet, Richard. "The fall and rise of William Byrd," in *Sundry sorts of music books: essays on the British Library collections, presented to O.W. Neighbour on his 70th birthday,* ed. Chris Banks, Arthur Searle and Malcolm Turner. London: British Library, 1993, pp. 119–28.

Describes how publication of Byrd's music dwindled after his death until the 1840s. After this a publishing revival took place and Byrd's work became re-established by the end of Queen Victoria's reign. See also XII.TUm and item 8 on pp. 101–02 of XII.TUbyr.

XII.TUfr   Turbet, Richard. "Francis Neilson, F.W. Dwelly and the first complete edition of Byrd." *Bulletin of the John Rylands University Library of Manchester* 77 (Summer 1995): 53–58.

Using Neilson's papers deposited in Manchester University Library, traces for the first time his involvement and that of Dwelly in the publishing history of C, Fellowes's complete edition. The correspondence establishes the edition's official title, the corrected dates of publication of the postwar volumes 10–17, and the size of the print run. It can now be presumed that Canon Dwelly's papers have been destroyed.

XII.TUj   Turbet, Richard. "Jubilate for Mr Bird's Service." *Annual Byrd newsletter* 6 (2000): 12.

Introduction to Robert Shenton's eighteenth-century adaptation of T 194c. See EMR in the list of editions *supra.*

XII.TUm   Turbet, Richard. "More early printed editions attributed to Byrd." *Brio* 35 (1998): 105.

Supplements XII.TUf and the relevant section of XII.TUbyr.

XII.TUmu Turbet, Richard. "The Musical Antiquarian Society, 1840–1848." *Brio* 29 (1992): 13–20.

Three of the Society's nineteen publications (all fully listed, along with the volumes of keyboard accompaniments published by Chappell) contained music by Byrd, and the Society can be credited with initiating the resurrection of William Byrd.

Note: The final date on page 19 should read 1843.

XII.TUs Turbet, Richard. "Stopped by the outbreak of war: the Byrd Festival of 1914." *Brio* 39 (Spring/Summer 2002): 24–25.

Cites the only surviving reference, and provides illustration of the only surviving document.

Note: Corrects footnote 3 in XI.Tby.

XII.TUt Turbet, Richard. "Two early printed attributions to Byrd in the Wighton Collection, Dundee." *Annual Byrd newsletter* 8 (2002): 10–13.

Notes two further appearances of *Non nobis Domine* attributed to Byrd, and reproduces one of them — an arrangement by James Oswald — in facsimile. An appendix to the article consists of an edition of an anthem by James Kempson, *circa* 1780, which begins with a "Canon by W. Bird": *Non nobis Domine* set to an English translation.

XII.TUw Turbet, Richard. "William Byrd and the English musical renaissance." *British Music Society newsletter* 45 (1990): 123–24.

Lists several quotations by or about composers of the early twentieth century that testify to the influence of the music of Byrd throughout this period.

XII.TUwi Turbet, Richard. "William Dyce and the Motett Society." *Aberdeen University review* 56 (1996): 442–46.

Account of shortlived but influential society 1841–52, with summary of its publishing activities, intended and actual. It made available much early music, including some by Byrd, in inexpensive, well-produced editions.

XII.TUws   Turbet, Richard. "W. Sterndale Bennett–Fugue on Byrd's *Bow thine ear.*" *Annual Byrd newsletter* 3 (1997): 12.

> Short introduction and first publication of musical text.

XII.W   *William Byrd Festival.*
            U.S. — Portland, OR, 1998–

> Programme of annual festival containing lists of all lectures, services and concerts, and of all the music being performed. Includes perceptive and informative notes on featured music.

XII.WIa   Wilson, Ruth. *Anglican chant and chanting in England, Scotland, and America 1660–1820.* Oxford: Clarendon, 1996.

> Draws attention to the adaptations for four voices in SD of T 192a; see especially pp. 49–51.

OBSOLESCENDA

Items in the first edition omitted from the second edition: 1, 2, 3, 4, 5, 6, 7, 8, 11, 12, 13, 14, 15, 16, 18, 19, 21, 22, 28, 29, 30, 32, 33, 34, 38, 40, 44, 45, 46, 47, 48, 50, 54, 55, 72, 73, 75, 76, 79, 81, 85, 86, 89, 98, 107, 108, 109, 111, 112, 113, 116, 117, 118, 120, 122, 123, 130, 135, 139, 140.

4

Byrd Discography 1995–2003

MICHAEL GREENHALGH

This discography is a comprehensive listing of Byrd recordings published from 1995 to 2003 inclusive. It therefore supplements the same author's "A Byrd discography" in *Byrd studies* edited by Alan Brown and Richard Turbet (Cambridge University Press, 1992), pp. 202–64, and "A Byrd discography supplement" in *Brio* (Vol. 33, No. 1, 1996), pp. 19–54. For an explanation of the order of entries, key to entries, and inclusion policy, which is consistent with the two previous Byrd discographies, see the introduction to the 1992 discography (pp. 202–4). One amendment to the order of entries has been made for this supplement. Five works listed in Grove as doubtful but in the main sequence of Richard Turbet's catalogue (see above) appear here in the Alphabetical list of Latin works: Domine Deus omnipotens; Reges Tharsis, 5vv; Sacris solemnis; Sanctus, 3vv; Vide, Domine, quoniam tribulor. Also listed by Grove as doubtful, Out of the deep, 6vv, appears here in Other English Music, as it has been authenticated by Richard Turbet, "Postscript," *Annual Byrd newsletter* 1 (1995): 4. The Lullaby [Keyboard adaptation] (EK 53) has been retained, as previously listed in Grove 6 as doubtful, though Grove 7 has changed its status to misattributed. Three new abbreviations appear in this supplement: '[ind]' (no date) indicates it has not been possible to verify the issue or reissue date of a recording (in the former case the entry is placed after the dated entries); the other abbreviations designate the new recording formats of super audio compact disc '(sacd)' and digital video disc '(dvd).' It should be noted '(sacd)' is a discrete format, incompatible with cd but '(sacd & cd)' is a hybrid format with a cd layer. Where the supplement entry merely records a different format or catalogue number, usually the result of reissue, from an entry in 1992 and/or 1996, only the entry number is normally cited, though when additional information has come to light this has been added. Some corrected entries also appear with the suffix '[corrected entry].' The assistance of Richard Turbet is gratefully acknowledged.

MASS SETTINGS

[3, 4, 5vv ordinary followed by Gradualia propers]
Mass, 3vv
  2.   Decca 4521702 (2 cds 1996).
  3.   Archiv 4394574 (mc), 4394572 (cd 1994).
  6.   Gimell 4548952 (4 cds 1988).
  9.   Nimbus NI 1762 (8 cds 1998).
 10.   Cardinall's Musick/Andrew Carwood [24'35]; ed Skinner, rec Fitzalan Chapel
        Arundel Castle 11/1999. ASV stereo digital CDGAU 206 (cd 2000).
 11.   Parthenia XVI/Mary Jane Newman 18'27; rec St Matthew's Episcopal Church Bedford New York 1999. Centaur stereo digital CRC 2471 (cd 2000).
 12.   Pro Arte Singers/Paul Hillier 17'27; ed Hillier; rec Auer Recital Hall Indiana University School of Music Bloomington 5/2000. Harmonia Mundi USA stereo digital HMU 907223 (cd 2002).

*Mass, 3vv: Kyrie, Sanctus & Agnus Dei
*3.   Downside Abbey Monks' & School Boys' Choirs [6'00]; rec Downside Abbey Bath 4/1996. Virgin stereo digital VTCD 99 (cd 1996).

*Mass, 3vv: Kyrie & Agnus Dei
*4.   Hilliard Ensemble/Paul Hillier (bar) [4'14]; rec St James Church Clerkenwell 10/1983. HMV stereo digital 5740362 [cd nd] [from 5].
*5.   Downside Abbey Monks' & School Boys' Choirs [3'50]; rec Downside Abbey Bath 4/1996. HMV stereo digital 5742392 [cd nd] [from *3].

*Mass, 3vv: Agnus Dei
*6.   Downside Abbey Monks' & School Boys' Choirs [3'12]; rec Downside Abbey Bath 4/1996. Universal stereo digital 4671402 (2 cds 2000) [from *3].

Mass, 4vv
  4.   Decca 4521702 (2 cds 1996).
 9+.   Arion ARN 58438 [cd nd].
 10.   Etcetera KTC 1031 (cd 1985).
 13.   Gimell 4548952 (4 cds 1988), 4549992 (CD 1991).

14. EMI 5740022 (cd 2000).
16. Virgin VBD 5620132 (2 cds 2002).
17. Nimbus NI 1762 (8 cds 1998).
18. Naxos 8505020 (5 cds 1994); 8553239 (cd 1995); 8505079 (5 cds 1998); 8503071 (3 cds 1999).
19. ECM 4391722 (cd 1994).
20. New College Oxford Choir Clerks/Edward Higginbottom [25'17]; rec Abbaye de Valloires Department de la Somme 4/1995. Collins stereo digital 14872 (cd 1996); CRD CRD 3499 (cd), CRD 5008 (5 cds 2003).
21. Children & Gentlemen of Her Majesty's Chapels Royal, St James's Palace/Richard Popplewell 31'16; rec St Alban's Church Holborn 22–24/ 7/1996. Griffin stereo digital GCCD 4011 (cd 1996).
22. BBC Singers/Bo Holten [22'19]; rec St Giles Cripplegate 7/2/1996. BBC Music Magazine stereo digital MM 70 (cd 1998).
23. Duodena Cantitans/Petr Danek 19'38; rec Korunni Street Prayer Hall Prague 10/9/1997. Supraphon stereo digital SU33282231 (cd 1998).
24. Cardinall's Musick/Andrew Carwood [22'51]; ed Skinner; rec Fitzalan Chapel Arundel Castle 11/1999. ASV stereo digital CDGAU 206 (cd 2000).
25. Parthenia XVI/Mary Jane Newman 24'32; rec St Matthew's Episcopal Church Bedford New York 1999. Centaur stereo digital CRC 2471 (cd 2000).
26. Pro Arte Singers/Paul Hillier 21'48; ed Hillier; rec Auer Recital Hall Indiana University School of Music Bloomington 5/2000. Harmonia Mundi USA stereo Digital HMU 907223 (cd 2002).

*Mass, 4vv: Sanctus, Benedictus & Agnus Dei
*1.   rec 21/7/1949. Testament SBT1121 (cd 1997).

*Mass, 4vv: Kyrie, Sanctus & Benedictus
*5.   Christ's College Cambridge Choir/David Rowland [5'23]; rec Downing College Chapel Cambridge 4/1995. Christ's College Choir stereo digital SP 1 (cd 1995).

*Mass, 4vv: Agnus Dei
*6.   Winchester Cathedral Choir/David Hill [4'10]; rec Winchester Cathedral 10/1989. Decca stereo digital 4674452 (cd 1994) [from 15].
*7.   Tallis Scholars/Peter Phillips 3'15; ed Phillips; rec Merton College Chapel Oxford 9/1983. Gimell stereo digital 1585T-999 (mc 1990) [from 13] [corrected entry].
*8.   Oxford Camerata/Jeremy Summerly 3'42; rec Hertford College Chapel Oxford 12/1991. Naxos stereo digital 8556701 (cd 1999) [from 18].

*9.   New College Oxford Choir Clerks/Edward Higginbottom 3'43; rec Abbaye de Valloires Department de la Somme 4/1995. Regis stereo digital RRC 1132 (cd 2003) [from 20].

*Mass, 4vv: Gloria
*10.   Hilliard Ensemble/Paul Hillier (bar) [6'15]; rec St James Church Clerkenwell 10/1983. HMV stereo digital 5740362 [cd nd] [from 12].

*Mass, 4vv: Kyrie
*11.   Washington National Cathedral Choir/Douglas Major 2'02. Gothic stereo digital CD 49126 (cd 2001).
*12.   St Edmundsbury Cathedral Choir/James Thomas 2'23; rec St Edmundsbury Cathedral 7/2001. Lammas [stereo digital] LAMM 135 (cd 2001).

*Mass, 5vv
3.   Decca 4521702 (2 cds 1996).
9.   rec 7/1980. EMI CDM 5652112 (cd 1995).
12.   Gimell 4548952 (4 cds 1988); 4549902 (2 cds 1998); Philips 4628622 (2 cds 1999); CDGIM 201 (2 cds 2003).
13.   EMI 5740022 (cd 2000).
14.   Virgin VER 5612972 (cd 1996). VBD 5620132 (2 cds 2002).
16.   Nimbus NI 1762 (8 cds 1998).
17.   Naxos 8505020 (5 cds 1994); 8553239 (cd 1995); 8505079 (5 cds 1998).
18.   Sarum Consort/Andrew Mackay [24'13]; rec Wardour Chapel Tisbury 28–30/8/1995. ASV stereo digital CDQS 6185 (cd 1996).
19.   Winchester Cathedral Choir/David Hill [23'47]; rec Winchester Cathedral 11/1995. Hyperion stereo digital CDA 66837 (cd 1996).
20.   Cardinall's Musick/Andrew Carwood [23'08]; ed Skinner; rec Fitzalan Chapel Arundel Castle 11/1999. ASV stereo digital CDGAU 206 (cd 2000).
21.   Parthenia XVI/Mary Jane Newman 21'58; rec St Matthew's Episcopal Church Bedford New York 1999. Centaur stereo digital CRC 2471 (cd 2000).
22.   Pro Arte Singers/Paul Hillier 20'38; ed Hillier; rec Auer Recital Hall Indiana University School of Music Bloomington 5/2000. Harmonia Mundi USA stereo digital HMU 907223 (cd 2002).
23.   Dunedin Consort [21'49]; rec Crichton Collegiate Church Midlothian 1/2003. Delphian stereo digital DCD 34008 (cd 2003).

*Mass, 5vv: Agnus Dei
*3.   Oxford Camerata/Jeremy Summerly 3'58; rec Hertford College Chapel Oxford 12/1991. Naxos stereo digital 8556701 (cd 1999) [from 17].

*Mass, 5vv: Credo
*4.   Hilliard Ensemble/Paul Hillier (bar) [10'37]; rec St James Church Clerkenwell 10/1983. HMV stereo digital 5740362 [cd nd] [from 11].

*Mass, 5vv: Gloria
*5.   Oxford Camerata/Jeremy Summerly 5'37; rec Hertford College Chapel Oxford 12/1991. Naxos stereo digital 8556702 (cd 1999) [from 17].
*6.   New College Oxford Choir/Edward Higginbottom [nt]; rec 2000. Erato stereo digital 8573802392 (cd 2000).

Annunciation of the BVM [before Easter]
1.   Hyperion CDH 55047 (cd 2002).

Annunciation of the BVM [after Easter (in Paschal time)]
1.   Hyperion CDH 55047 (cd 2002).

Assumption of the BVM
2.   Hyperion CDH 55047 (cd 2002).

Corpus Christi
1.   Nimbus NI 1762 (8 cds 1998).
2.   ECM 4391722 (cd 1994).
3.   Winchester Cathedral Choir/David Hill [26'00]; rec Winchester Cathedral 11/1995. Hyperion stereo digital CDA 66837 (cd 1996).

Easter Day
3.   Cardinall's Musick/Andrew Carwood [14'21]; ed Skinner; rec Fitzalan Chapel Arundel Castle 2/2000. ASV stereo digital CDGAU 214 (cd 2001).

*Easter Day: Resurrexi, Haec dies, 5vv, Victimae paschali laudes & Pascha nostrum . . . veritatis.
*1.   St James's Consort/Robin Kimber [14'34]; rec St Mary Magdalen Church Little Venice London 9/2000. Priory stereo digital PRCD 679 (cd 2000).

*Easter Day: Resurrexi, Haec does, 5vv, Terra tremuit & Pascha nostrum . . . veritatis.
*2.   Queen's College Oxford Choir/Owen Rees [12'27]; rec Queen's College Chapel 4/2001. Guild stereo digital GMCD 7222 (cd 2001).

Epiphany
1.   Cardinall's Musick/Andrew Carwood [11'19]; ed Skinner; rec Fitzalan Chapel Arundel Castle 11/1997. ASV stereo digital CDGAU 179 (cd 1999).

*Epiphany: Reges Tharsis, Vidimus stellam & Surge, illuminare, Jerusalem
*1.   Canterbury Cathedral Lay Clerks/David Flood [7'22]; rec Canterbury
       Cathedral [3/2000]. York Ambisonic stereo digital YORKCD 158 (cd
       2000).

Feast of All Saints
   1.   Virgin VER 5612972 (cd 1996); VBD 5620132 (2 cds 2002).
   2.   Nimbus NI 1762 (8 cds 1998).

Feast of SS Peter and Paul
   1.   Virgin VBD 5620132 (2 cds 2002).

Nativity of our Lord Jesus Christ
   3.   Nimbus NI 1762 (8 cds 1998).
   4.   Cardinall's Musick/Andrew Carwood [10'24]; ed Skinner; rec Fitzalan
         Chapel Arundel Castle 1996. ASV stereo digital CDGAU 178 (cd 1998).

Nativity of the BVM
   1.   Hyperion CDH 55047 (cd 2002).

Purification of the BVM [before Septuagesima]
   1.   Hyperion CDH 55047 (cd 2002).
   2.   Cardinall's Musick/Andrew Carwood [23'55]; ed Skinner; rec Fitzalan
         Chapel Arundel Castle 15/11/2000. ASV stereo digital CDGAU 309 (cd
         2002).

Purification of the BVM [after Septuagesima]
   1.   Hyperion CDH 55047 (cd 2002).
   2.   Cardinall's Musick/Andrew Carwood [26'41]; ed Skinner; rec Fitzalan
         Chapel Arundel Castle 15/11/2000. ASV stereo digital CDGAU 309
         (2002).

Saturday Lady Masses from Christmas to Purification [before Septuagesima]
   1.   Hyperion CDH 55047 (cd 2002).
   2.   Cardinall's Musick/Andrew Carwood [12'40]; ed Skinner; rec Fitzalan
         Chapel Arundel Castle 1/3/1999. ASV stereo digital CDGAU 224 (cd
         2001).

Saturday Lady Masses from Christmas to Purification [after Septuagesima]
   1.   Hyperion CDH 55047 (cd 2002).
   2.   Cardinall's Musick/Andrew Carwood [13'31]; ed Skinner; rec Fitzalan
         Chapel Arundel Castle 1/3/1999. ASV stereo digital CDGAU 224 (cd
         2001).

Saturday Lady Masses from Pentecost to Advent
1. Hyperion CDH 55047 (cd 2002).

Saturday Lady Masses from Purification to Easter [before Septuagesima]
1. Hyperion CDH 55047 (cd 2002).

Saturday Lady Masses from Purification to Easter [after Septuagesima]
1. Hyperion CDH 55047 (cd 2002).

Saturday Lady Masses in Advent
1. Hyperion CDH 55047 (cd 2002).
2. Cardinall's Musick/Andrew Carwood [8'25]; ed Skinner; rec Fitzalan Chapel Arundel Castle 10–11/1996. ASV stereo digital CDGAU 170 (cd 1997).

Saturday Lady Masses in Paschal Time
1. Hyperion CDH 55047 (cd 2002).

Vigil of the Assumption of the BVM
1. Hyperion CDH 55047 (cd 2002).

ALPHABETICAL LIST OF LATIN WORKS

Ab ortu solis
1. Winchester Cathedral Choir/David Hill 6'17; rec Winchester Cathedral 11/1995. Hyperion stereo digital CDA 66837 (cd 1996).

Ad Dominum cum tribularer
2. Virgin VBD 5620132 (2 cds 2002).
3. I Fagiolini/Robert Hollingworth 8'55; rec The Warehouse Waterloo 11/ 1994. Chandos stereo digital CHAN 0578 (cd 1995).
4. Cardinall's Musick/Andrew Carwood 10'02; ed Skinner; rec Fitzalan Chapel Arundel Castle 1996. ASV stereo digital CDGAU 178 (cd 1998).

Adoramus te, Christe
1. Robin Tyson (ct), Patrick Russill (cha org) 1'38; ed Skinner; rec Fitzalan Chapel Arundel Castle 20/7/2000. ASV stereo digital CDGAU 214 (cd 2001).

Adorna thalamum tuum
1. Cardinall's Musick/Andrew Carwood 3'35; ed Skinner; rec Fitzalan Chapel Arundel Castle 15/11/2000. ASV stereo digital CDGAU 309 (cd 2002).

Alleluia, Ascendit Deus
3.   Ionian Singers/Timothy Salter 1'16; rec St Silas' Church Chalk Farm
      1997. Usk [stereo digital] USK 1222 CD (cd 1997).
4.   Durham Cathedral Choir/James Lancelot 1'18; rec Nine Altars Chapel
      Durham Cathedral 5/2002. Priory stereo digital PRCD 801 (cd 2003).

Alleluia, Ave Maria . . . in mulieribus. Alleluia, Virga Jesse
1.   Hyperion CDH 55047 (cd 2002).
2.   Collegium CSCD 508 (cd 2002).

Alleluia, Cognoverunt. Alleluia, Caro mea.
2.   Winchester Cathedral Choir/David Hill 4'15; rec Winchester Cathedral
      11/1995. Hyperion stereo digital CDA 66837 (cd 1996).

Alleluia, Confitemini Domino
1.   Cardinall's Musick/Andrew Carwood 1'21; ed Skinner; rec Fitzalan
      Chapel Arundel Castle 1996. ASV stereo digital CDGAU 178 (cd 1998).

Alleluia, Laudata pueri Dominum [not listed separately in Grove 7, originally
thought to be part of Alleluia, Confitemini Domino]
1.   Cardinall's Musick/Andrew Carwood 1'28; ed Skinner; rec Fitzalan
      Chapel Arundel Castle 1996. ASV stereo digital CDGAU 178 (cd 1998).

Alleluia, [Vespere autem sabbati] quae lucescit
1.   Cardinall's Musick/Andrew Carwood [7'30]; ed Skinner; rec Fitzalan
      Chapel Arundel Castle 2/2000. ASV stereo digital CDGAU 214 (cd
      2001).

Alma Redemptoris mater
1.   Cardinall's Musick/Andrew Carwood 4'04; ed Skinner; rec Fitzalan
      Chapel Arundel Castle 10–11/1996. ASV stereo digital CDGAU 170 (cd
      1997).

Angelus Domini descendit de coelo
1.   Cardinall's Musick/Andrew Carwood 1'15; ed Skinner; rec Fitzalan
      Chapel Arundel Castle 2/2000. ASV stereo digital CDGAU 214 (cd
      2001).

Aspice, Domine, de sede sancta tua
1.   CRD CRD 5003 (3 cds 2002); Regis RRC 1132 (cd 2003).
2.   Cardinall's Musick/Andrew Carwood 5'42; ed Skinner; rec Fitzalan
      Chapel Arundel Castle 2/2001. ASV stereo digital CDGAU 309 (cd
      2002).

Aspice, Domine, quia facta est desolata civitas
3. New College Oxford Choir/Edward Higginbottom 5'48; rec New College Chapel 7/1994. CRD stereo digital CRD 3492 (cd 1997); CRD 5003 (3 cds 2002).
4. Cardinall's Musick/Andrew Carwood 5'19; ed Skinner; rec Fitzalan Chapel Arundel Castle 3/1999. ASV stereo digital CDGAU 197 (cd 1999).

Assumpta est Maria . . . Dominum. Alleluia
4. Hyperion CDH 55047 (cd 2002).

Attollite portas
3. Collegium COLCD 301 (2 cds 1995); CSCD 507 (cd 2002).
4. I Fagiolini/Robert Hollingworth 4'35; rec The Warehouse Waterloo 11/1994. Chandos stereo digital CHAN 0578 (cd 1995).
5. New College Oxford Choir/Edward Higginbottom 5'12; rec New College Chapel 7/1994. CRD stereo digital CRD 3492 (cd 1997); CRD 5003 (3 cds 2002).
6. St John's College Oxford Choir/Simon Jones 4'38; rec Merton College Oxford Chapel 6/1996. ThM stereo digital ThM 1 CD [cd 1997].
7. Cardinall's Musick/Andrew Carwood 4'19; ed Skinner; rec Fitzalan Chapel Arundel Castle 3/1999. ASV stereo digital CDGAU 197 (cd 1999).

Audivi vocem
1. Cardinall's Musick/Andrew Carwood 3'47; ed Skinner; rec Fitzalan Chapel Arundel Castle 10–11/1996. ASV stereo digital CDGAU 170 (cd 1997).

Ave Maria . . . fructus ventris tui
3. Hyperion CDH 55047 (cd 2002).
4. Canterbury Cathedral Lay Clerks/David Flood 2'02; rec Canterbury Cathedral [3/2000]. York Ambisonic stereo digital YORKCD 158 (cd 2000).

*Ave maris stella: Ave maris stella [1st section], Vitam praesta [6th section], Sit laus Deo [7th section]
*1. Ghent Madrigal Choir/Johan Duijck 3'03; rec Sound Recording Centre Steurbaut Ghent. Eufoda stereo digital EUF 1055 (1p 1980); EUF 1197 (cd 1988).

Ave regina, 4vv
4. Cardinall's Musick/Andrew Carwood 3'11; ed Skinner; rec Fitzalan Chapel Arundel Castle 1/3/1999. ASV stereo digital CDGAU 309 (cd 2002).

Ave regina caelorum
1.   Cardinall's Musick/Andrew Carwood 4'33; ed Skinner; rec Fitzalan Chapel Arundel Castle 1996. ASV stereo digital CDGAU 178 (cd 1998).

Ave verum corpus
4.   rec 19/7/1950. Testament SBT 1121 (cd 1997).
7.   rec 1959. Decca 4521702 (2 cds 1996), 4529492 [2 cds 1998].
9.   EMI TC-CFP4481 (mc), EMI 7672652 (cd 1991).
26.   HMV 5740362 [cd nd].
28.   rec 9/1983. Gimell 4548952 (4 cds 1988).
29.   Etcetera KTC 1031 (cd 1985).
35.   Collegium COLCD 302 (2 cds 1995).
37.   Collegium COLCD 301 (2 cds 1995); CSCD 507 (cd 2002).
40.   Nimbus NI 1762 (8 cds 1998).
41.   Westminster Choir/Joseph Flummerfeldt 4'28; rec St Mary the Virgin Church New York City 1992. Chesky stereo digital JD 83 (cd 1992).
43.   Voices of Ascension/Dennis Keene 4'19; rec Church of the Ascension New York City 3/1994. Delos stereo digital DE 3165 (cd 1994).
44.   Christ's College Cambridge Choir/David Rowland 4'16; rec Downing College Chapel Cambridge 4/1995. Christ's College Choir stereo digital SP 1 (cd 1995).
45.   Clare College Cambridge Choir/Timothy Brown 3'54; rec Clare College Chapel 3/1991. Guild stereo digital GMCD 7109 (cd 1995).
46.   Christ Church Cathedral Oxford Choir/Stephen Darlington 4'04; rec Christ Church Cathedral 4/1994. Nimbus stereo digital NI 5440 (cd 1995).
47.   King's Singers 4'28; rec CTS Studio 2 London 1994. RCA stereo 09026680042 (cd 1995).
48.   Clare College Cambridge Choir/Timothy Brown 4'16; ed Morris; rec St George's Church Chesterton 6/1993. Guild stereo digital GMCD 7115 (cd 1996).
49.   Winchester Cathedral Choir/David Hill 4'33; rec Winchester Cathedral 11/1995. Hyperion stereo digital CDA 66837 (cd 1996).
50.   Christ's Hospital Choir/Peter Allwood [nt]; rec 1996. Carlton stereo digital 3036600852 (cd 1997).
51.   St Patrick's Cathedral New York City Choir/John-Michael Caprio 3'15; rec St Patrick's Cathedral New York City. Gothic stereo digital CD 49091 (cd 1997).
52.   Downside Abbey Monks' & School Boys' Choirs [nt]; rec Downside Abbey Bath 7/1997. Virgin stereo digital VTMC 171 (2 mcs), VTCD 171 (2 cds 1997).

53. Westminster Cathedral Choir/James O'Donnell 4'15; rec Westminster Cathedral 6/1995. Hyperion stereo digital CDA 66850 (cd 1996); WCC 100 (cd 1998).
54. BBC Singers/Bo Holten 4'22; rec St Giles Cripplegate 7/2/1996. BBC Music Magazine stereo digital MM 70 (cd 1998).
55. New College Oxford Choir/Edward Higginbottom 4'29; rec New College Chapel 1/1998. Erato stereo digital 3984216592 (cd), 3984295882 (2 cds 1998).
56. Truro Cathedral Choir/Andrew Nethsingha 4'41; rec Truro Cathedral 1/1997. Priory stereo digital PRCD 614 (cd 1998).
57. Keble College Oxford Choir/Philip Stopford 4'14; rec Keble College Chapel 6/1998. Priory stereo digital PRCD 657 (cd 1998).
58. Laudibus/Michael Brewer 3'25; rec Westminster Cathedral 7/1998. Hyperion stereo digital CDA 67076 (cd 1999).
59. Wells Cathedral Choir/Malcolm Archer [nt]. Griffin stereo digital GCMC 4019 (mc), GCCD 4019 [cd 2001].
60. St Thomas Church New York Choir/Gerre Hancock 4'03; rec St Thomas Church New York Priory stereo PRCD 910 (cd 2001).
61. Gents/Peter Dijkstra 4'17; rec Old Catholic Church the Hague 5/2002. Channel Classics stereo digital CCS 18998 (cd), CCS SA 18902 (sacd 2002).
62. Guildford Cathedral Choirs/Stephen Farr & Louise Reid 3'44; rec Guildford Cathedral 6/2003. Herald stereo digital HAVPC 288 (mc), HAVPCD 288 (cd 2003).
63. Durham Cathedral Choir/James Lancelot 4'11; rec Nine Altars Chapel Durham Cathedral 5/2002. Priory stereo digital PRCD 801 (cd 2003).

Beata es, virgo Maria
3. Hyperion CDH 55047 (cd 2002).

Beata viscera
3. Hyperion CDH 55047 (cd 2002).
4. Farm Street Church Choir/Nicholas Danby 2'01; ed Brett; rec Farm Street Church London 11/1993. Priory stereo digital PRCD 455 (cd 1993).
5. London Oriana Choir/Leon Lovett 2'17; ed Petti; rec St Giles' Church Cripplegate 2/1995. ASV stereo digital CDWHL 2096 (cd 1995).
6. King's Singers 1'53; rec CTS Studio 2 London 1994. RCA stereo 09026680042 (cd 1995).
7. Cardinall's Musick/Andrew Carwood 1'22; ed Skinner; rec Fitzalan Chapel Arundel Castle 1/3/1999. ASV stereo digital CDGAU 224 (cd 2001).

Beati mundo corde
2.　Virgin VBD 5620132 (2 cds 2002).
3.　Nimbus NI 1762 (8 cds 1998).

Benedicta et venerabilis
2.　Hyperion CDH 55047 (cd 2002).
3.　Lincoln College Oxford Choir/David Terry 3'56; rec Exeter College Chapel Oxford. Guild stereo digital GMCD 7158 (cd 1999).

Benigne fac, Domine
1.　Cardinall's Musick/Andrew Carwood 2'50; ed Skinner; rec Fitzalan Chapel Arundel Castle 3/3/1999. ASV stereo digital CDGAU 179 (cd 1999).

Cantate Domino
2.　Sarum Consort/Andrew Mackay 2'28; rec Milton Abbey 9/1996. ASV stereo digital CDQS 6211 (cd 1997).

Christe qui lux es . . . praedicans/Precamur
1.　rec 4/1927. Amphion PHICD 138 (cd 1996) [sung to English words 'O Christ who art the light and day'].
5.　Priory PRCD 006 (cd 1995).
6.　HMV 5740362 [cd nd].
7.　St Mary's Scottish Episcopal Cathedral Edinburgh Choir/Timothy Byram-Wigfield 3'37; rec St Mary's Scottish Episcopal Cathedral 2/1996. Priory stereo digital PRC 557 (mc), PRCD 557 (cd 1997).
8.　Cardinall's Musick/Andrew Carwood 3'59; ed Skinner; rec Fitzalan Chapel Arundel Castle 10–11/1996. ASV stereo digital CDGAU 170 (cd 1997); CDGAU 1004 (cd 1998).
9.　Gaudium/Mark Levett 4'26; rec St John-at-Hackney Church London 5/2001. Karuna [stereo digital] Karuna 109 [cd 2002].

Christus resurgens
1.　Collegium COLCD 301 (2 cds 1995); CSCD 507 (cd 2002).
2.　Cardinall's Musick/Andrew Carwood 5'33; ed Skinner; rec Fitzalan Chapel Arundel Castle 2/2000. ASV stereo digital CDGAU 214 (cd 2001).

Cibavit eos
3.　Etcetera KTC 1031 (cd 1985).
4.　Nimbus NI 1762 (8 cds 1998).
5.　ECM 4391722 (cd 1994).
6.　Winchester Cathedral Choir/David Hill 3'55; rec Winchester Cathedral 11/1995. Hyperion stereo digital CDA 66837 (cd 1996).
7.　Con Brio 3'22. Euridice Turn Left stereo digital EUCD 013 (cd 1999).

Circumdederent me dolores mortis
1.   CRD CRD 5003 (3 cds 2002).

Circumspice, Hierusalem.
1.   Cardinall's Musick/Andrew Carwood 4'11; ed Skinner, rec Fitzalan Chapel Arundel Castle 11/1997. ASV stereo digital CDGAU 179 (cd 1999).

Confirma hoc, Deus
2.   Etcetera KTC 1031 (cd 1985)
3.   Douai Singers/John Rowntree 1'23; rec Douai Abbey Berkshire 10/2002. Herald stereo digital HAVPC 285 (mc), HAVPCD 285 (cd 2002).

Constitues eos
1.   Virgin VBD 5620132 (2 cds 2002).

Cunctis diebus
1.   CRD CRD 5003 (3 cds 2002).

Da mihi auxilium
2.   I Fagiolini/Robert Hollingworth 6'33; rec The Warehouse Waterloo 11/ 1994. Chandos stereo digital CHAN 0578 (cd 1995).
3.   Cardinall's Musick/Andrew Carwood 5'56; ed Skinner; rec Fitzalan Chapel Arundel Castle 3/1999. ASV stereo digital CDGAU 197 (cd 1999).

Defecit in dolore
2.   Alpha CACA 944 (mc 1993).
3.   Cardinall's Musick/Andrew Carwood 6'26; ed Skinner; rec Fitzalan Chapel Arundel Castle 14/2/2001. ASV stereo digital CDGAU 224 (cd 2001).

De lamentatione Hieremiae
4.   New College Oxford Choir Clerks/Edward Higginbottom [12'14]; rec Abbaye de Valloires Department de la Somme 4/1995. Collins stereo digital 14872 (cd 1996); CRD CRD 3499 (cd), CRD 5008 (5 cds 2003).
5.   Cardinall's Musick/Andrew Carwood 11'25; ed Skinner; rec Fitzalan Chapel Arundel Castle 10–11/1996. ASV stereo digital CDGAU 170 (cd 1997).

Deus, in adiutorium meum intende
1.   Cardinall's Musick/Andrew Carwood 10'12; ed Skinner; rec Fitzalan Chapel Arundel Castle 1996. ASV stereo digital CDGAU 178 (cd 1998).

Deus, venerunt gentes
1.   I Fagiolini 12'53; rec The Warehouse Waterloo 6/1996. Chandos stereo digital CHAN 0609 (cd 1997).
2.   Cardinall's Musick/Andrew Carwood 11'59; ed Skinner; rec Fitzalan Chapel Arundel Castle 11/2000. ASV stereo digital CDGAU 224 (cd 2001).
3.   Sixteen/Harry Christophers 13'25; ed Fellowes; rec All Saints' Church Tooting 5/2003. Coro stereo digital CORDVD 1 (dvd), CORSACD 16016 (sacd & cd 2003).

Dies sanctificatus
2.   Nimbus NI 1762 (8 cds 1998).
3.   Cardinall's Musick/Andrew Carwood [1'20]; ed Skinner; rec Fitzalan Chapel Arundel Castle 1996. ASV stereo digital CDGAU 178 (cd 1998).

Diffusa est gratia
1.   Hyperion CDH 55047 (cd 2002).
2.   Cardinall's Musick/Andrew Carwood 1'22; ed Skinner; rec Fitzalan Chapel Arundel Castle 15/11/2000. ASV stereo digital CDGAU 309 (cd 2002).

Diliges Dominum
2.   Virgin VER 5612972 (cd 1996); VBD 5620132 (2 cds 2002).
3.   Cardinall's Musick/Andrew Carwood 2'52; ed Skinner; rec Fitzalan Chapel Arundel Castle 3/1999. ASV stereo digital CDGAU 197 (cd 1999).

Domine, ante te omne desiderium
1.   Cardinall's Musick/Andrew Carwood 4'10; ed Skinner; rec Fitzalan Chapel Arundel Castle 11/1997. ASV stereo digital CDGAU 179 (cd 1999).

Domine Deus omnipotens
1.   Cardinall's Music/Andrew Carwood 8'18; ed Skinner; rec Fitzalan Chapel Arundel Castle 3/3/1999. ASV stereo digital CDGAU 179 (cd 1999).

Domine, non sum dignus
1.   CRD CRD 5003 (3 cds 2002).

Domine, praestolamur
1.   Cardinall's Musick/Andrew Carwood 5'46; ed Skinner; rec Fitzalan Chapel Arundel Castle 11/2000. ASV stereo digital CDGAU 224 (cd 2001).

Domine, quis habitabit
1. Cardinall's Musick/Andrew Carwood 8'34; ed Skinner; rec Fitzalan Chapel Arundel Castle 10–11/1996. ASV stereo digital CDGAU 170 (cd 1997).

Domine, salva nos
2. CRD CRD 5003 (3 cds 2002).

Domine, secundum actum meum
2. I Fagiolini/Robert Hollingworth 7'26; rec The Warehouse Waterloo 11/ 1994. Chandos stereo digital CHAN 0578 (cd 1995).
3. New College Oxford Choir/Edward Higginbottom 7'52, rec New College Chapel 7/1994. CRD stereo digital CRD 3492 (cd 1997); CRD 5003 (3 cds 2002).
4. Cardinall's Musick/Andrew Carwood 6'32; ed Skinner; rec Fitzalan Chapel Arundel Castle 17/9/1999. ASV stereo digital CDGAU 197 (cd 1999).

Domine, secundum multitudinem dolorum meum
1. CRD CRD 5003 (3 cds 2002).
2. Cardinall's Musick/Andrew Carwood 3'15; ed Skinner; rec Fitzalan Chapel Arundel Castle 2/2001. ASV stereo digital CDGAU 309 (cd 2002).

Domine, tu iurasti
1. CRD CRD 5003 (3 cds 2002); Regis RRC 1132 (cd 2003).
2. I Fagiolini/Robert Hollingworth 4'49; rec The Warehouse Waterloo 6/ 1996. Chandos stereo digital CHAN 0609 (cd 1997).
3. Cardinall's Musick/Andrew Carwood 4'11; ed Skinner; rec Fitzalan Chapel Arundel Castle 11/2000 ASV stereo digital CDGAU 224 (cd 2001).

Ecce advenit dominator Dominus
1. King's College Cambridge Choral Scholars 1'40; rec Jesus College Chapel Cambridge 20/1/1998. Quilisma stereo digital QUIL 401 (cd 1998).
2. Cardinall's Musick/Andrew Carwood 4'54, ed Skinner, rec Fitzalan Chapel Arundel Castle 11/1997. ASV stereo digital CDGAU 179 (cd 1999).

Ecce virgo concipiet
1. Hyperion CDH 55047 (cd 2002).
2. Cardinall's Musick/Andrew Carwood 1'21; ed Skinner; rec Fitzalan Chapel Arundel Castle 10–11/1996. ASV stereo digital CDGAU 170 (ed 1997).

Ego sum panis vivus
4.   Winchester Cathedral Choir/David Hill 2'32; rec Winchester Cathedral
      11/1995. Hyperion stereo digital CDA 66837 (cd 1996).
5.   Durham Cathedral Choir/James Lancelot 2'13; rec Nine Altars Chapel
      Durham Cathedral 5/2002. Priory stereo digital PRCD 801 (cd 2003).

Emendemus in melius
5.   King's School Canterbury Crypt Choir/Michael Harris 3'11; rec St Mar-
      tin's Church Canterbury [3/1995]. York Ambisonic stereo digital
      YORKCD 121 (cd 1995).
6.   Collegium COLCD 301 (2 cds 1995); CSCD 507 (cd 2002).
7.   Cardinall's Musick/Andrew Carwood 3'15; ed Skinner; rec Fitzalan
      Chapel Arundel Castle 3/1999. ASV stereo digital CDGAU 197 (cd 1999).
8.   St Thomas Church New York Choir/Gerre Hancock 3'53; rec St Thomas
      Church New York. Priory stereo PRCD 910 (cd 2001).

Exsurge, quare obdormis, Domine?
8.   CRD CRD 5003 (3 cds 2002).
9.   Sarum Consort/Andrew Mackay 4'34; rec Milton Abbey 9/1996. ASV
      stereo digital CDQS 6211 (cd 1997).
10.   Hereford Cathedral Choir/Roy Massey 4'08, rec Hereford Cathedral 5/
      1996. Priory stereo digital PRCD 585 (cd 1997).
11.   Canterbury Cathedral Choir/David Flood 4'50; rec Canterbury Cathedral
      [2/1998]. York Ambisonic stereo digital YORKCD 136 (cd 1998).

Fac cum servo tuo
1.   CRD CRD 5003 (3 cds 2002).

Factus est repente de coelo sonus
2.   Canterbury Cathedral Lay Clerks/David Flood 2'00; rec Canterbury
      Cathedral [3/2000]. York Ambisonic stereo digital YORKCD 158 (cd
      2000).
3.   Douai Singers/John Rowntree 1'45; rec Douai Abbey Berkshire 10/2002.
      Herald stereo digital HAVPC 285 (mc), HAVPCD 285 (cd 2002).

Felix es, sacra virgo
2.   Hyperion CDH 55047 (cd 2002).
3.   Durham Cathedral Choir/James Lancelot 1'47; rec Nine Altars Chapel
      Durham Cathedral 5/2002. Priory stereo digital PRCD 801 (cd 2003).

Felix namque es
1.   Hyperion CDH 55047 (cd 2002).

2.   Cardinall's Musick/Andrew Carwood 1'33; ed Skinner; rec Fitzalan Chapel Arundel Castle 1/3/1999. ASV stereo digital CDGAU 224 (cd 2001).

Gaudeamus omnes . . . beatae Mariae
2.   Hyperion CDH 55047 (cd 2002).
3.   Dunedin Consort 5'17; rec Crichton Collegiate Church Midlothian 1/ 2003. Delphian stereo digital DCD 34008 (cd 2003).

Gaudeamus omnes . . . Sanctorum omnium
2.   Collegium COLCD 301 (2 cds 1995); CSCD 507 (cd 2002).
3.   Virgin VBD 5620132 (2 cds 2002).
4.   Nimbus NI 1762 (8 cds 1998).

Gaude Maria
1.   Hyperion CDH 55047 (cd 2002).
2.   Cardinall's Musick/Andrew Carwood 2'46; ed Skinner; rec Fitzalan Chapel Arundel Castle 1/3/1999. ASV stereo digital CDGAU 224 (cd 2001).

Haec dicit Dominus
2.   CRD CRD 5003 (3 cds 2002).
4.   Jesus College Cambridge Mixed Choir/Duncan Aspden 6'53; rec Jesus College Chapel. Lammas [stereo digital] LAMM 086D (cd 1995).

Haec dies, 3vv
1.   Cardinall's Musick/Andrew Carwood 1'15, ed Skinner, rec Fitzalan Chapel Arundel Castle 2/2000. ASV stereo digital CDGAU 214 (cd 2001).

Haec dies, 5vv
3.   St James's Consort/Robin Kimber 2'03; rec St Mary Magdalen Church Little Venice London 9/2000. Priory stereo digital PRCD 679 (cd 2000).
4.   Cardinall's Musick/Andrew Carwood 1'51, ed Skinner, rec Fitzalan Chapel Arundel Castle 2/2000. ASV stereo digital CDGAU 214 (cd 2001).
5.   Queen's College Oxford Choir/Owen Rees 1'54; rec Queen's College Chapel 4/2001. Guild stereo digital GMCD 7222 (cd 2001).

Haec dies, 6vv
2.   rec 1958. Belart 4614542 [cd nd].
4.   EMI TC-CFP 4481 (mc), EMI 7672652 (cd 1991).
5.   His Master's Voice mono CLP 3525 (lp 1966).
11.   Collegium COLCD 302 (2 cds 1995).

12.   CRD CRD 5003 (3 cds 2002).

15.   St Mary's Collegiate Church Warwick Choir/Simon Lole [2'23]; rec
       St Mary's Church Warwick 1/1989. Alpha stereo digital CACA 592 (mc),
       CDCA 592 (cd 1989) [corrected numbering].

16.   Wells Cathedral Choir/Anthony Crossland 1'32; rec Wells Cathedral
       1/3/1991. Priory stereo digital PRCD 362 (cd 1991).

17.   Clare College Cambridge Choir/Timothy Brown 2'02. Gamut stereo digi-
       tal IMCD 701 (cd 1993) [corrected numbering].

18.   Jesus College Cambridge Mixed Choir/Duncan Aspden 2'45; rec Jesus
       College Chapel. Lammas [stereo digital] LAMM 086D (cd 1995).

19.   King's Singers 2'04; rec CTS Studio 2 London 1994. RCA stereo
       09026680042 (cd 1995).

20.   King's School Canterbury Crypt Choir/Michael Harris 2'21; rec
       St Martin's Church Canterbury [3/1995]. York Ambisonic stereo digital
       YORKCD 121 (cd 1995).

21.   Clare College Cambridge Choir/Timothy Brown 2'01; ed Morris; rec
       St George's Church Chesterton 6/1993. Guild stereo digital GMCD 7115
       (cd 1996).

22.   Westminster Cathedral Choir/James O'Donnell 2'42; rec Westminster
       Cathedral 6/1995. Hyperion stereo digital CDA 66850 (cd 1996).

23.   Sarum Consort/Andrew Mackay 2'42; rec Milton Abbey 9/1996. ASV
       stereo digital CDQS 6211 (cd 1997).

24.   Ionian Singers/Timothy Salter 2'27; rec St Silas' Church Chalk Farm
       1997. Usk [stereo digital] USK 1222 CD (cd 1997).

25.   New Company/Harry Bicket 2'32; rec Temple Church London 4/1998.
       Classic FM stereo digital (cd 1999).

26.   Canterbury Cathedral Choir/David Flood 2'56; rec Canterbury Cathedral
       [3/2000]. York Ambisonic stereo digital YORKCD 162 (cd 2000).

27.   Salisbury Cathedral Choir/Douglas Guest 3'05; rec Salisbury Cathedral
       11/12/1953. Salisbury Cathedral Archive Recordings mono SCS 276502
       (cd 2002).

28.   Sheffield Cathedral Choir Girls and Men/Neil Taylor 2'09; rec Sheffield
       Cathedral 9/2002. Lammas [stereo digital] LAMM 147 (cd 2003).

29.   Durham Cathedral Choir/James Lancelot 2'50; rec Nine Altars Chapel
       Durham Cathedral 5/2002. Priory stereo digital PRCD 801 (cd 2003).

Hodie Beata Virgo Maria
1.   OxRecs OXCD 5287 (cd 2000).

2.   EMI CDM 5662442 (cd 1996).

4.   Cardinall's Musick/Andrew Carwood 2'22; ed Skinner; rec Fitzalan
       Chapel Arundel Castle 2/2001. ASV stereo digital CDGAU 309 (cd 2002).

Hodie Christus natus est
3. Nimbus NI 1762 (8 cds 1998).
4. Cardinall's Musick/Andrew Carwood 2'13; ed Skinner; rec Fitzalan Chapel Arundel Castle 1996. ASV stereo digital CDGAU 178 (cd 1998).

Hodie Simon Petrus
1. Virgin VBD 5620132 (2 cds 2002).

Infelix ego
1. Gimell 4548952 (4 cds 1988).
2. Oxford Camerata/Jeremy Summerly 13'42; rec Hertford College Chapel Oxford 12/1991. Naxos stereo digital 8550574 (cd 1992) [corrected entry], 8505020 (5 cds 1994), 8505079 (5 cds 1998).
3. Jesus College Cambridge Mixed Choir/Duncan Aspden 14'23; rec Jesus College Chapel. Lammas [stereo digital] LAMM 086D (cd 1995).
4. Sarum Consort/Andrew Mackay 12'35; rec Wardour Chapel Tisbury 8/1995. ASV stereo digital CDQS 6185 (cd 1996).
5. Ars Nova/Paul Hillier 12'43; rec Roskilde Gammel Vor Frue Kirke 8/ 1999. Ars Nova stereo digital VANCD 01 (cd 2002).

In resurrectione tua
2. CRD CRD 5003 (3 cds 2002); Regis RRC 1132 (cd 2003).
3. Sarum Consort/Andrew Mackay 1'41; rec Milton Abbey 9/1996. ASV stereo digital CDQS 6211 (cd 1997).
4. Cardinall's Musick/Andrew Carwood 1'36; ed Skinner; rec Fitzalan Chapel Arundel Castle 17/2/2000. ASV stereo digital CDGAU 309 (cd 2002).

Iustorum animae
2. rec 11/12/1952. Testament SBT1121 (cd 1997).
5. EMI TC-CFP 4481 (mc), 7672652 (cd 1991); HMV 5721662 [cd nd], 5732232 [cd nd].
12. Etcetera KTC 1031 (cd 1985).
14. York Minster Chapter House Choir/Peter Young 2'57; [rec York Minster Chapter House 1987].
15. Collegium COLCD 301 (2 cds 1995); CSCD 502 (cd 1996), CSCD 507 (cd 2002).
16. Virgin VBD 5620132 (2 cds 2002).
17. Nimbus NI 1762 (8 cds 1998).
20. Christ's College Cambridge Choir/David Rowland 2'55; rec Downing College Chapel Cambridge 4/1995. Christ's College Choir stereo digital SP1 (cd 1995).
21. Voices of Ascension/Dennis Keene 3'01; rec Church of the Ascension New York City 1994. Delos stereo digital DE 3174 (cd 1995).

22. Dorian Choir/Peter Godfrey 3'41; rec Auckland Grammar School Hall. Kiwi Pacific stereo CDSLD 109 (cd 1998).
23. Clare College Cambridge Choir/Timothy Brown 2'50; rec Ely Cathedral Lady Chapel 3/2000. Collegium stereo digital COLCD 127 (cd 2000).
24. Dunedin Consort 2'44; rec Crichton Collegiate Church Midlothian 1/2003. Delphian stereo digital DCD 34008 (cd 2003).

Laetentur coeli
7. Christ's College Cambridge Choir/David Rowland 3'46; rec Downing College Chapel Cambridge 4/1995. Christ's College Choir stereo digital SP 1 (cd 1995).
8. Winchester Cathedral Choir/David Hill [nt]; rec Winchester Cathedral 1/1996. Virgin stereo digital VM 5613142 (cd 1996).
9. Sarum Consort [soloists: Alison Bullock (s), Andrew Stewart (ct), Colin Howard (t)]/ Andrew Stewart 3'38; rec Milton Abbey 9/1996. ASV stereo digital CDQS 6211 (cd 1997).
10. St Paul's Cathedral Choir/John Scott 3'21; rec St Paul's Cathedral London 6/1997. Hyperion stereo digital CDA 66994 (cd 1997).
11. Ionian Singers/Timothy Salter 3'38; rec St Silas' Church Chalk Farm 1997. Usk [stereo digital] USK 1222 CD (cd 1997).
12. Wellington Cathedral Choir/Philip Walsh 3'18; rec Wellington Cathedral NZ 5/1998. Herald stereo digital HAVPC 224 (mc), HAVPCD 224 (cd 1998).
13. Canterbury Cathedral Choir/David Flood 4'03; rec Canterbury Cathedral [2/1998]. York Ambisonic stereo digital YORKCD 136 (cd 1998).
14. King's College London Choir/David Trendell 3'33; rec St Mary Magdalen Church Paddington 6/2000. Proudsound stereo digital PROUCD 149 (cd 2000).
15. Cardinall's Musick/Andrew Carwood 3'42; ed Skinner; rec Fitzalan Chapel Arundel Castle 2/2001. ASV stereo digital CDGAU 309 (cd 2002).
16. Dunedin Consort 2'59; rec Crichton Collegiate Church Midlothian 1/2003. Delphian stereo digital DCD 34008 (cd 2003).
17. Durham Cathedral Choir/James Lancelot 3'31; rec Nine Altars Chapel Durham Cathedral 5/2002. Priory stereo digital PRCD 801 (cd 2003).

Laudate Dominum omnes gentes
1. Nimbus NI 1762 (8 cds 1998).

Laudate, peuri, Dominum
3. Nimbus NI 1762 (8 cds 1998).
4. Sarum Consort/Andrew Mackay 4'34; rec Milton Abbey 9/1996. ASV stereo digital CDQS 6211 (cd 1997).

5.   Cardinall's Musick/Andrew Carwood 4/18; ed Skinner; rec Fitzalan Chapel Arundel Castle 3/1999. ASV stereo digital CDGAU 197 (cd 1999).

Laudibus in sanctis
9.   Brilliant 99937 (6 cds 2002); CRD CRD 5003 (3 cds 2002).
10.   Collegium COLCD 301 (2 cds 1995); CSCD 507 (cd 2002).
12.   Nimbus NI 1762 (8 cds 1998).
14.   Oxford Camerata/Jeremy Summerly 5'53; rec Hertford College Chapel Oxford 4/1993. Naxos stereo digital 8550843 (cd 1994) [corrected entry].
15.   Jesus College Cambridge Mixed Choir/Duncan Aspden 5'58; rec Jesus College Chapel. Lammas [stereo digital] LAMM 086D (cd 1995).
16.   King's Singers 4'39; rec CTS Studio 2 London 1994. RCA stereo 09026680042 (cd 1995).
17.   I Fagiolini/Robert Hollingworth 4'55; rec The Warehouse Waterloo 6/1996. Chandos stereo digital CHAN 0609 (cd 1997).
18.   St Thomas Church New York Choir/Gerre Hancock 6'02; rec St Thomas Church New York. Priory stereo PRCD 910 (cd 2001).
19.   Ars Nova/Paul Hillier 4'55; rec Roskilde Gammel Vor Frue Kirke 8/1999. Ars Nova stereo digital VANCD 01 (cd 2002).
20.   Durham Cathedral Choir/James Lancelot 6'00; rec Nine Altars Chapel Durham Cathedral 5/2002. Priory stereo digital PRCD 801 (cd 2003).

Libera me, Domine, de morte aeterna
2.   Cardinall's Musick/Andrew Carwood 3'57; ed Skinner; rec Fitzalan Chapel Arundel Castle 3/1999. ASV stereo digital CDGAU 197 (cd 1999).

Libera me, Domine, et pone me iuxta te
4.   Cardinall's Musick/Andrew Carwood 6'52; ed Skinner; rec Fitzalan Chapel Arundel Castle 3/1999. ASV stereo digital CDGAU 197 (cd 1999).

Memento, Domine
1.   Cardinall's Musick/Andrew Carwood 4'19; ed Skinner; rec Fitzalan Chapel Arundel Castle 11/2000. ASV stereo digital CDGAU 224 (cd 2001).

Memento, homo
3.   Cardinall's Musick/Andrew Carwood 2'25; ed Skinner; rec Fitzalan Chapel Arundel Castle 3/1999. ASV stereo digital CDGAU 197 (cd 1999).

Miserere mei, Deus
2.   EMI TC-CFP 4481 (mc), 7672652 (cd 1991).
3.   Guild GMCD 7131 (cd 1997).
6.   Brilliant 99937 (6 cds 2002), CRD CRD 5003 (3 cds 2002).
7.   Collegium COLCD 301 (2 cds 1995).
8.   Christ's College Cambridge Choir/David Rowland 3'24; rec Downing College Chapel Cambridge 4/1995. Christ's College Choir stereo digital SP 1 (cd 1995).
9.   Voices of Ascension/Dennis Keene 3'25; rec Church of the Ascension New York City 1994. Delos stereo digital DE 3174 (cd 1995).
10. Jesus College Cambridge Mixed Choir/Duncan Aspden 3'49; rec Jesus College Chapel. Lammas [stereo digital] LAMM 086D (cd 1995).
11. St Thomas-on-the-Bourne Choir/David Swinson 3'03; rec Charterhouse Chapel Surrey 5/1999. Herald stereo digital HAVPC 235 (mc), HAVPCD 235 (cd 1999).
12. Gaudium/Mark Levett 3'46; rec St John-at-Hackney Church London 5/2001. Karuna [stereo digital] Karuna 109 [cd 2002].
13. Durham Cathedral Choir/James Lancelot 3'02; rec Nine Altars Chapel Durham Cathedral 5/2002. Priory stereo digital PRCD 801 (cd 2003).

Miserere mihi, Domine
2.   rec 6/1991. Guild GMCD 7108 (cd 1996).
3.   I Fagiolini/Robert Hollingworth 2'12; rec The Warehouse Waterloo 11/1994. Chandos stereo digital CHAN 0578 (cd 1995).
4.   New College Oxford Choir/Edward Higginbottom 2'20; rec New College Chapel 7/1994. CRD stereo digital CRD 3492 (cd 1997); CRD 5003 (3 cds 2002).
5.   Cardinall's Musick/Andrew Carwood 2'11, ed Skinner; rec Fitzalan Chapel Arundel Castle 17/9/1999. ASV stereo digital CDGAU 197 (cd 1999).

Ne irascaris [see also O Lord, turn Thy wrath]
3.   CRD CRD 5003 (3 cds 2002).
6.   Jesus College Cambridge Mixed Choir/Duncan Aspden 8'55; rec Jesus College Chapel. Lammas [stereo digital] LAMM 086D (cd 1995).
7.   Sarum Consort/Andrew Mackay 9'41; rec Milton Abbey 9/1996. ASV stereo digital CDQS 6211 (cd 1997).
8.   Cardinall's Musick/Andrew Carwood 8'36; ed Skinner; rec Fitzalan Chapel Arundel Castle 2/2001. ASV stereo digital CDGAU 309 (cd 2002).
9.   Durham Cathedral Choir/James Lancelot [8'30]; rec Nine Altars Chapel Durham Cathedral 5/2002. Priory stereo digital PRCD 801 (cd 2003).

*Ne irascaris: Civitas sancti tui [2nd section: see also Bow Thine ear]
  *6.   Westminster Cathedral Choir/James O'Donnell 5'13; rec Westminster Cathedral 6/1995. Hyperion stereo digital CDA 66850 (cd 1996).
  *7.   Downside Abbey Monks' & Scholboys' Choirs 4'44; rec Downside Abbey Bath 4/1996. Virgin stereo digital VTCD 99 (cd 1996), HMV 5742392 [cd nd].
  *8.   Canterbury Cathedral Choir/David Flood 4'49; rec Canterbury Cathedral [3/2000]. York Ambisonic stereo digital YORKCD 162 (cd 2000).
  *9.   Gaudium/Mark Levett 6'02; rec St John-at-Hackney Church London 5/2001. Karuna [stereo digital] Karuna 109 [cd 2002].
  *10. RSCM Millennium Youth Choir/Gordon Stewart 3'45; rec Jesus College Chapel Cambridge 4/2002. Lammas [stereo digital] LAMM 140 (cd 2002).
  *11. Manchester Cathedral Choir/Christopher Stokes 4'21; rec Manchester Cathedral 2002. Naxos stereo digital 8557025 (cd 2002).

Ne Perdas
  1.   Cardinall's Musick/Andrew Carwood 3'53; ed Skinner; rec Fitzalan Chapel Arundel Castle 10–11/1996. ASV stereo digital CDGAU 170 (cd 1997).

Non vos relinquam orphanos
  6.   Collegium CSC 500 (mc), CSCD 500 (cd 1990); COLCD 301 (2 cds 1995); CSCD 507 (cd 2002).
  7.   All Saints' Episcopal Church Beverly Hills Choir/Thomas Foster 1'40; rec All Saints' Episcopal Church Beverly Hills California 1993. Gothic stereo digital CD 49064 (cd 1993).
  8.   Durham Cathedral Choir/James Lancelot 1'34; rec Nine Altars Chapel Durham Cathedral 5/2002. Priory stereo digital PRCD 801 (cd 2003).

Nunc dimittis servum tuum
  1.   Hyperion CDH 55047 (cd 2002).
  2.   Cardinall's Musick/Andrew Carwood 4'22; ed Skinner; rec Fitzalan Chapel Arundel Castle 15/11/2000. ASV stereo digital CDGAU 309 (cd 2002).

Nunc scio vere
  1.   Virgin VBD 5620132 (2 cds 2002).

O admirabile commercium
  2.   Nimbus NI 1762 (8 cds 1998).
  3.   Cardinall's Musick/Andrew Carwood 3'17; ed Skinner; rec Fitzalan Chapel Arundel Castle 1996. ASV stereo digital CDGAU 178 (cd 1998).

Oculi omnium
2.   Nimbus NI 1762 (8 cds 1998).
3.   ECM 4391722 (cd 1994).
4.   Winchester Cathedral Choir/David Hill 4'50; rec Winchester Cathedral
      11/1995. Hyperion stereo digital CDA 66837 (cd 1996).

O Domine, adiuva me
1.   Cardinall's Musick/Andrew Carwood 3'47; ed Skinner; rec Fitzalan Chapel
      Arundel Castle 11/2000. ASV stereo digital CDGAU 224 (cd 2001).

O lux, beata Trinitas
3.   rec 6/1991. Guild GMCD 7108 (cd 1996).
4.   New College Oxford Choir/Edward Higginbottom 5'13; rec New College
      Chapel 7/1994. CRD stereo digital CRD 3492 (cd 1997); CRD 3507 (cd
      1998); CRD 5003 (3 cds 2002).
5.   Sarum Consort/Andrew Mackay 4'07; rec Milton Abbey 9/1996. ASV
      stereo digital CDQS 6211 (cd 1997).
6.   Cardinall's Musick/Andrew Carwood 4'27; ed Skinner; rec Fitzalan
      Chapel Arundel Castle 3/1999. ASV stereo digital CDGAU 197 (cd
      1999).
7.   Clare College Cambridge Choir/Timothy Brown 4'54; rec Ely Cathedral
      Lady Chapel 6/1999. Collegium stereo digital COLCD 125 (cd 1999).

O magnum misterium
7.   Collegium COLCD 301 (2 cds 1995); CSCD 507 (cd 2002).
8.   CRCD 4162 (mc 1989); CRD 5001 (3 cds 2002).
9.   Nimbus NI 1762 (8 cds 1998).
10.   Cardinall's Musick/Andrew Carwood 4'44; ed Skinner; rec Fitzalan
      Chapel Arundel Castle 1996. ASV stereo digital CDGAU 178 (cd 1998).
11.   Monteverdi Choir/Sir John Eliot Gardiner 3'36; rec St Peter & St Paul
      Church Salle 5/1998. Philips stereo digital 4620502 (cd 1998).
12.   King's College Cambridge Choral Scholars 5'41; ed Elias; rec Jesus Col-
      lege Chapel Cambridge 20/1/1998. Quilisma stereo digital QUIL 401 (cd
      1998).
13.   Durham Cathedral Choir/James Lancelot 5'18; rec Nine Altars Chapel
      Durham Cathedral 5/2002. Priory stereo digital PRCD 801 (cd 2003).

Omni tempore benedic Deum
1.   Cardinall's Musick/Andrew Carwood 5'40; ed Skinner; rec Fitzalan Chapel
      Arundel Castle 10–11/1996. ASV stereo digital CDGAU 170 (cd 1997).

Optimam partem elegit.
2.   Hyperion CDH 55047 (cd 2002).

O quam gloriosum est regnum
1. EMI TC-CFP 4481 (mc), 7672652 (cd 1991).
3. CRD CRD 5003 (3 cds 2002); Regis RRC 1132 (cd 2003).
4. Sarum Consort/Andrew Mackay 4'50; rec Milton Abbey 9/1996. ASV stereo digital CDQS 6211 (cd 1997).
5. I Fagiolini/Robert Hollingworth 3'41; rec The Warehouse Waterloo 6/1996. Chandos stereo digital CHAN 0609 (cd 1997).
6. Cardinall's Musick/Andrew Carwood 5'00; ed Skinner; rec Fitzalan Chapel Arundel Castle 2/2001. ASV stereo digital CDGAU 309 (cd 2002).
7. Durham Cathedral Choir/James Lancelot 5'08; rec Nine Altars Chapel Durham Cathedral 5/2002. Priory stereo digital PRCD 801 (cd 2003).

O quam suavis est
2. Collegium COLCD 301 (2 cds 1995), CSCD 502 (cd 1996), CSCD 507 (cd 2002).

O sacrum convivium
4. Winchester Cathedral Choir/David Hill 3'51; rec Winchester Cathedral 11/1995. Hyperion stereo digital CDA 66837 (cd 1996).

O salutaris hostia, 4vv
1. Nimbus NI 1762 (8 cds 1998).
2. Winchester Cathedral Choir/David Hill 3'38; rec Winchester Cathedral 11/1995. Hyperion stereo digital CDA 66837 (cd 1996).

O salutaris hostia, 6vv
1. Ionian Singers/Timothy Salter 3'01; rec St Silas' Church Chalk Farm 1997. Usk [stereo digital] USK 1222 CD (cd 1997).
2. Cardinall's Musick/Andrew Carwood 2'44; ed Skinner; rec Fitzalan Chapel Arundel Castle 1996. ASV stereo digital CDGAU 178 (cd), CDGAU 1004 (cd 1998).

[Pange linguia . . . misterium] Nobis datus
2. Nimbus NI 1762 (8 cds 1998).

Pascha nostrum . . . veritatis
1. His Master's Voice mono CLP 3525 (1p 1966).
2+. Wells Cathedral Choir/Anthony Crossland 1'32; rec Wells Cathedral 1/3/1991. Priory stereo digital PRCD 362 (cd 1991).
4. St James's Consort/Robin Kimber 1'59; rec St Mary Magdalen Church Little Venice London 9/2000. Priory stereo digital PRCD 679 (cd 2000).

5.   Cardinall's Musick/Andrew Carwood 1'39; ed Skinner; rec Fitzalan
      Chapel Arundel Castle 2/2000. ASV stereo digital CDGAU 214 (cd
      2001).
6.   Queen's College Oxford Choir/Owen Rees 1'36; rec Queen's College
      Chapel 4/2001. Guild stereo digital GMCD 7222 (cd 2001).

Peccavi super numerum
1.   Cardinall's Musick/Andrew Carwood 6'25; ed Skinner; rec Fitzalan
      Chapel Arundel Castle 10–11/1996. ASV stereo digital CDGAU 170 (cd
      1997).

Petrus beatus
1.   Cardinall's Musick/Andrew Carwood 6'35; ed Skinner; rec Fitzalan
      Chapel Arundel Castle 11/1997. ASV stereo digital CDGAU 179 (cd
      1999).

Plorans ploravit
1.   Collegium COLCD 301 (2 cds 1995); CSCD 507 (cd 2002).
2.   Cardinall's Musick/Andrew Carwood 4'58; ed Skinner; rec Fitzalan
      Chapel Arundel Castle 2/2000. ASV stereo digital CDGAU 214 (cd
      2001).

Post dies octo
1.   Cardinall's Musick/Andrew Carwood [1'41]; ed Skinner [places Mane
      vobiscum, the second part as published (timing 0'47), on a separate
      track before Post dies octo (timing 0'54) with different voices, observ-
      ing its correct liturgical position and distinctiveness]; rec Fitzalan
      Chapel Arundel Castle 2/2000. ASV stereo digital CDGAU 214 (cd
      2001).

Post partum, virgo
1.   Hyperion CDH 55047 (cd 2002).
2.   Cardinall's Musick/Andrew Carwood 1'54; ed Skinner; rec Fitzalan
      Chapel Arundel Castle 1/3/1999. ASV stereo digital CDGAU 224 (cd
      2001).

Psallite Domino
4.   Ionian Singers/Timothy Salter 1'04; rec St Silas' Church Chalk Farm
      1997. Usk [stereo digital] USK 1222 CD (cd 1997).

Puer natus est
2.   Nimbus NI 1762 (8 cds 1998).

3. Pomerium/Alexander Blachly 8'13; rec 1996. Archiv stereo digital 4498192 (cd 1997); 4745572 (cd 2003).
4. Cardinall's Musick/Andrew Carwood 4'44; ed Skinner; rec Fitzalan Chapel Arundel Castle 1996. ASV stereo digital CDGAU 178 (cd 1998).

*Quem terra, Pontus, aethera; Gloria tibi, Domine
*1. St Mary's Scottish Episcopal Cathedral Edinburgh Choir/Dennis Town-hill [1'30]; rec St Mary's Scottish Episcopal Cathedral Edinburgh. Criterion stereo CRS 253 (lp 1975).
*2. Durham Cathedral Choir/James Lancelot 1'41; rec Nine Altars Chapel Durham Cathedral 5/2002. Priory stereo digital PRCD 801 (cd 2003).

Quis me statim
2. Gérard Lesne (ct), Ensemble Orlando Gibbons 2'55; rec Royal Abbey of Fontevraud Grand réfectoire 1/1996. Virgin stereo digital VC 5452642 (cd 1998).
3. Catherine King (ms), Rose Consort of Viols 2'29, rec St Andrew's Church Toddington Gloucestershire 9/1997. Naxos stereo digital 8554284 (cd 1999).
4. James Bowman (ct), Ricercar Consort 2'27; rec St Apollainaire Church Bolland 9/1998. Ricercar [stereo digital] 206442 (cd 1999).

Quodcunque ligaveris
1. Virgin VBD 5620132 (2 cds 2002).

Quomodo cantabimus?
1. Virgin VBD 5620132 (2 cds 2002).
2. I Fagiolini/Robert Hollingworth 5'57; rec The Warehouse Waterloo 6/1996. Chandos stereo digital CHAN 0609 (cd 1997).
3. Cardinall's Musick/Andrew Carwood 8'54; ed Skinner; rec Fitzalan Chapel Arundel Castle 11/1997. ASV stereo digital CDGAU 179 (cd 1999).
4. Sixteen/Harry Christophers 6'07. Coro stereo digital COR 16001 (cd 2001).

Quotiescunque manducabitis
1. Nimbus NI 1762 (8 cds 1998).
2. ECM 4391722 (cd 1994).
3. Winchester Cathedral Choir/David Hill 3'30; rec Winchester Cathedral 11/1995. Hyperion stereo digital CDA 66837 (cd 1996).

Recordare, Domine
1. Sarum Consort/Andrew Mackay 6'42; rec Milton Abbey 9/1996. ASV stereo digital CDQS 6211 (cd 1997).

Reges Tharsis, 4vv
1. Pomerium/Alexander Blachly 4'18; rec 1996. Archiv stereo digital
    4498192 (cd 1997); 4745572 (cd 2003).
2. Cardinall's Musick/Andrew Carwood 2'43; ed Skinner; rec Fitzalan
    Chapel Arundel Castle 11/1997. ASV stereo digital CDGAU 179 (cd
    1999).
3. Canterbury Cathedral Lay Clerks/David Flood 3'09; rec Canterbury
    Cathedral [3/2000]. York Ambisonic stereo digital YORKCD 158 (cd
    2000).

Reges Tharsis, 5vv
1. Cardinall's Musick/Andrew Carwood 2'33; ed Skinner; rec Fitzalan
    Chapel Arundel Castle 30/10/1996. ASV stereo digital CDGAU 179 (cd
    1999).

Regina coeli
2. Ars Nova/Paul Hillier 5'22; rec Roskilde Gammel Vor Frue Kirke 8/1999.
    Ars Nova stereo digital VANCD 01 (cd 2002).

Responsum accepit Simeon
1. Hyperion CDH 55047 (cd 2002).
2. Cardinall's Musick/Andrew Carwood 3'00; ed Skinner; rec Fitzalan
    Chapel Arundel Castle 15/11/2000. ASV stereo digital CDGAU 309 (cd
    2002).

Resurrexi
3. St James's Consort/Robin Kimber 4'10; rec St Mary Magdalen Church
    Little Venice London 9/2000. Priory stereo digital PRCD 679 (cd
    2000).
4. Cardinall's Musick/Andrew Carwood 4'57; ed Skinner; rec Fitzalan
    Chapel Arundel Castle 2/2000. ASV stereo digital CDGAU 214 (cd
    2001).
5. Queen's College Oxford Choir/Owen Rees 4'56; rec Queen's College
    Chapel 4/2001. Guild stereo digital GMCD 7222 (cd 2001).

Rorate coeli
2. Hyperion CDH 55047 (cd 2002).
3. Cardinall's Musick/Andrew Carwood 3'55; ed Skinner; rec Fitzalan
    Chapel Arundel Castle 1996. ASV stereo digital CDGAU 170 (1997).
4. Bath Abbey Choir of Boys & Men/Peter King 4'18; rec Bath Abbey
    3/1998. Priory stereo digital PRCD 666 (cd 1998).

5.   St Mary's Scottish Episcopal Cathedral Edinburgh Choir/Matthew Owens 4'28; rec St Mary's Cathedral 1/2000. Lammas [stereo digital] LAMM 122D (cd 2000).

6.   Durham Cathedral Choir/James Lancelot 4'04; rec Nine Altars Chapel Durham Cathedral 5/2002. Priory stereo digital PRCD 801 (cd 2003).

Sacerdotes Domini

3.   Cantoris CRCD 6059 (cd 2002).

9.   Nimbus NI 1762 (8 cds 1998).

11.   ECM 4391722 (cd 1994).

12.   Clare College Cambridge Choir/Timothy Brown 1'19; rec Clare College Chapel 3/1991. Guild stereo digital GMCD 7109 (cd 1995).

13.   Belfast Cathedral Choir/David Drinkell 1'24; rec Belfast Cathedral 1996. Guild stereo digital GMCD 7126 (cd 1996).

14.   Winchester Cathedral Choir/David Hill 1'34; rec Winchester Cathedral 11/1995. Hyperion stereo digital CDA 66837 (cd 1996).

15.   Guildford Cathedral Choir/Andrew Millington 1'32; rec Guildford Cathedral 1996. Lammas [stereo digital] LAMM 087C (mc), LAMM 087D (cd 1996).

16.   Durham Cathedral Choir/James Lancelot 1'20; rec Nine Altars Chapel Durham Cathedral 5/2002. Priory stereo digital PRCD 801 (cd 2003).

Sacris solemniis [listed in Grove 7 as Noctis recolitur]

1.   Cardinall's Musick/Andrew Carwood 7'44; ed Skinner; rec Fitzalan Chapel Arundel Castle 3/3/1999. ASV stereo digital CDGAU 179 (cd 1999).

Salve regina, 5vv

1.   Jesus College Cambridge Mixed Choir/Duncan Aspden 9'07; rec Jesus College Chapel. Lammas [stereo digital] LAMM 086D (cd 1995).

2.   Sarum Consort [soloists Deborah Mackay (a), Julian Podger(t) Richard Brett (b)]/Andrew Mackay 9'29; rec Milton Abbey 9/1996. ASV stereo digital CDQS 6211 (cd 1997).

3.   Ars Nova/Paul Hillier 7'17; rec Roskilde Gammel Vor Frue Kirke 8/1999. Ars Nova stereo digital VANCD 01 (cd 2002).

Salve sancta parens

3.   Hyperion CDH 55047 (cd 2002).

Sanctus, 3vv

1.   Frideswide Consort 0'51; ed Skinner; rec Fitzalan Chapel Arundel Castle 1996. ASV stereo digital CDGAU 170 (cd 1997).

Senex puerum portabat . . . adoravit
3.   EMI CDM 5662442 (cd 1996).
4.   Cantoris CRCD 6059 (cd 2002).
9.   St Edmundsbury Cathedral Choir/James Thomas 2'53; rec St Edmundsbury Cathedral 2/1999. Lammas [stereo digital] LAMM 115D (cd 1999).
10. Cardinall's Musick/Andrew Carwood 1'49; ed Skinner; rec Fitzalan Chapel Arundel Castle 2/2001. ASV stereo digital CDGAU 309 (cd 2002).
11. Durham Cathedral Choir/James Lancelot 2'17; rec Nine Altars Chapel Durham Cathedral 5/2002. Priory stereo digital PRCD 801 (cd 2003).

Senex puerum portabat . . . regebat
1.   rec 11/12/1952. Testament SBT1121 (cd 1997).
2.   Hyperion CDH 55047 (cd 2002).
3.   Cardinall's Musick/Andrew Carwood 1'35; ed Skinner; rec Fitzalan Chapel Arundel Castle 15/11/2000. ASV stereo digital CDGAU 309 (cd 2002).
4.   Durham Cathedral Choir/James Lancelot 1'26; rec Nine Altars Chapel Durham Cathedral 5/2002. Priory stereo digital PRCD 801 (cd 2003).

Sicut audivimus
1.   Hyperion CDH 55047 (cd 2002).

Siderum rector
4.   Collegium COLCD 301 (2 cds 1995); CSCD 507 (cd 2002).
5.   New College Oxford Choir/Edward Higginbottom 3'20; rec New College Chapel 7/1994. CRD stereo digital CRD 3492 (cd 1997); CRD 5003 (3 cds 2002).
6.   Cardinall's Musick/Andrew Carwood 3'02; ed Skinner; rec Fitzalan Chapel Arundel Castle 3/1999. ASV stereo digital CDGAU 197 (cd 1999).

Similes illis fiant
1.   Cardinall's Musick/Andrew Carwood [2'28]; ed Skinner [3 plainsong verses (2, 4, 6) alternate with Byrd's 3 verses, total performance time 3'36]; rec Fitzalan Chapel Arundel Castle 1996. ASV stereo digital CDGAU 178 (cd 1998).

Solve iubente Deo
1.   Collegium COLCD 301 (2 cds 1995); CSCD 507 (cd 2002).

Speciosus forma
1.   Hyperion CDH 55047 (cd 2002).

2. Cardinall's Musick/Andrew Carwood 2'59; ed Skinner; rec Fitzalan Chapel Arundel Castle 1/3/1999. ASV stereo digital CDGAU 224 (cd 2001).

Surge, illuminare, Ierusalem
2. Cardinall's Musick/Andrew Carwood 1'51; ed Skinner; rec Fitzalan Chapel Arundel Castle 11/1997. ASV stereo digital CDGAU 179 (cd 1999).
3. Canterbury Cathedral Lay Clerks/David Flood 2'11; rec Canterbury Cathedral [3/2000]. York Ambisonic stereo digital YORKCD 158 (cd 2000).

Suscepimus Deus
1. Hyperion CDH 55047 (cd 2002).
2. Cardinall's Musick/Andrew Carwood [6'15]; ed Skinner; rec Fitzalan Chapel Arundel Castle 15/11/2000. ASV stereo digital CDGAU 309 (cd 2002).

Terra tremuit
4. Christ's College Cambridge Choir/David Rowland 0'50; rec Downing College Chapel Cambridge 4/1995. Christ's College Choir stereo digital SP 1 (cd 1995).
5. Cardinall's Musick/Andrew Carwood 0'48; ed Skinner; rec Fitzalan Chapel Arundel Castle 2/2000. ASV stereo digital CDGAU 214 (cd 2001).
6. Queen's College Oxford Choir/Owen Rees 0'47; rec Queen's College Chapel 4/2001. Guild stereo digital GMCD 7222 (cd 2001).
7. Durham Cathedral Choir/James Lancelot 0'46; rec Nine Altars Chapel Durham Cathedral 5/2002. Priory stereo digital PRCD 801 (cd 2003).

Timete Dominum
1. Virgin VBD 5620132 (2 cds 2002).
2. Nimbus NI 1762 (8 cds 1998).

Tollite portas
2. Hyperion CDH 55047 (cd 2002).
3. Cardinall's Musick/Andrew Carwood 3'22; ed Skinner; rec Fitzalan Chapel Arundel Castle 10–11/1996. ASV stereo digital CDGAU 170 (cd 1997).

Tribue, Domine
3. New College Oxford Choir/Edward Higginbottom 12'42; rec New College Chapel 7/1994. CRD stereo digital CRD 3492 (cd 1997); CRD 5003 (3 cds 2002).

4.   Sarum Consort/Andrew Mackay 12'09; rec Milton Abbey 9/1996. ASV
      stereo digital CDQS 6211 (cd 1997).
5.   Tallis Scholars/Peter Philips 11'41; rec Merton College Oxford Chapel
      concert 1997. Gimell stereo digital 4549982 (cd 1998); CDGIM 998 (cd
      2001).
6.   Cardinall's Musick/Andrew Carwood 11'35; ed Skinner; rec Fitzalan
      Chapel Arundel Castle 3/1999. ASV stereo digital CDGAU 197 (cd
      1999).

Tribulationes civitatum
2.   Sarum Consort/Andrew Mackay 8'12; rec Milton Abbey 9/1996. ASV
      stereo digital CDQS 6211 (cd 1997).
3.   Cardinall's Musick/Andrew Carwood 8'14; ed Skinner; rec Fitzalan
      Chapel Arundel Castle 2/2001. ASV stereo digital CDGAU 309 (cd
      2002).

Tribulatio proxima est
1.   CRD CRD 5003 (3 cds 2002).

Tristitia et anxietas
1.   CRD CRD 5003 (3 cds 2002).
3.   King's College London Choir/David Trendell 10'15; rec St Mary
      Magdalen Church Paddington 6/2000. Proudsound stereo digital PROUCD
      149 (cd 2000).
4.   Cardinall's Musick/Andrew Carwood 8'27; ed Skinner; rec Fitzalan
      Chapel Arundel Castle 11/2000. ASV stereo digital CDGAU 224 (cd
      2001).
5.   Ars Nova/Paul Hillier 8'56; rec Roskilde Gammel Vor Frue Kirke 8/1999.
      Ars Nova stereo digital VANCD 01 (cd 2002).

Tu es pastor ovium
1.   Virgin VBD 5620132 (2 cds 2002).

Tu es Petrus
1.   EMI TC-CFP 4481 (mc), EMI 7672652 (cd 1991).
3.   Virgin VBD 5620132 (2 cds 2002).

Tui sunt coeli
2.   Nimbus NI 1762 (8 cds 1998).
3.   Cardinall's Musick/Andrew Carwood 1'18; ed Skinner; rec Fitzalan
      Chapel Arundel Castle 1996. ASV stereo digital CDGAU 178 (cd 1998).

Turbarum voces in passione Domini secundum Ioannem
1. Cardinall's Musick/Andrew Carwood [4'20, total performance time including plainchant of Passion setting 35'31]; ed Skinner; rec Fitzalan Chapel Arundel Castle 2/2000. ASV stereo digital CDGAU 214 (cd 2001).

Unam petii a Domino
1. Ionian Singers/Timothy Salter 3'50; rec St Silas' Church Chalk Farm 1997. Usk [stereo digital] USK 1222 CD (cd 1997).

Veni, Sancte Spiritus, et emitte
1. Cambridge Singers/John Rutter 5'45; rec Great Hall University College School London. Collegium stereo digital COLC 110 (mc), COLCD 110 (cd 1989); COLCD 301 (2 cds 1995); CSCD 507 (cd 2002) [corrected entry].

Veni, Sancte Spiritus, reple
1. Cantoris CRCD 6059 (cd 2002).
2. Durham Cathedral Choir/James Lancelot 1'19; rec Nine Altars Chapel Durham Cathedral 5/2002. Priory stereo digital PRCD 801 (cd 2003).

Victimae paschali laudes
4. St James's Consort/Robin Kimber 6'22; rec St Mary Magdalen Church Little Venice London 9/2000. Priory stereo digital PRCD 679 (cd 2000).
5. Cardinall's Musick/Andrew Carwood 5'11; ed Skinner; rec Fitzalan Chapel Arundel Castle 2/2000. ASV stereo digital CDGAU 214 (cd 2001).
6. Durham Cathedral Choir/James Lancelot 5'09; rec Nine Altars Chapel Durham Cathedral 5/2002. Priory stereo digital PRCD 801 (cd 2003).

Vide, Domine, afflictionem nostram
1. CRD CRD 5003 (3 cds 2002).
2. Cardinall's Musick/Andrew Carwood 6'40; ed Skinner; rec Fitzalan Chapel Arundel Castle 11/2000. ASV stereo digital CDGAU 224 (cd 2001).

Vide, Domine, quoniam tribulor
1. King's Singers [3'22]; rec EMI studios Abbey Road London 1976. His Master's Voice stereo/quad CSD 3779 (lp), TC-CSD 3779 (mc 1977).
2. Cardinall's Musick/Andrew Carwood 3'48; ed Skinner; rec Fitzalan Chapel Arundel Castle 1996. ASV stereo digital CDGAU 170 (cd 1997).

Viderunt . . . Dei nostri
2. Nimbus NI 1762 (8 cds 1998).

3.   Cardinall's Musick/Andrew Carwood 1'00; ed Skinner; rec Fitzalan Chapel Arundel Castle 1996. ASV stereo digital CDGAU 178 (cd 1998).

Vidimus stellam
2.   Cardinall's Musick/Andrew Carwood 1'58; ed Skinner; rec Fitzalan Chapel Arundel Castle 11/1997. ASV stereo digital CDGAU 179 (cd 1999).
3.   Canterbury Cathedral Lay Clerks/David Flood 2'07; rec Canterbury Cathedral [3/2000]. York ambisonic stereo digital YORKCD 158 (cd 2000).

Vigilate
1.   CRD CRD 5003 (3 cds 2002).
3.   Lincoln Cathedral Choir/David Flood 4'26; rec Lincoln Cathedral [10/1987]. York Ambisonic stereo digital YORKMC 105 (mc 1988) [corrected entry].
4.   Bath Abbey Choir/Peter King 4'41; rec Bath Abbey 3/1992. Priory stereo digital PRCD 421 (cd 1992).
5.   Jesus College Cambridge Mixed Choir/Duncan Aspden 4'15; rec Jesus College Chapel. Lammas [stereo digital] LAMM 086D (cd 1995).
6.   King's Singers 4'24; rec CTS Studio 2 London 1994. RCA stereo 09026680042 (cd 1995).
7.   St Thomas-on-the-Bourne Choir/David Swinson 4'23; rec Charterhouse Chapel Surrey 5/1996. Herald stereo digital HAVPC 196 (mc), HAVPCD 196 (cd 1996).
8.   I Fagiolini/Robert Hollingworth 3'44; rec The Warehouse Waterloo 6/1996. Chandos stereo digital CHAN 0609 (cd 1997).
9.   Canterbury Cathedral Choir/David Flood 5'06; rec Canterbury Cathedral [2/1998]. York Ambisonic stereo digital YORKCD 136 (cd 1998).
10.   Salisbury Cathedral Choir/Simon Lole [nt]. Griffin stereo digital GCMC 4030 (mc), GCCD 4030 (cd 2001).
11.   Cardinall's Musick/Andrew Carwood 4'32, ed Skinner; rec Fitzalan Chapel Arundel Castle 2/2001. ASV stereo digital CDGAU 309 (cd 2002).

Viri Galilaei
3.   Cambridge Singers/John Rutter 3'40; rec Great Hall University College School London 5/1993. Collegium stereo digital COLC 124 (mc), COLCD 124 (cd 1995).
4.   Durham Cathedral Choir/James Lancelot 4'40; rec Nine Altars Chapel Durham Cathedral 5/2002. Priory stereo digital PRCD 801 (cd 2003).

Vista quaesumus, Domine
2.   Collegium COLCD 301 (2 cds 1995); CSCD 502 (cd 1996), CSCD 507 (cd 2002).

Vultum tuum
1.   Hyperion CDH 55047 (cd 2002).
2.   Cardinall's Musick/Andrew Carwood 4'55; ed Skinner; rec Fitzalan Chapel Arundel Castle 1/3/1999. ASV stereo digital CDGAU 224 (cd 2001).

ENGLISH LITURGICAL MUSIC

*Great Service: Venite, Te Deum, Benedictus, Creed, Magnificat & Nunc Dimittis
*1.   Gimmel 4549112 [cd nd].

*Great Service: Magnificat & Nunc Dimittis
*2.   rec 1959. Decca 4480564 [mc], 4480562 [cd nd]; 4521702 (2 cds 1996).

*Great Service: Magnificat
*8.   New College Oxford Choir/Edward Higginbottom [14'40]; rec New College Chapel 7/1996. Priory stereo digital PRCD 596 (cd 1996); PRCD 1MNSET (21 cds 2002).

*Great Service: Nunc Dimittis
*9.   King's College Cambridge Choir/David Willcocks [6'01]; ed Fellowes; rec King's College Chapel 1959. Decca stereo 4608402 [cd nd]; 4674312 [cd nd].

*Second Preces and Psalms 114, 55, 119, 24: Psalms 55 & 119
*10.   St Edmundsbury Cathedral Choir/Mervyn Cousins [6'25]; rec St Edmundsbury Cathedral 1995. Priory stereo digital PRC 554 (mc), PRCD 554 (cd 1996); PRCD 1MNSET (21 cds 2002) [alternating plainsong with full sections of Psalm 119 sung to the Magnificat text and with sections of Psalm 55 sung to the Nunc Dimittis text].

*Second Preces and Psalms 114, 55, 119, 24: Psalm 119
*5.   Regis RRC 2030 (2 cds), RRC 4001 (4 cds 2000).
*9.   Priory PRC 454 (mc 1993).
*11.   Dora Kemp (s), Christ's College Cambridge Choir/David Rowland, Michael Bawtree (org) 3'32; rec Downing College Cambridge 4/1995. Christ's College Choir stereo digital SP 1 (cd 1995).

*12.   Alex Shephard (s), Clare College Cambridge Choir/Timothy Brown, Dominic Wheeler (cha org) 3'06; rec Clare College Chapel 3/1991. Guild stereo digital GMCD 7109 (cd 1995).
*13.   Blackburn Cathedral Choir/Richard Tanner, Ian Pattinson (org) 3'07; rec Blackburn Cathedral 1999. Lammas [stereo digital] LAMM 119D (cd 2000).
*14.   St Paul's Rock Creek Parish Choir/Graham Elliott, Neil Weston (org) 3'31; rec St Paul's Rock Creek Episcopal Church Washington DC 5/2002. Lammas [stereo digital] LAMM 142 (cd 2002).
*15.   St Bartholomew's Church New York City Boy & Girl Choristers & Members of St Bartholomew's Choir/Vincent Edwards, Stephen Tharp (org) [nt]. Pro Organo Stereo digital CD 7150 [cd nd].

Second Service
4.   St George's Church Belfast Choir/Nigel McClintock [6'48]; rec St George's Church Belfast 1998. Priory stereo digital PRCD 633 (cd 1999); PRCD 1MNSET (21 cds 2002).

*Short Service: Venite
4.   IMP 3036700422 [cd nd].

*Short Service: Magnificat & Nunc dimittis
*5.   Truro Cathedral Choir/Andrew Nethsingha, Simon Morley (org) [5'36]; rec Truro Cathedral 7/1996. Priory stereo digital PRCD 553 (cd 1997); PRCD 1MNSET (21 cds 2002).

Third Preces and Responses
3.   Eton College Chapel Choir/Ralph Allwood [2'41]; rec Eton College Chapel 3/1996. Herald stereo digital HAVPC 202 (mc), HAVPCD 202 (cd 1997).

*Third Service: Magnificat
*1.   St Mary Magdalen Church Oxford Choir, Voces Sacrae/Judy Martin, Peter Parshall (org) 3'47; rec Exeter College Chapel Oxford 1999. Metier stereo digital SMM 1 (cd 1999).

OTHER ENGLISH MUSIC

Ah silly soul
3.   Virgin VBD 5615612 (2 cds 1999).
4.   Timothy Penrose (ct), English Consort of Viols 4'02; rec Evangelical Church Honrath 8/1990. Musicaphon stereo digital M 56815 (cd 1995).

5.   David Cordier (ct), Royabl Consort 3'23; rec Utrecht 9/1996. Globe stereo digital GLO 5159 (cd 1998).
6.   Daniel Taylor (ct), Voix Humaines 3'18; ed Little; rec St Augustine's Church Montreal 10/1999. Atma stereo digital ACD 22207 (cd 2001).

All as a sea
2.   Decca 4750492 (cd 2003).

Ambitious love
1.   †David Cordier (ct), Royal Consort 1'48; rec Utrecht 9/1996. Globe stereo digital GLO 5159 (cd 1998).

An aged dame
1.   Drew Minster (ct), Newberry Consort [nt]; rec 1998. Harmonia Mundi stereo digital HMU 907140 (cd 2001).

Blame I confess
2.   Gérard Lesne (ct), Ensemble Orlando Gibbons 2'41; rec Royal Abbey of Fontevraud Grand réfectoire 1/1996. Virgin stereo digital VC 5452642 (cd 1998).
3.   Daniel Taylor (ct), Voix Humaines 2/57; ed Napper; rec St Augustine's Church Montreal 10/1999. Alma stereo digital ACD 22207 (cd 2001).

Blessed is he that fears the Lord
1.   Lyrichord LEMS 8014 (cd 1995).

Bow thine ear [contrafactum]
4.   Collegium COLCD 302 (2 cds 1995).

Care for thy soul
1.   Decca 4750492 (cd 2003).

Christ rising again [Church anthem version] (BE11)
1.   Zoe Milton Brown, Abigail Williams (ss), Christ's College Cambridge Choir/David Rowland, Michael Bawtree (org) [5'59]; rec Downing College Chapel Cambridge 4/1995.
2.   Jennifer Bacon, Alice Gribbin (ss), Queen's College Oxford Choir/Owen Rees 6'02, rec Queen's College Chapel 4/2001. Guild stereo digital GMCD 7222 (cd 2001).

Come help, O God
2.   Etcetera KTC 1031 (cd 1985).

Come pretty babe
3.   David Cordier (ct), Royal Consort 3'12; rec Utrecht 9/1996. Globe stereo
       digital GLO Globe stereo digital GLO 5159 (cd 1998).
4.   Montserrat Figueras (s), Hesperion XXI 2'45; rec Monastery of St Pere de
       Casserres Catalogne 14/7/2002. Alia Vox stereo digital AV 9826 (cd 2002).

Come to me, grief, for ever
4.   Decca 4750492 (cd 2003).
5.   Etcetera KTC 1031 (cd 1985).
6.   HMV 5740362 [cd nd].
7.   Harmonia Mundi HMX 2958001–5 [5 cds nd].
8.   Virgin VBD 5618212 [2 cds nd].
11.   Cambridge Taverner Choir/Owen Rees 4'37; rec Charterhouse Chapel
       Surrey 3/1995. Herald stereo digital HAVPC 187 (mc), HAVPCD 187 (cd
       1996).
12.   †Maarten Koningsberger (bar), Brist [nt]; rec 1997. Globe stereo digital
       GLO 5163 [cd 1997].
13.   Trinity Consort/Clare Wilkinson (c) 1'00; rec St Paul's Church Rusthall
       8/1998. Beulah stereo digital 1RF2 (cd 1998).
14.   †Daniel Taylor (ct), Stephen Stubbs (lt), Voix Humaines 8'12; ed Little;
       rec St Augustine's Church Montreal 10/1999. Atma stereo digital ACD
       22207 (cd 2001).

Come, woeful Orpheus
5.   †Ellen Hargis (s), Newberry Consort [nt]; rec 1998. Harmonia Mundi ste-
       reo digital HMU 907140 (cd 2001).

Constant Penelope
2.   Meridian KE 77271 (mc 1993).
3.   Trinity Consort/Clare Wilkinson (c) 2'56; rec St Paul's Church Rusthall
       8/1998. Beulah stereo digital 1RF2 (cd 1998).
4.   †David Cordier (ct), Royal Consort 2'31; rec Utrecht 9/1996. Globe ste-
       reo digital GLO 5159 (cd 1998).

Content is rich
2.   Meridian KE 77271 (mc 1993).

Crowned with flowers and lilies
1.   Anna Crookes (s), Concordia 5'08; rec The Warehouse Waterloo 6/1996.
       Chandos stereo digital CHAN 0609 (cd 1997).

Delight is dead
1.   Tamara Crout (s), Lawrence Lipnik (ct), New York Consort of Viols 4'06; rec Studio Dufay Leverett 1993. Lyrichord stereo digital LEMS 8015 (cd 1995).
2.   Ines Villanueva (s), Jaye-Consort Berlin 5'17; rec Kapelle Klein-Glienicke concert 7/2/2001. Jaye-Consort Berlin stereo digital 'Farewell all ioyes' (cd 2001) [performed as a solo song].
3.   James Bowman, Paul Esswood (cts), English Consort of Viols 4'29; [rec concert]. Regis [stereo] RRC 1065 (cd 2001).

Exalt thyself, O God
2.   Alpha CACA 901 (mc 1990); Regis RRC 2030 (2 cds), RRC 4001 (4 cds 2000).

Fair Britain isle
3.   David Cordier (ct), Royal Consort 5'52; rec Utrecht 9/1996. Globe stereo digital GLO 5159 (cd 1998).
4.   Gérard Lesne (ct), Ensemble Orlando Gibbons 6'08; rec Royal Abbey of Fontevraud Grand réfectoire 1/1996. Virgin stereo digital VC 5452642 (cd 1998).
5.   James Bowman (ct), Ricercar Consort 6'34; rec St Apollainaire Church Bolland 9/1998. Ricercar [stereo digital] 206442 (cd 1999).
6.   Geraldine McGreevy (s), Phantasm 6'39; rec St Bartholomew's Church Orford 8/1998. Simax stereo [digital] PSC 1191 (cd 1999).

Farewell, false love
2.   †Robin Blaze (ct), Fretwork 6'55; rec The Warehouse Waterloo 11/1994. Chandos stereo digital CHAN 0578 (cd 1995).
3.   †Lawrence Lipnik (ct), New York Consort of Viols 5'26; rec Studio Dufay Leverett 1993. Lyrichord stereo digital LEMS 8015 (cd 1995).

*From Virgin's womb: Rejoice, rejoice [chorus]
*4.   Trinity College Cambridge Choir/Richard Marlow [nt]; rec 1993. Conifer stereo digital 75605513532 [2 cds 1993].
*5.   Voices of Ascension/Dennis Keene 0'57; rec Church of the Ascension New York City Delos stereo digital DE 3174 (cd 1995).

Have mercy upon me, O God
4.   Naxos 8551203 (cd 1995).

How vain the toils
1.   Timothy Penrose (ct), English Consort of Viols 2'24; rec Evangelical Church Honrath 8/1990. Musicaphon stereo digital M 56815 (cd 1995).

2.   James Bowman (ct), English Consort of Viols 2'27, [rec concert]. Regis
        [stereo] RRC 1065 (cd 2001).

If women could be fair
1.   Decca 4750492 (cd 2003).
2.   Virgin VBD 5615612 (2 cds 1999).
3.   †David Cordier (ct), Royal Consort 3'06; rec Utrecht 9/1996. Globe ste-
        reo digital GLO 5159 (cd 1998).

In angel's weed
4.   Sara Stowe [(s)], Elizabethan Consort [3'24]. Classical Communications
        [stereo digital] CCLCDG 1052 (cd 2003).

In fields abroad
2.   Decca 4750492 (cd 2003).
5.   †Ian Partridge (t), Phantasm 5'27; rec St Bartholomew's Church Orford
        8/1998. Simax stereo [digital] PSC 1191 (cd 1999).

Is love a boy?
2.   rec 1981. HMV 5734642 (cd 2000).

La virginella
1.   Lyrichord LEMS 8014 (cd 1995).
5.   †Geraldine McGreevy (s), Phantasm 2'28; rec St Bartholomew's Church
        Orford 8/1998. Simax stereo [digital] PSC 1191 (cd 1999).

Lord, hear my prayer
2.   Guild GMCD 7131 (cd 1997).

Lord, in thy rage
1.   †Sara Stowe [(s)], Elizabethan Consort [2'27]. Classical Communica-
        tions [stereo digital] CCLCDG 1052 (cd 2003).

Lullaby, my sweet little baby
7.   Decca 4750492 (cd 2003).
9.   Timothy Wilson (ct), Tallis Scholars/Peter Phillips 6'27; rec St Peter & St
        Paul Church Salle. Gimell stereo digital CDGIM 010 (cd 1986); 4549104
        [mc], 4549102 [cd nd] [corrected entry].
12.   Amon Ra CSAR 46 (mc 1990).
13.   Virgin VBD 5615612 (2 cds 1999).
14.   Herald HAVPCD 252 (cd 1993).
15.   Sixteen/Harry Christophers 6'30; rec All Hallows Church Hampstead
        5/1996. Collins stereo digital 14922 (cd 1996).

16. Monteverdi Choir/Sir John Eliot Gardener 1'49; rec St Peter & St Paul Church Salle 5/1998. Philips stereo digital 4620502 (cd 1998).
17. †James Bowman (ct), Ricercar Consort 5'45; rec St Apollainaire Church Bolland 9/1998. Ricercar [stereo digital] 206442 (cd 1999).
18. †Geraldine McGreevy (s), Phantasm 12'36; rec St Bartholomew's Church Orford 8/1998. Simax stereo [digital] PSC 1191 (cd 1999).
19. †Suzie LeBlanc (s), Sylvain Bergeron (lt), Voix Humaines [nt]. Atma stereo digital ACD 22166, ACD 22190 (cd 2001).

*Lullaby, my sweet little baby [chorus]
*5. Collegium COLCD 105 (cd 1987).

My mind to me a kingdom is
1. †Carys Lane (s), Fretwork 5'57; rec The Warehouse Waterloo 11/1994. Chandos stereo digital CHAN 0578 (cd 1995).

My mistress had a little dog
3. Tamara Crout (s), New York Consort of Viols 6'09; rec Studio Dufay Leverett 1993. Lyrichord stereo digital LEMS 8015 (cd 1995).
4. Ian Partridge (t), Phantasm 6'47; rec St Bartholomew's Church Orford 8/1998. Simax stereo [digital] PSC 1191 (cd 1999).

O dear life
3. Trinity Consort/Clare Wilkinson (c) 2'52; rec St Paul's Church Rusthall 8/1998. Beulah stereo digital 1RF2 (cd 1998).

O God, give ear
1. Decca 4750492 (cd 2003).
2. †Alice Downing (c), Lynda Sayce (lt) 2'57; rec Downing College Chapel Cambridge 4/1995. Christ's College Choir stereo digital SP 1 (cd 1995).

O God, the proud are risen against me
1. Gimell 4549112 [cd nd].

O Lord, bow down
1. Ines Villanueva (s), Jaye-Consort Berlin 4'43; rec Kapelle Klein-Glienicke concert 7/2/2001. Jaye-Consort Berlin stereo digital 'Farewell all ioyes' (cd 2001).

O Lord, give ear [contrafactum]
2. rec 6/1991. Guild GMCD 7108 (cd 1996).

O Lord, how long wilt thou forget?
1. Lyrichord LEMS 8014 (cd 1995).
2. Decca 4750492 (cd 2003).
3. †James Griffett (t), English Consort of Viols 2'14; [rec concert]. Regis [stereo] RRC 1065 (cd 2001).

O Lord, how vain
5. Anna Crookes (s), Fretwork 6'49; rec The Warehouse Waterloo 11/1994. Chandos stereo digital CHAN 0578 (cd 1995).
6. Ian Partridge (t), Phantasm 7'42; rec St Bartholomew's Church Orford 8/1998. Simax stereo [digital] PSC 1191 (cd 1999).
7. Barbara Bonney (s), Phantasm 7'22; rec Henry Wood Hall London 10/1998. Decca stereo digital 4661322 (cd 2001).

O Lord, make thy servant
3. Guild GMCD 7118 (cd 1996).
5. Gimell 4549112 [cd nd]; 4549992 (cd 1991).
7. King's Singers 3'41; rec CTS Studio 2 London 1994. RCA stereo 09026680042 (cd 1995).
8. Choir of Her Majesty's Chapels Royal, St Peter ad Vincula & St John the Evangelist/Stephen Tilton [nt]; rec 1996. Isis stereo digital CD 021 [cd 1996].
9. St Mary's Scottish Episcopal Cathedral Edinburgh Choir/Timothy Byram-Wigfield 3'01; rec St Mary's Scottish Episcopal Cathedral 2/1996. Priory stereo digital PRCD 557 (cd 1997).
10. St Edmundsbury Cathedral Choir/James Thomas 2'51; rec St Edmundsbury Cathedral 7/2001. Lammas [stereo digital] LAMM 135 (cd 2001).
11. Ars Nova/Paul Hillier 2'53; rec Roskilde Gammel Vor Frue Kirke 8/1999. Ars Nova stereo digital VANCD 01 (cd 2002).
12. Christ Church Cathedral Oxford Singers/Robert Webb 2'53; rec Christ Church Cathedral concert 7/9/2002. OxRecs stereo digital OXCD 93 (cd 2003).

O Lord, rebuke me not
1. Salisbury Cathedral Archive Recordings SCS 276501 (cd 2000).
1+. Gay Walker (s), St John the Evangelist's Scottish Episcopal Church Edinburgh Choir/Robert D Kidd, Richard Walker (org) [nt]; rec St John the Evangelist's Scottish Episcopal Church Edinburgh 1975. St John's Church stereo SJC 101 (mc), SJC 101 (1p 1976).

O Lord, turn thy wrath [contrafactum]
1. Regis RRC 2030 (2 cds), RRC 4001 (4 cds 2000).

O Lord, within thy tabernacle
1.　Gérard Lesne (ct), Ensemble Orlando Gibbons 4'10; rec Royal Abbey of Fontevraud Grand réfectoire 1/1996. Virgin stereo digital VC 5452642 (cd 1998).

O that most rare breast
1.　Decca 4750492 (cd 2003).
3.　Trinity Consort/Clare Wilkinson (c) 8'15; rec St Paul's Church Rusthall 8/1998. Beulah stereo digital 1RF2 (cd 1998).

Out of the deep, 6vv
1.　Trinity College Cambridge Choir/Richard Marlow 5'26; rec Trinity College Chapel 3/1994. Conifer stereo digital 75605512312 (cd 1995).
2.　Oxford Camerata/Jeremy Summerly, Laurence Cummings (cha org) 5'59; rec Hertford College Chapel Oxford 7/1994. Naxos stereo digital 4553130 (mc), 8553130 (cd 1995).

Out of the orient crystal skies
4.　Ella Thomas (s), Choir of Her Majesty's Chapels Royal, Tower of London/Stephen Tilton 3'52; rec St Peter ad Vincula Chapel Tower of London 6/2001. Quilisma stereo digital QUIL 404 (cd 2001).
5.　Sara Stowe [(s)], Elizabethan Consort [3'44]. Classical Communications [stereo digital] CCLCDG 1052 (cd 2003).
6.　Eva Nievergelt (s), Katharina Beidler (s), Klaus Haffke (ct), Viola da Gamba Consort of Vienna/Jose Vazquez. Amati [stereo digital] AMI 96041 [cd nd].

O you that hear this voice
2.　Trinity Consort/Clare Wilkinson (c) 1'55; rec St Paul's Church Rusthall 8/1998. Beulah stereo digital 1RF2 (cd 1998).

Penelope that longed
1.　Trinity Consort/Clare Wilkinson (c); rec St Paul's Church Rusthall 8/1998. Beulah stereo digital 1RF2 (cd 1998).
2.　†Catherine King (ms), Rose Consort of Viols 3'17; rec St Andrew's Church Toddington Gloucestershire 9/1997. Naxos stereo digital 8554284 (cd 1999).

Praise our Lord, all ye Gentiles
8.　Collegium CSCD 507 (cd 2002), COLCD 301 (2 cds 1995).
9.　Lincoln College Choir/Alexander Chaplin 2'55; rec St John's Church St Stephen's House Oxford 7/1994. Regent stereo digital REGCD 110 (cd 1994).

Prevent us, O Lord
5.   Etcetera KTC 1031 (cd 1985).
6.   Holy Trinity Cathedral Auckland Choir/Anthony Jennings 2'52; rec
       Holy Trinity Cathedral 1980. Kiwi Pacific stereo CDSLD 87 (cd
       1991).
7.   Choir of Her Majesty's Chapels Royal, St Peter ad Vincula & St John the
       Evangelist/Stephen Tilton [nt], rec 1996. Isis stereo digital CD 021 [cd
       1996].
8.   Lichfield Cathedral Choir/Andrew Lumsden 2'36; rec Lichfield Cathe-
       dral 2/1998. Lammas [stereo digital] LAMM 104D (cd 1998).
9.   Ars Nova/Paul Hillier 2'36; rec Roskilde Gammel Vor Frue Kirke 8/1999.
       Ars Nova stereo digital VANCD 01 (cd 2002).
10.   Episcopal Church of the Incarnation Dallas Chancel Choir/Kevin M.
       Clarke [nt]. Pro Organo stereo digital CD 7091 [cd nd].

Rejoice unto the Lord
3.   Tamara Crout (s), New York Consort of Viols 4'08; rec Studio Dufay
       Leverett 1993. Lyrichord stereo digital LEMS 8015 (cd 1995).
4.   Robin Blaze (ct), Concordia 4'42; rec The Warehouse Waterloo 6/1996.
       Chandos stereo digital CHAN 0609 (cd 1997).
5.   Gérard Lesne (ct), Ensemble Orlando Gibbons 3'16; rec Royal Abbey of
       Fontevraud Grand réfectoire 1/1996. Virgin stereo digital VC5452642 (cd
       1998).
6.   James Bowman (ct), Ricercar Consort 3'33; rec St Apollainaire Church
       Bolland 9/1998. Ricercar [stereo digital] 206442 (cd 1999).
7.   Geraldine McGreevy (s), Phantasm 3'04; rec St Bartholomew's Church
       Orford 8/1998. Simax stereo [digital] PSC 1191 (cd 1999).
8.   Sara Stowe [(s)], Elizabethan Consort [3'57]. Classical Communications
       [stereo digital] CCLCDG 1052 (cd 2003).

Retire, my soul
1.   Etcetera KTC 1031 (cd 1985).
2.   Ars Nova/Paul Hillier 3'18; rec Roskilde Gammel Vor Frue Kirke 8/1999.
       Ars Nova stereo digital VANCD 01 (cd 2002).

Sing joyfully unto God our strength
12.   Regis RRC 2030 (2 cds), RRC 4001 (4 cds 2000).
16.   [rec 6/1986] Gimell 4549112 [cd nd].
18.   Collegium CSC 500 (mc), CSCD 500 (cd 1990); COLCD 301 (2 cds
       1995); CSCD 507 (cd 2002).
21.   Christ's College Cambridge Choir/David Rowland 2'39; rec Downing
       College Chapel Cambridge 4/1995. Christ's College Choir stereo digital
       SP 1 (cd 1995).

22. Voices of Ascension/Dennis Keene 2'09; rec Church of the Ascension New York City 1994. Delos stereo digital DE 3174 (cd 1995).
23. King's Singers 2'14; rec CTS Studio 2 London 1994. RCA stereo 09026680042 (cd 1995).
24. Clare College Cambridge Choir/Timothy Brown 2'31; ed Morris; rec St George's Church Chesterton 6/1993. Guild stereo digital GMCD 7115 (cd 1996).
25. Ars Nova/Paul Hillier 2'21; rec Roskilde Gammel Vor Frue Kirke 8/1999. Ars Nova stereo digital VANCD 01 (cd 2002).
26. St Paul's Rock Creek Parish Choir/Graham Elliott 2'53; rec St Paul's Rock Creek Episcopal Church Washington DC 5/2002. Lammas [stereo digital] LAMM 142 (cd 2002).
27. St Paul's Indianapolis Episcopal Church Choir/Frank Boles [nt]; rec concert Great Britain. Pro Organo stereo digital CD 7174 [cd nd].

Susanna fair, 5vv
4. Decca 4750492 (cd 2002).
7. †Geraldine McGreevy (s), Phantasm 2'27; rec St Bartholomew's Church Orford 8/1998. Simax stereo [digital] PSC 1191 (cd 1999).
8. †Sara Stowe [(s)], Elizabethan Consort [3'16]. Classical Communications [stereo digital] CCLCDG 1052 (cd 2003).

The man is blest
1. Lyrichord LEMS 8014 (cd 1995).

The match that's made
1. Decca 4750492 (cd 2003).

The noble famous queen
2. BBC CORO (cd 2002).
3. Anna Crookes (s), Concordia 1'41; rec The Warehouse Waterloo 6/1996. Chandos stereo digital CHAN 0609 (cd 1997).

This day Christ was born
2. York Minster Choir/Edward Bairstow rec York Minster 4/1927. Amphion PHICD 138 (cd 1996).
7. Herald HAVPCD 252 (cd 1993).
8. Clare College Cambridge Choir/Timothy Brown 2'06; ed Morris; rec St George's Church Chesterton 6/1993. Guild stereo digital GMCD 7115 (cd 1996).
9. Felicity Lott, Emily Woolf, Clare Porter, Helen Semple (ss), Andy Mackinder (bar), Joyful Company of Singers/Peter Broadbent 2'42; rec Champs Hill Pullborough 11/2002. ASV stereo digital CDWHL 2150 (cd 2003).

This sweet and merry month of May, 6vv
8.   rec 1981. HMV 5734642 (cd 2000).
9.   Collegium COLCD 105 (cd 1987).
10.   Magdalen College Oxford Choir/Grayston Ives [nt], rec 1999. Debonair stereo digital CDDEB 1012 (cd 2000).

Though Amaryllis dance in green
3.   Lyrichord LEMS 8014 (cd 1995).
14.   IMP 3036701752 (cd 1987).
18.   †Geraldine McGreevy (s), Phantasm 4'59; rec St Bartholomew's Church Orford 8/1998. Simax stereo [digital] PSC 1191 (cd 1999).
19.   †Barbara Bonney (s), Phantasm 3'05; rec Henry Wood Hall London 10/1998. Decca stereo digital 4661322 (cd 2001).

Though I be Brown
2.   Geraldine McGreevy (s), Phantasm 4'17; rec St Bartholomew's Church Orford 8/1998. Simax stereo [digital] PSC 1191 (cd 1999).

Thou poet's friend
1.   Timothy Penrose (ct), English Consort of Viols 1'45; rec Evangelical Church Honrath 8/1990. Musicaphon stereo digital M 56815 (cd 1995).

Triumph with pleasant melody
2.   Richard Wyn Roberts, Robin Blaze (cts), Fretwork 3'32; rec The Warehouse Waterloo 11/1994. Chandos stereo digital CHAN 0578 (cd 1995).
3.   James Bowman (ct), Ricercar Consort 3'42; rec St Apollainaire Church Bolland 9/1998. Ricercar [stereo digital] 206442 (cd 1999).
4.   Katharine Beidler, Haida Housseini (ss), Klaus Haffke (ct), Bernard Hunziker (t), Viola da Gamba Consort of Vienna/Jose Vazquez. Amati [stereo digital] AMI 96051 [cd nd].

Truth at the first
1.   Carys Lane (s), Fretwork 2'55; rec The Warehouse Waterloo 11/1994. Chandos stereo digital CHAN 0578 (cd 1995).

Turn our captivity, O Lord
5.   Collegium CSCD 507 (cd 2002); COLCD 301 (2 cds 1995).

Weeping full sore
1.   Trinity Consort/Clare Wilkinson (c) 6'28; rec St Paul's Church Rusthall 8/1998. Beulah stereo digital 1RF2 (cd 1998).

What pleasure have great princes?
1.   Lyrachord LEMS 8014 (cd 1995).
4.   Decca 4750492 (cd 2003).

Who likes to love
2.   †Anna Crookes (s), Fretwork 4'37; rec The Warehouse Waterloo 11/1994. Chandos stereo digital CHAN 0578 (cd 1995).

Who made thee, Hob, forsake the plough?
5.   Tamara Crout (s), Lawrence Lipnik (ct), New York Consort of Viols 3'43; rec Studio Dufay Leverett 1993. Lyrichord stereo digital LEMS 8015 (cd 1995).

Why do I use my paper, ink and pen?
2.   Lyrichord LEMS 8014 (cd 1995).
3.   †Robert Hollingworth, Richard Wyn Roberts, Robin Blaze (cts), Concordia 6'47; rec The Warehouse Waterloo 6/1996. Chandos stereo digital CHAN 0609 (cd 1997).

With lilies white
1.   Connor Burrowes (tr), Amsterdam Loeki Stardust Quartet 2'35. Channel Classics stereo digital CCS 9196 (cd 1996).
2.   Gérard Lesne (ct), Ensemble Orlando Gibbons 4'50; rec Royal Abbey of Fontevraud Grand réfectoire 1/1996. Virgin stereo digital VC 5452642 (cd 1998).

Wretched Albinus
1.   Connor Burrowes (tr), Amsterdam Loeki Stardust Quartet 2'28. Channel Classics stereo digital CCS 9196 (cd 1996).
2.   Gérard Lesne (ct), Ensemble Orlando Gibbons 2'51; rec Royal Abbey of Fontevraud Grand réfectoire 1/1996. Virgin stereo digital VC 5452642 (cd 1998).
3.   James Bowman (ct), Ricercar Consort 3'27; rec St Apollainaire Church Bolland 9/1998. Ricercar [stereo digital] 206442 (cd 1999).

Ye sacred muses
6.   HMV 5740362 [cd nd].
8.   Virgin VBD 5615612 (2 cds 1999).
11.   Tamara Crout (s), New York Consort of Viols 3'09; rec Studio Dufay Leverett 1993. Lyrichord stereo digital LEMS 8015 (cd 1995).
12.   Maarten Koningsberger (bar), Mike Fentross (lt) [nt]; rec 1997. Globe stereo digital GLO 5163 [cd 1997].
13.   David Cordier (ct), Royal Consort 3'57; rec Utrecht 9/1996. Globe stereo digital GLO 5159 (cd 1998).
14.   Gérard Lesne (ct), Ensemble Orlando Gibbons 3'38; rec Royal Abbey of Fontevraud Grand réfectoire 1/1996. Virgin stereo digital VC 5452642 (cd 1998). 15. Catherine King (ms), Rose Consort of Viols 3'52; rec

St Andrew's Church Toddington Glouchestershire 9/1997. Naxos stereo
digital 8554284 (cd 1999).

16.   James Bowman (ct), Ricercar Consort 3'56; rec St Apollainaire Church
      Bolland 9/1998. Ricercar [stereo digital] 206442 (cd 1999).

17.   Ian Partridge (t), Phantasm 4'14; re St Bartholomew's Church Orford 8/
      1998. Simax stereo [digital] PSC 1191 (cd 1999).

18.   Daniel Taylor (ct), Voix Humaines 4'12; ed Napper; rec St August-
      ine's Church Montreal 10/1999. Atma stereo digital ACD 22207 (cd
      2001).

19.   Ines Villanueva (s & drum), Jaye-Consort Berlin 3'51; rec Kapelle Klein-
      Glienicke concert 7/2/2001. Jaye-Consort Berlin stereo 'Farewell
      all ioyes' (cd 2001) [s beats funereally on a drum in the instrumental
      introduction].

20.   Matthew White (ct), Voix Baroques 3'15; rec St Augustine's Church
      Montreal 9/2002. Analekta stereo digital AN 29902 (cd 2003).

CONSORT MUSIC

Fantasias, Grounds, and Dances

Browning à 5

7.   Bis CD 8 (cd 1992); CD 57 (cd 1993).

9.   Virgin VBD 5615612 (2 cds 1999).

10+. Marlon Verbruggen (rec), Flanders Recorder Quartet; rec 1992. Vox
      Temporis Productions VTPCD 90212 [cd 1992].

10++. King's Noyse/David Douglas [nt]. Harmonia Mundi stereo digital HMU
      907101 [cd 1994].

12.   New York Consort of Viols [4'45]; rec Studio Dufay Leverett 1993. Lyri-
      chord stereo digital LEMS 8015 (cd 1995) [preceded by one unaccompa-
      nied verse of the vocalization, 'The leaves be green,' sung by Lawrence
      Lipnik (ct), additional timing 0'16].

13.   Capriccio Stravagante 3'50; rec Temple de l'Ascension Paris 3/1997.
      Audivis stereo digital E 8611 (cd 1997).

14.   Phantasm with Martha McGaughey (t vl) 4'15; rec St Bartholomew's
      Church Orford 8/1996. Simax stereo [digital] PSC 1143 (cd 1997).

15.   Royal Consort 3'43; rec Ulrecht 9/1996. Globe stereo digital GLO 5159
      (cd 1998). 16. Ensemble Orlando Gibbons 4'23; rec Royal Abbey of
      Fontevraud Grand réfectoire 1/1996. Virgin stereo digital VC 5452642
      (cd 1998).

17.   Calefax Reed Quintet 3'34; ed Hekkema; rec 2000. MDG stereo digital
      61910432 (cd 2001).

Fantasia à 3 in C, no 1
1.   Virgin VBD 5615612 (2 cds 1999).

Fantasia à 3 in C, no 2
3.   RCA 09026615832 (28 cds 1993, part 3).
4.   Virgin VBD 5615612 (2 cds 1999).
6.   New York Consort of Viols 1'59; rec Studio Dufay Leverett 1993. Lyrichord stereo digital LEMS 8015 (cd 1995).
7.   Sara Stowe [(s)], Elizabethan Consort [2'39]. Classical Communications [stereo digital] CCLCDG 1052 (cd 2003) [tr vl part vocalized as 'sol-fa'].

Fantasia à 3 in C, no 3
2.   Virgin VBD 5615612 (2 cds 1999).
3.   New York Consort of Viols 0'52; rec Studio Dufay Leverett 1993. Lyrichord stereo digital LEMS 8015 (cd 1995).

Fantasia à 4 in A minor
1.   Jaye-Consort Berlin 3'12; rec Kapelle Klein-Glienicke concert 7/2/2001. Jaye-Consort Berlin stereo digital 'Farewell all ioyes' (cd 2001).

Fantasia à 4 in G minor
5.   Virgin VBD 5615612 (2 cds 1999); VBD 5618212 [2 cds nd].
8.   New York Consort of Viols 2'43; rec Studio Dufay Leverett 1993. Lyrichord stereo digital LEMS 8015 (cd 1995).
9.   Phantasm/Laurence Dreyfus (tr vl) 2'18; rec St Bartholomew's Church Orford 8/1998. Simax stereo [digital] PSC 1191 (cd 1999).
10. Elizabethan Consort [3'07]. Classical Communications [stereo digital] CCLCDG 1052 (cd 2003).

Fantasia à 5 in C
6+. English Consort of Viols 5'52; ed Elliott; rec Boxgrove Priory 1986. Musicaphon stereo digital M 56808 (cd 1994).
8.   Phantasm with Martha McGaughey (t vl) 5'39; rec St Bartholomew's Church Orford 8/1996. Simax stereo [digital] PSC 1143 (cd 1997).
9.   Ensemble Orlando Gibbons 6'53; rec Royal Abbey of Fontevraud Grand réfectoire 1/1996. Virgin stereo digital VC 5452642 (cd 1998).

Fantasia à 6 in G minor, no. 1
1.   Lyrichord LEMS 8014 (cd 1995).
6.   Virgin VBD 5615612 (2 cds 1999).
7.   Capriccio Stravagante 5'52; rec Temple de l'Ascension Paris 3/1997. Audivis stereo digital E 8611 (cd 1997).

8.   Phantasm with Martha McGaughey (t vl), Alison McGillivray (b vl)
     5'04; rec St Bartholomew's Church Orford 8/1996. Simax stereo [digital]
     PSC 1143 (cd 1997).
9.   Ricercar Consort/Philippe Pierlot (tr vl) 5'53; rec St Apollainaire Church
     Bolland 9/1998. Ricercar [stereo digital] 206442 (cd 1999).

Fantasia à 6 in G minor, no. 2
5.   Virgin VBD 5615612 (2 cds 1999).
7.   Phantasm with Martha McGaughey (t vl), Alison McGillivray (b vl)
     4'10; rec St Bartholomew's Church Orford 8/1996. Simax Stereo [digital]
     PSC 1143 (cd 1997).

Pavan à 5 in C minor
2+. English Consort of Viols 3'09; ed Elliott; rec Boxgrove Priory 1986.
     Musicaphon stereo digital M 56808 (cd 1994).
4.   Capriccio Stravagante 3'50; rec Temple de l'Ascension Paris 3/1997.
     Audivis stereo digital E 8611 (cd 1997).

Pavan and Galliard à 6 in C
4.   Virgin VBD 5615612 (2 cds 1999).
5.   Naxos 8554064 (cd 1997); 8553199–20 (2 cds & book 2000).
6.   Capriccio Stravagante [3'59]; rec Temple de l'Ascension Paris 3/1997.
     Audivis stereo digital E 8611 (cd 1997).

Prelude [and Ground]
1.   Lyrichord LEMS 8014 (cd 1995).
2+. English Consort of Viols 6'18; ed Elliott; rec Boxgrove Priory 1986.
     Musicaphon stereo digital M 56808 (cd 1994).
4.   Capriccio Stravagante 6'16; rec Temple de l'Ascension Paris 3/1997.
     Audivis stereo digital E 8611 (cd 1997).
5.   Parley of Instruments/Peter Holman 5'27; rec St Jude-on-the-Hill
     Church Hampstead 10/1996. Hyperion stereo digital CDA 66929 (cd
     1997).
6.   Ensemble Orlando Gibbons 5'53; rec Royal Abbey of Fontevraud Grand
     réfectoire 1/1996. Virgin stereo digital VC 5452642 (cd 1998).
7.   Newberry Consort/Mary Springfels [nt]; rec 1998 Harmonia Mundi ste-
     reo digital HMU 907140 (cd 2001).
8.   Calefax Reed Quintet 4'14; ed Hekkema; rec 2000. MDG stereo digital
     61910432 (cd 2001).

IN NOMINES

In Nomine à 4, no 1
7. Royal Consort 2'47; rec Ulrecht 9/1996. Globe stereo digital GLO 5159 (cd 1998).
8. Ricercar Consort/Philippe Pierlot (tr vl) 2'27; rec St Apollainaire Church Bolland 9/1998. Ricercar [stereo digital] 206442 (cd 1999).
9. Phantasm/Laurence Dreyfus (tr vl) 2'28; rec St Bartholomew's Church Orford 8/1998. Simax stereo [digital] PSC 1191 (cd 1999).

In Nomine à 4, no 2
11. Phantasm/Laurence Dreyfus (tr vl) 2'21; rec St Bartholomew's Church Orford 8/1998. Simax stereo [digital] PSC 1191 (cd 1999).

In Nomine à 5, no 1
1. Virgin VBD 5615612 (2 cds 1999).
2. Marlon Verbruggen (rec), Flanders Recorder Quartet; rec 1992. Vox Temporis Productions VTPCD 90212 [cd 1992].
3. Ensemble Orlando Gibbons 3'07; rec Royal Abbey of Fontevraud Grand réfectoire 1/1996. Virgin stereo digital VC 5452642 (cd 1998).

In Nomine à 5, no 2, 'on the sharpe'
3. Virgin VBD 5615612 (2 cds 1999).
5. Phantasm with Martha McGaughey (t vl) 2'26; rec St Bartholomew's Church Orford 8/1996. Simax stereo [digital] PSC 1143 (cd 1997).
6. Ensemble Orlando Gibbons 3'23; rec Royal Abbey of Fontevraud Grand réfectoire 1/1996.Virgin stereo digital VC 5452642 (cd 1998).

In Nomine à 5, no 3
1. Virgin VBD 5615612 (2 cds 1999).
3. Phantasm with Martha McGaughey (t vl) 2'29; rec St Bartholomew's Church Orford 8/1996. Simax stereo [digital] PSC 1143 (cd 1997).
4. Ensemble Orlando Gibbons 3'04; rec Royal Abbey of Fontevraud Grand réfectoire 1/1996.Virgin stereo digital VC 5452642 (cd 1998).

In Nomine à 5, no 4
2. Virgin VBD 5615612 (2 cds 1999).
3+. Marlon Verbruggen (rec), Flanders Recorder Quartet; rec 1992. Vox Temporis Productions VTPCD 90212 [cd 1992].
6. Phantasm with Martha McGaughey (t vl) 2'17; rec St Bartholomew's Church Orford 8/1996. Simax stereo [digital] PSC 1143 (cd 1997).
7. Ensemble Orlando Gibbons 2'50; rec Royal Abbey of Fontevraud Grand réfectoire 1/1996. Virgin stereo digital VC 5452642 (cd 1998).

In Nomine à 5, no 5
1.   Lyrichord LEMS 8014 (cd 1995).
3.   Virgin VBD 5615612 (2 cds 1999).
7.   His Majesty's Sagbutts & Cornetts 2'27; rec St Jude-on-the-Hill
       Church Hampstead 1996. Hyperion stereo digital CDA 66894
       (cd 1997).
8.   Phantasm with Martha McGaughy (t vl) 2'43; rec St Bartholomew's
       Church Orford 8/1996. Simax stereo [digital] PSC 1143 (cd 1997).
9.   Ensemble Orlando Gibbons 3'04; rec Royal Abbey of Fontevraud Grand
       réfectoire 1/1996. Virgin stereo digital VC 5452642 (cd 1998).

HYMN AND MISERERE SETTINGS

Christe qui lux es à 4, no 2
2.   Cardinall's Musick/Andrew Carwood [2'44]; ed Skinner [vocalized with
       3 plainsong verses (1, 3, 5) alternating with Byrd's 3 verses, total perfor-
       mance time 4'34]; rec Fitzalan Chapel Arundel Castle 30/10/1996. ASV
       stereo digital CDGAU 179 (cd 1999).

Christe qui lux es à 4, no 3
5.   Frideswide Consort 1'03; ed Skinner; rec Fitzalan Chapel Arundel Castle
       1996. ASV stereo digital CDGAU 170 (cd 1997).

Christe Redemptor à 4
5.   Cardinall's Musick/Andrew Carwood [2'38]; ed Skinner [vocalized with
       3 plainsong verses (1, 3, 5) alternating with Byrd's 2 verses, total perfor-
       mance time 4'26]; rec Fitzalan Chapel Arundel Castle 1996. ASV stereo
       digital CDGAU 170 (cd 1997).

Miserere à 4
3.   Frideswide Consort 1'19; ed Skinner; rec Fitzalan Chapel Arundel Castle
       1996. ASV stereo digital CDGAU 170 (cd 1997).

Sermone blando à 4, no 2
3.   Frideswide Consort 1'44; ed Skinner; rec Fitzalan Chapel Arundel Castle
       1996. ASV stereo digital CDGAU 170 (cd 1997).

*Te lucis ante terminum à 4: verse 10
*1.   Fretwork 1'21; rec Maltings Snape 3/1993. Virgin stereo digital VC
       5450312 (cd 1994) [corrected entry].
*2.   Cardinall's Musick/Andrew Carwood [1'15]; ed Skinner [vocalized with
       a plainsong verse before and after Byrd's verse, total performance time

2'15]; rec Fitzalan Chapel Arundel Castle 30/10/1996. ASV stereo digital CDGAU 179 (cd 1999).

KEYBOARD MUSIC

Fantasias, preludes, hymns and antiphons

Christe qui lux
2. Davitt Moroney (org) 2'26; ed Brown; rec Eglise-Musée des Augustins Toulouse 9/1991. Hyperion stereo digital CDA 66551–7 (7 cds 1999); CDA 66558 (cd 2001).

Clarifica me, Pater, setting 1
3. ECM 4391722 (cd 1994).
5. Davitt Moroney (org) 1'44; ed Brown; rec Eglise-Musée des Augustins Toulouse 9/1991. Hyperion stereo digital CDA 66551–7 (7 cds 1999).

Clarifica me, Pater, setting 2
3. ECM 4391722 (cd 1994).
5. Davitt Moroney (org) 1'34; ed Brown; rec Eglise-Musée des Augustins Toulouse 9/1991. Hyperion stereo digital CDA 66551–7 (7 cds 1999).

Clarifica me, Pater, setting 3
6. Bis CD 140–141 (2 cds 1996).
9. ECM 4391722 (cd 1996).
11. Davitt Moroney (org) 3'15; ed Brown; rec Eglise-Musée des Augustins Toulouse 9/1991. Hyperion stereo digital CDA 66551–7 (7 cds 1999).
12. John Kitchen (org) 2'34; rec Crichton Collegiate Church Midlothian 1/2003. Delphian stereo digital DCD 34008 (cd 2003).

Fantasia in A minor
4. Talent DOM 291022 (cd 1996).
5+. Ton Koopman (hpsc) 7'44; rec Maria Minor Utrecht 12/1986. Capriccio stereo digital 10211 (cd 1988).
8. Anne Page (hist org) 7'26; rec Pembroke College Cambridge Chapel 1993. OxRecs stereo digital OXCASS 59 (mc), OXCD 59 (cd 1994).
9. Laurent Stewart (hpsc) 7'19; rec Chateau de Vicq Pas-de-Calais 11/1994. Pierre Verany stereo digital PV 795051 (cd 1995).
10. Sophie Yates (virg) 7'04; rec Forde Abbey 4/1994. Chandos stereo digital CHAN 0574 (cd 1995).
11. Charles Harrison (org) 7'53; rec Jesus College Cambridge Chapel. Lammas [stereo digital] LAMM 086D (cd 1995).

12.   David Leigh (hist hpsc) 7'04; [ed Brown]; rec [Leigh's house] Charlbury
       Oxfordshire 27/10/1998. Acanthus [stereo digital] 94010 (cd 1998).
13.   Davitt Moroney (org) 8'05; ed Brown; rec Royal Abbey of Fontevraud
       2/1997. Hyperion stereo digital CDA 66551–7 (7 cds 1999); CDA 66558
       (cd 2001).
14.   Aapo Hakkinen (hist hpsc) 7'43; ed Brown; rec Brussels 6/1999. Alba
       stereo digital ABCD 148 (cd 2000).
15.   Andreas Staier (hpsc) 7'12; ed Brown; rec DeutschlandRadio Cologne
       8/2001. Teldec stereo digital 0927422052 (cd 2001).

Fantasia in C, no 1
2.   Davitt Moroney (msr) 6'17; ed Brown; rec Ingatestone Hall Essex 3/1992.
       Hyperion stereo digital CDA 66551–7 (7 cds 1999).

Fantasia in C, no 2
7.   Bis CD 140–141 (2 cds 1996).
15.   Charles Harrison (org) 5'29; rec Jesus College Cambridge Chapel.
       Lammas [stereo digital] LAMM 086D (cd 1995).
16.   Skip Sempé (hpsc) 4'53; rec Temple de l'Ascension Paris 3/1997.
       Audivis stereo digital E 8611 (cd 1997).
17.   Timothy Morris (org) 5'38; rec New College Chapel 7/1994. CRD stereo
       digital CRD 3492 (cd 1997); CRD 5003 (3 cds 2002).
18.   Andrew Cyprian Love (org) [nt]; rec Glenstal Abbey. SDG Recordings
       stereo digital SDG CD 607 (cd 1998).
19.   Davitt Moroney (org) 5'45; ed Brown; rec Eglise-Musée des Augustins
       Toulouse 9/1991. Hyperion stereo digital CDA 66551–7 (7 cds 1999).
20.   Davitt Moroney (hpsc) 5'34; ed Brown; rec Royal Abbey of Fontevraud
       12/1996. Hyperion stereo digital CDA 66551–7 (7 cds 1999).
21.   Patrick Russill (cha org) 5'35; ed Skinner; rec Fitzalan Chapel Arundel
       Castle 20/7/2000. ASV stereo digital CDGAU 206 (cd 2000).
22.   Christopher Stembridge (hist org) 5'44; rec Church of the Ospedaletto
       Venice 5/1999. Quilisma stereo digital QUIL 302 (cd 2000).
23.   Andreas Staier (hpsc) 6'18; ed Brown; rec DeutschlandRadio Cologne
       8/2001. Teldec stereo digital 0927422052 (cd 2001).
24.   Siebe Henstra (org) 5'54; rec Old Catholic Church the Hague 5/2002. Chan-
       nel Classics stereo digital CCS 18998 (cd), CCS SA 18902 (sacd 2002).
25.   Martin Souter (hist virg) [5'29]; rec Hill Music Room Ashmolean
       Museum Oxford. Classical Communications [stereo digital] CCLCD 832
       (cd 2003).

Fantasia in C, no 3
3.   Davitt Moroney (org) 5'36; ed Brown; rec Eglise-Musée des Augustins
       Toulouse 9/1991. Hyperion stereo digital CDA 66551–7 (7 cds 1999).

*Fantasia in C, no 3: [bar 46 to end]
*4.	Patrick Russill (cha org) 2'52; ed Skinner; rec Fitzalan Chapel Arundel Castle 20/7/2000. ASV stereo digital CDGAU 206 (cd 2000).

Fantasia in D minor
9.	Timothy Morris (org) 4'53; rec New College Chapel 7/1994. CRD stereo digital CRD 3492 (cd 1997); CRD 5003 (3 cds 2002).
10.	John Scott (org) 4'52; rec St Jude-on-the-Hill Church Hampstead. Guild stereo digital GMCD 7150 (cd 1998).
11.	Davitt Moroney (org) 5'14; ed Brown; rec Eglise-Musée des Augustins Toulouse 9/1991. Hyperion stereo digital CDA 66551–7 (7 cds 1999).
12.	Davitt Moroney (hpsc) 4'12; ed Brown; rec Ingatestone Hall Essex 3/1992. Hyperion stereo digital CDA 66551–7 (7 cds 1999).
13.	Aapo Hakkinen (hist hpsc) 5'24; ed Brown; rec Brussels 6/1999. Alba stereo digital ABCD 148 (cd 2000).
14.	Patrick Russill (cha org) 5'05; ed Skinner; rec Fitzalan Chapel Arundel Castle 20/7/2000. ASV stereo digital CDGAU 206 (cd 2000).
15.	Martin Souter (hist virg) [4'50]; rec Hill Music Room Ashmolean Museum Oxford. Classical Communications [stereo digital] CCLCD 832 (cd 2003).

Fantasia in G, no 2
3.	Claddagh CSM 59CD [cd nd].
6.	Robert Quinney (hist cha org) 7'08; rec Eton College Chapel. OxRecs stereo digital OXCASS 65 (mc), OXCD 65 (cd 1996).
7.	Davitt Moroney (hpsc) 7'19; ed Brown; rec Ingatestone Hall Essex 3/1992. Hyperion stereo digital CDA 66551–7 (7 cds 1999).
8.	Davitt Moroney (org) 9'06; ed Brown; rec Eglise-Musée des Augustins Toulouse 9/1991. Hyperion stereo digital CDA 66551–7 (7 cds 1999).

Fantasia in G, no 3
3.	Davitt Moroney (hpsc) 4'32; ed Brown; rec Ingatestone Hall Essex 3/1992. Hyperion stereo digital CDA 66551–7 (7 cds 1999).

Gloria tibi Trinitas
1.	ECM 4391722 (cd 1994).
3.	Davitt Moroney (org) 1'46; ed Brown; rec Eglise-Musée des Augustins Toulouse 9/1991. Hyperion stereo digital CDA 66551–7 (7 cds 1999).

Miserere, setting 1
2.	Davitt Moroney (org) 0'57; ed Brown; rec Eglise-Musée des Augustins Toulouse 9/1991. Hyperion stereo digital CDA 66551–7 (7 cds 1999).

3.   Davitt Moroney (clvc) 1'00; ed Brown; rec Royal Abbey of Fontevraud
      2/1997. Hyperion stereo digital CDA 66551–7 (7 cds 1999); CDA 66558
      (cd 2001).

Miserere, setting 2
3.   Davitt Moroney (clvc) 1'28; ed Brown; rec Eglise-Musée des Augustins
      Toulouse 9/1991. Hyperion stereo digital CDA 66551–7 (7 cds 1999).
4.   Davitt Moroney (clvc) 1'21; ed Brown; rec Royal Abbey of Fontevraud
      2/1997. Hyperion stereo digital CDA 66551–7 (7 cds 1999); CDA 66558
      (cd 2001).

Prelude in A minor
3.   Talent DOM 291022 (cd 1996).
7.   Laurent Stewart (hpsc) 0'47; rec Chateau de Vicq Pas-de-Calais 11/1994.
      Pierre Verany stereo digital PV 795051 (cd 1995).
8.   Sophie Yates (virg) 0'50; rec Forde Abbey 4/1994. Chandos stereo digital
      CHAN 0574 (cd 1995).
9.   Davitt Moroney (org) 0'58; ed Brown; rec Eglise-Musée des
      Augustins Toulouse 9/1991. Hyperion stereo digital CDA 66551–7
      (7 cds 1999).
10.   Davitt Moroney (clvc) 0'42; ed Brown; rec Royal Abbey of Fontevraud
      2/1997. Hyperion stereo digital CDA 66551–7 (7 cds 1999).
11.   Davitt Moroney (hpsc) 0'43; ed Brown; rec Royal Abbey of Fontevraud
      2/1997. Hyperion stereo digital CDA 66551–7 (7 cds 1999).
12.   Davitt Moroney (hpsc) 0'40; ed Brown; rec Royal Abbey of Fontevraud
      2/1997. Hyperion stereo digital CDA 66551–7 (7 cds 1999), CDA 66558
      (cd 2001).
13.   Davitt Moroney (msr) 0'48; ed Brown; rec Royal Abbey of Fontevraud
      2/1997. Hyperion stereo digital CDA 66551–7 (7 cds 1999).
14.   Aapo Hakkinen (hist hpsc) 0'46; ed Brown; rec Brussels 6/1999. Alba
      stereo digital ABCD 148 (cd 2000).
15.   Andreas Staier (hpsc) 1'01; ed Brown; rec DeutschlandRadio Cologne
      8/2001. Teldec stereo digital 0927422052 (cd 2001).

Prelude in C
6.   Davitt Moroney (clvc) 1'08; ed Brown; rec Royal Abbey of Fontevraud
      2/1997. Hyperion stereo digital CDA 66551–7 (7 cds 1999).
7.   John Kitchen (org) 1'06; rec Crichton Collegiate Church Midlothian
      1/2003. Delphian stereo digital DCD 34008 (cd 2003).

Prelude in F
2.   Louis Bagger (hpsc) [0'42]; rec Studio Dufay Leverett 1993. Lyrichord
      stereo digital LEMS 8015 (cd 1995).

3. Davitt Moroney (msr) 1'08; ed Brown; rec Royal Abbey of Fontevraud 2/1997. Hyperion stereo digital CDA 66551–7 (7 cds 1999).
4. Aapo Hakkinen (hist hpsc) 1'07; ed Brown; rec Brussels 6/1999. Alba stereo digital ABCD 148 (cd 2000).

Prelude in G
2. Davitt Moroney (hpsc) 1'29; ed Brown; rec Royal Abbey of Fontevraud 2/1997. Hyperion stereo digital CDA 66551–7 (7 cds 1999).
3. Aapo Hakkinen (hist hpsc) 1'24; ed Brown; rec Brussels 6/1999. Alba stereo digital ABCD 148 (cd 2000).

Prelude in G minor
3. Talent DOM 291022 (cd 1996).
6. Davitt Moroney (hpsc) 0'40; ed Brown; rec Royal Abbey of Fontevraud 2/1997. Hyperion stereo digital CDA 66551–7 (7 cds 1999).

Salvator mundi, setting 1
2. Andrew Cyprian Love (org) [nt]; rec Glenstal Abbey. SDG Recording stereo digital SDG CD 604 (cd 1997).
3. Davitt Moroney (org) 1'15; ed Brown; rec Eglise-Musée des Augustins Toulouse 9/1991. Hyperion stereo digital CDA 66551–7 (7 cds 1999).

Salvator mundi, setting 2
2. Timothy Morris (org) 1'27; rec New College Chapel 7/1994. CRD stereo digital CRD 3492 (cd 1997); CRD 5003 (3 cds 2002).
3. Davitt Moroney (org) 1'25; ed Brown; rec Eglise-Musée des Augustins Toulouse 9/1991. Hyperion stereo digital CDA 66551–7 (7 cds 1999).

Ut mi re, in G
1. Davitt Moroney (org) 7'51; ed Brown; rec Eglise-Musée des Augustins Toulouse 9/1991. Hyperion stereo digital CDA 66551–7 (7 cds 1999).

Ut re mi fa sol la, in G
2. Talent DOM 291022 (cd 1996).
6. Louis Bagger (hpsc) 6'18; rec Studio Dufay Leverett 1993. Lyrichord stereo digital LEMS 8015 (cd 1995).
7. Davitt Moroney (org) 8'28; ed Brown; rec Eglise-Musée des Augustins Toulouse 9/1991. Hyperion stereo digital CDA 66551–7 (7 cds 1999); CDA 66558 (cd 2001).
8. Martin Souter (hist virg) [8'02]; rec Hill Music Room Ashmolean Museum Oxford. Classical Communications [stereo digital] CCLCD 832 (cd 2003).

Verse [Fantasia in C, no 4]
3.   Davitt Moroney (org) 1'46; ed Brown; rec Eglise-Musée des Augustins Toulouse 9/1991. Hyperion stereo digital CDA 66551–7 (7 cds 1999).

Voluntary for my Lady Nevell [Fantasia in G, no 1]
1.   rec 30th Street Studio New York City 5/1967. Philips 4568082 (2 cds 1999).
3.   Davitt Moroney (org) 4'52; ed Brown; rec Eglise-Musée des Augustins Toulouse 9/1991. Hyperion stereo digital CDA 66551–7 (7 cds 1999).
4.   Davitt Moroney (hpsc) 4'54; ed Brown; rec Royal Abbey of Fontevraud 12/1996. Hyperion stereo digital CDA 66551–7 (7 cds 1999).
5.   Martin Souter (hist virg) [5'16]; rec Hill Music Room Ashmolean Museum Oxford. Classical Communications [stereo digital] CCLCD 832 (cd 2003).

Grounds and related pieces

Hornpipe
1.   John Whitelaw (hpsc) [6'01]. Talent stereo digital DOM 291022 (cd 1996).
2.   Davitt Moroney (hpsc) 6'17; ed Brown; rec Ingatestone Hall Essex 3/1992. Hyperion stereo digital CDA 66551–7 (7 cds 1999).

Hugh Aston's Ground
2.   rec Eaton's Auditorium Toronto 18/4/1971. Philips 4568082 (2 cds 1999).
5.   Sophie Yates (virg) 7'07; rec Forde Abbey 4/1994. Chandos stereo digital CHAN 0574 (cd 1995).
6.   Rachelle Taylor (hpsc) 9'52; rec St Alphonse de Rodriguez Church Quebec 4/1999. Atma stereo digital ACD 22197 (cd 1999).
7.   Davitt Moroney (msr) 8'04; ed Brown; rec Ingatestone Hall Essex 3/1992. Hyperion stereo digital CDA 66551–7 (7 cds 1999).
8.   Joanna MacGregor (pf) 7'15. SoundCircus stereo digital SC 007 (cd 2001).
9.   Andreas Staier (hpsc) 7'21; ed Brown; rec DeutschlandRadio Cologne 8/2001. Teldec stereo digital 0927422052 (cd 2001).

*Hugh Aston's Ground [variations 1–9]
*1.   Joanna MacGregor (pf) [nt]. SoundCircus stereo digital SCPCD (cd 1998).

My Lady Nevell's Ground
7.   Laurent Stewart (hpsc) 5'09; rec Chateau de Vicq Pas-de-Calais 11/1994. Pierre Verany digital PV 795051 (cd 1995).

8.   Davitt Moroney (hpsc) 5'18; ed Brown; rec Royal Abbey of Fontevraud 12/1996. Hyperion stereo digital CDA 66551–7 (7 cds 1999); CDA 66558 (2001).

9.   Andreas Staier (hpsc) 5'00; ed Brown; rec DeutschlandRadio Cologne 8/2001. Teldec stereo digital 0927422052 (cd 2001).

10. Martin Souter (hist virg) [5'21]; rec Hill Music Room Ashmolean Museum Oxford. Classical Communications [stereo digital] CCLCD 832 (cd 2003).

Qui pass [Chi passa] for my Lady Nevell

4.   Davitt Moroney (hpsc) 3'43; ed Brown; rec Royal Abbey of Fontevraud 12/1996. Hyperion stereo digital CDA 66551–7 (7 cds 1999).

5.   Andreas Staier (hpsc) 4'14; ed Brown; rec DeutschlandRadio Cologne 8/2001. Teldec stereo digital 0927422052 (cd 2001).

6.   Martin Souter (hist virg) [4'57]; rec Hill Music Room Ashmolean Museum Oxford. Classical Communications [stereo digital] CCLCD 832 (cd 2003).

[Short] Ground in C

2.   Davitt Moroney (org) 2'59; ed Brown; rec Eglise-Musée des Augustins Toulouse 9/1991. Hyperion stereo digital CDA 66551–7 (7 cds 1999). CDA 66558 (cd 2001).

[Short] Ground in G

2.   Davitt Moroney (msr) 5'49; ed Brown; rec Ingatestone Hall Essex 3/1992. Hyperion stereo digital CDA 66551–7 (7 cds 1999).

[Short] Ground in G minor

2.   Davitt Moroney (org) 4'30; ed Brown; rec Eglise-Musée des Augustins Toulouse 9/1991. Hyperion stereo digital CDA 66551–7 (7 cds 1999).

3.   Davitt Moroney (hpsc) 4'18; ed Brown; rec Royal Abbey of Fontevraud 2/1997. Hyperion stereo digital CDA 66551–7 (7 cds 1999).

The Bells

6.   Talent DOM 291022 (cd 1996).

12. Sophie Yates (virg) 5'40; rec Forde Abbey 4/1994. Chandos stereo digital CHAN 0574 (cd 1995).

13. David Leigh (hist hpsc) 6'20; rec [Leigh's house] Charlbury Oxfordshire 27/10/1998. Acanthus [stereo digital] 94010 (cd 1998).

14. Davitt Moroney (hpsc) 5'37; ed Brown; rec Ingatestone Hall Essex 3/1992. Hyperion stereo digital CDA 66551–7 (7 cds 1999); CDA 66558 (cd 2001).

15. Andreas Staier (hpsc) 5'49; ed Brown; rec DeutschlandRadio Cologne 8/2001. Teldec stereo digital 0927422052 (cd 2001).

The Hunt's Up, or Pescodd Time
4.   Davitt Moroney (hpsc) 7'19; ed Brown; rec Ingatestone Hall Essex 3/1992.
      Hyperion stereo digital CDA 66551–7 (7 cds 1999).
5.   Martin Souter (hist virg) [8'21]; rec Hill Music Room Ashmolean Museum
      Oxford. Classical Communications [stereo digital] CCLCD 832 (cd 2003)
      [omits variation 5b, Bars 81–96, only in the Fitzwilliam Virginal Book].

The seconde grownde, in C
2.   Davitt Moroney (hpsc) 8'56; ed Brown; rec Ingatestone Hall Essex 3/1992.
      Hyperion stereo digital CDA 66551–7 (7 cds 1999).
3.   Aapo Hakkinen (hist hpsc) 8'36; ed Brown; rec Brussels 6/1999. Alba
      stereo digital ABCD 148 (cd 2000).

Ut re mi fa sol la, in F
1.   Davitt Moroney, Oliver Neighbour (msr) 3'03; ed Brown, rec Ingatestone
      Hall Essex 3/1992. Hyperion stereo digital CDA 66551–7 (7 cds 1999).

Variations

All in a garden green
3.   Sophie Yates (virg) 4'02; rec Forde Abbey 17/11/1994. Chandos stereo
      digital CHAN 0578 (cd 1995).
4.   Martin Souter (hpsc) 4'30; rec Greenacre Studios Oxford 1996. Isis ste-
      reo digital CD 020 (cd 1996).
5.   Davitt Moroney (hpsc) 4'52; ed Brown; rec Royal Abbey of Fontevraud
      12/1996. Hyperion stereo digital CDA 66551–7 (7 cds 1999).

Callino casturame
10.   Davitt Moroney (hpsc) 1'58; ed Brown; rec Ingatestone Hall Essex 3/1992.
      Hyperion stereo digital CDA 66551–7 (7 cds 1999).
11.   Andreas Staier (hpsc) 1'32; ed Brown; rec DeutschlandRadio Cologne
      8/2001. Teldec stereo digital 0927422052 (cd 2001).
12.   Byron Schenkman (hpsc) [nt]. Centaur stereo digital CRC 2638 (cd
      2003).

Fortune
7.   David Leigh (hist hpsc) 4'09; rec [Leigh's house] Charlbury Oxfordshire
      26/10/1998. Acanthus [stereo digital] 94010 (cd 1998).
8.   Rachelle Taylor (virg) 3'57; rec St Alphonse de Rodriguez Church Que-
      bec 4/1999. Atma stereo digital ACD 22197 (cd 1999).
9.   Davitt Moroney (hpsc) 3'57; ed Brown; rec Ingatestone Hall Essex 3/1992.
      Hyperion stereo digital CDA 66551–7 (7 cds 1999).

Gipsies' Round
2.   Davitt Moroney (hpsc) 4'43; ed Brown; rec Royal Abbey of Fontevraud
     2/1997. Hyperion stereo digital CDA 66551–7 (7 cds 1999).

Go from my window
1.   Davitt Moroney (hpsc) 4'17; ed Brown; rec Ingatestone Hall Essex 3/1992.
     Hyperion stereo digital CDA 66551–7 (7 cds 1999); CDA 66558 (cd
     2001).

John come kiss me now
4.   Talent DOM 291022 (cd 1996).
10. Davitt Moroney (hpsc) 5'37; ed Brown; rec Royal Abbey of Fontevraud
     2/1997. Hyperion stereo digital CDA 66551–7 (7 cds 1999).
11. Zora Paterova (hpsc) 5'58; rec Studio Martinek Prague 4/1997. Prague
     Divox stereo digital CDX 79804 (cd 2000).
12. Andreas Staier (hpsc) 5'20; ed Brown; rec DeutschlandRadio Cologne
     8/2001. Teldec stereo digital 0927422052 (cd 2001).

O mistress mine, I must
5.   Gerhard Gnann (cha org) 5'24; rec St Sebastian Bombach 10/1994. Ars
     Musici stereo digital AM 11352 (cd 1995).
6.   Sophie Yates (virg) 4'34; rec Forde Abbey 17/11/1994. Chandos stereo
     digital CHAN 0578 (cd 1995).
7.   Gary Cooper (virg) [nt]; rec 1995. Philips stereo digital 4466874 (mc),
     4466872 (cd 1997).
8.   Davitt Moroney (hpsc) 6'21; ed Brown; rec Royal Abbey of Fontevraud
     2/1997. Hyperion stereo digital CDA 66551–7 (7 cds 1999).
9.   Byron Schenkman (hpsc) [nt]. Centaur stereo digital CRC 2638 (cd
     2003).

Rowland, or Lord Willoughby's Welcome home
14. Laurent Stewart (hpsc) 2'47; rec Chateau de Vicq Pas-de-Calais 11/1994.
     Pierre Verany stereo digital PV 795051 (cd 1995).
15. Sophie Yates (virg) 2'00; rec Forde Abbey 25/8/1996. Chandos stereo
     digital CHAN 0609 (cd 1997).
16. David Leigh (hist hpsc) 2'00; [ed Brown]; rec [Leigh's house] Charlbury
     Oxfordshire 26/10/1998. Acanthus [stereo digital] 94010 (cd 1998).
17. Davitt Moroney (msr) 2'38; ed Brown; rec Ingatestone Hall Essex 3/1992.
     Hyperion stereo digital CDA 66551–7 (7 cds 1999).
18. Adam Skeaping (hpsc) 2'10; ed Skeaping; rec ARC Music Studios
     East Grinstead 1/9/2000. ARC Music stereo digital EUCD 1616 (cd
     2000).

19.   Peter Watchorn (hpsc) 2'45; ed Brown; rec St Stephen's Episcopal
       Church Belvedere 2/2/2001. Musica Omnia stereo digital MO 0104
       (3 cds 2001).
20.   Martin Souter (hist virg) [2'42]; rec Hill Music Room Ashmolean
       Museum Oxford Classical Communications [stereo digital] CCLCD 832
       (cd 2003).

Sellinger's Round
1.   rec Eaton's Auditorium Toronto 18/4/1971. Philips 4568082 (2 cds
       1999).
8.   Davitt Moroney (hpsc) 6'11; ed Brown; rec Ingatestone Hall Essex 3/1992.
       Hyperion stereo digital CDA 66551–7 (7 cds 1999).
9.   Andreas Staier (hpsc) 5'29; ed Brown; rec DeutschlandRadio Cologne
       8/2001. Teldec stereo digital 0927422052 (cd 2001).
10.   Martin Souter (hist virg) [6'41]; rec Hill Music Room Ashmolean
       Museum Oxford Classical Communications [stereo digital] CCLCD 832
       (cd 2003).

The Carman's Whistle
9.   Virgin VBD 5618212 [2 cds nd].
16.   Skip Sempé (hpsc) 5'14; rec Temple de l'Ascension Paris 3/1997. Audi-
       vis stereo digital E 8611 (cd 1997).
17.   David Leigh (hist hpsc) 4'09; rec [Leigh's house] Charlbury Oxfordshire
       27/10/1998. Acanthus [stereo digital] 94010 (cd 1998).
18.   Davitt Moroney (cha org) 4'14; ed Brown; rec Ingatestone Hall Essex
       3/1992. Hyperion stereo digital CDA 66551–7 (7 cds 1999); CDA 66558
       (cd 2001).
19.   Sophie Yates (virg) 4'03; rec Forde Abbey 5/2002. Chandos stereo digital
       CHAN 0699 (cd 2003).

*The Carman's Whistle: [variations 1, 3-end]
*2.   Martin Jones (pf) 5'22; ed Grainger; rec the Ballroom Wyastone Leys
       20/4/1989. Nimbus stereo digital NI 5286 (cd 1991); NI 1767 (5 cds
       1997).
*3.   Piers Lane (pf) 4'21; ed Grainger; rec Henry Wood Hall London 4/2001.
       Hyperion stereo digital CDA 67279 (cd 2002).

The Maiden's Song
5.   Louis Bagger (hpsc) 4'44; rec Studio Dufay Leverett 1993. Lyrichord ste-
       reo digital LEMS 8015 (cd 1995).
6.   John Whitelaw (hpsc) [5'12]. Talent stereo digital DOM 291022 (cd
       1996).

7.   Davitt Moroney (cha org) 5'28; ed Brown; rec Ingatestone Hall Essex 3/1992. Hyperion stereo digital CDA 66551–7 (7 cds 1999).

The woods so wild
6.   Sophie Yates (virg) 4'00; rec Forde Abbey 4/1994. Chandos stereo digital CHAN 0574 (cd 1995).
7.   Davitt Moroney (msr) 4'36; ed Brown; rec Ingatestone Hall Essex 3/1992. Hyperion stereo digital CDA 66551–7 (7 cds 1999).
8.   Andreas Staier (hpsc) 3'28; ed Brown; rec DeutschlandRadio Cologne 8/2001. Teldec stereo digital 0927422052 (cd 2001).
9.   Martin Souter (hist virg) [4'29]; rec Hill Music Room Ashmolean Museum Oxford Classical Communications [stereo digital] CCLCD 832 (cd 2003).

Walsingham
10.   Martin Souter (hpsc) 9'15; rec Greenacre Studios Oxford 1996. Isis stereo digital CD 020 (cd 1996).
11.   Sophie Yates (hpsc) 8'19; rec Forde Abbey 25/8/1996. Chandos stereo digital CHAN 0609 (cd 1997).
12.   David Leigh (hist hpsc) 9'18; rec [Leigh's house] Charlbury Oxfordshire 26/10/1998. Acanthus [stereo digital] 94010 (cd 1998).
13.   Davitt Moroney (hpsc) 9'23; ed Brown; rec Royal Abbey of Fontevraud 2/1997. Hyperion stereo digital CDA 66551–7 (7 cds 1999); CDA 66558 (cd 2001).
14.   Aapo Hakkinen (hist hpsc) 8'49; ed Brown; rec Brussels 6/1999. Alba stereo digital ABCD 148 (cd 2000).
15.   Andreas Staier (hpsc) 8'31; ed Brown; rec DeutschlandRadio Cologne 8/2001. Teldec stereo digital 0927422052 (cd 2001).

Wilson's wild
1.   Biddulph LHW 016 (cd 1994).
5+.   Igor Kipnis (hpsc) [nt]; re 1986. Music & Arts stereo digital CD 4243 [cd 1986].
8.   Sophie Yates (virg) 1'14; re Forde Abbey 17/11/1994. Chandos stereo digital CHAN 0578 (cd 1995).
9.   Ronan de Burca (org) [nt]; rec 1996. Isis digital ISIS CD 021 [cd 1996].
10.   David Leigh (hist hpsc) 1'27; [ed Brown] rec [Leigh's house] Charlbury Oxfordshire 10/1998. Acanthus [stereo digital] 94010 (cd 1998).
11.   Davitt Moroney (hpsc) 1'23; ed Brown; rec Royal Abbey of Fontevraud 12/1996. Hyperion stereo digital CDA 66551–7 (7 cds 1999); HYP 20 (2cds 2000).

Pavans and Galliards

Echo Pavan and Galliard in G, no. 5

2.   Davitt Moroney (hpsc) [6'09]; ed Brown; rec Royal Abbey of Fontevraud
      2/1997. Hyperion stereo digital CDA 66551–7 (7 cds 1999).

*Echo Pavan and Galliard in G, no 5 Galliard

*1.   Aapo Hakkinen (hist hpsc) 1'44; ed Brown; rec Brussels 6/1999. Alba
      stereo digital ABCD 148 (cd 2000).

Galliard in C, no 4, Mistess Mary Brownlow

6.   Davitt Moroney (clvc) 3'11; ed Brown; rec Royal Abbey of Fontevraud
      2/1997. Hyperion stereo digital CDA 66551–7 (7 cds 1999).

Galliard in D minor, no 2

4.   Davitt Moroney (hpsc) 1'44; ed Brown; rec Royal Abbey of Fontevraud
      2/1997. Hyperion stereo digital CDA 66551–7 (7 cds 1999).

Galliard in G, no 9

2.   Davitt Moroney (msr) 1'03; ed Brown; rec Royal Abbey of Fontevraud
      12/1996 Hyperion stereo digital CDA 66551–7 (7 cds 1999).

Lady Monteagle's Pavan in G, no 7

1.   Davitt Moroney (hpsc) 2'59; ed Brown; rec Royal Abbey of Fontevraud
      2/1997 Hyperion stereo digital CDA 66551–7 (7 cds 1999).

Passamezzo Pavan and Galliard

6.   John Whitelaw (hpsc) [10'30]. Talent stereo digital DOM 291022 (cd
      1996).

7.   Davitt Moroney (hpsc) [11'41]; ed Brown; rec Royal Abbey of Fon-
      tevraud 12/1996. Hyperion stereo digital CDA 66551–7 (7 cds 1999).

Pavan and Galliard in A minor, no 1

4.   Talent DOM 291022 (cd 1996).

7.   Skip Sempé (hpsc) [5'31]; rec Temple de l'Ascension Paris 3/1997.
      Audivis stereo digital E 8611 (cd 1997).

8.   [Alexander Rosenblatt] (hpsc) [6'13] Holyland Records stereo digital CD
      14 (cd 1999).

9.   Davitt Moroney (msr) [6'45]; ed Brown; rec Royal Abbey of Fontevraud
      12/1996. Hyperion stereo digital CDA 66551–7 (7 cds 1999).

10.   Peter Watchorn (hpsc) [6'36]; rec Southern Vermont College Old Ben-
      nington 6/1998. Musica Omnia stereo digital MO 0104 (3 cds 2001).

Pavan and Galliard in A minor, no 3
1.   Davitt Moroney (msr) [5'41]; ed Brown; rec Royal Abbey of Fontevraud 2/1997. Hyperion stereo digital CDA 66551–7 (7 cds 1999).

Pavan and Galliard in B♭
1.   Davitt Moroney (msr) [6'19]; ed Brown; rec Royal Abbey of Fontevraud 12/1996. Hyperion stereo digital CDA 66551–7 (7 cds 1999); CDA 66558 (cd 2001).

Pavan and Galliard in C, no 1
3.   Davitt Moroney (hpsc) [4'32]; ed Brown; rec Royal Abbey of Fontevraud 12/1996. Hyperion stereo digital CDA 66551–7 (7 cds 1999).

Pavan and Galliard in C, no 2, Kinborough Good
1.   rec 30th Street Studio New York City 5/1967. Philips 4568082 (2 cds 1999).
4.   Skip Sempé (hpsc) [5'33]; rec Temple de l'Ascension Paris 3/1997. Audivis stereo digital E 8611 (cd 1997).
5.   Davitt Moroney (hpsc) [6'25]; ed Brown; rec Royal Abbey of Fontevraud 12/1996. Hyperion stereo digital CDA 66551–7 (7 cds 1999).

Pavan and Galliard in C, no 3
2.   Davitt Moroney (hpsc) [6'38]; ed Brown; rec Royal Abbey of Fontevraud 2/1997. Hyperion stereo digital CDA 66551–7 (7 cds 1999).

Pavan and Galliard in C minor, no 1
2.   rec 30th Street Studio New York City 6/1967. Philips 4568082 (2 cds 1999).
6.   Davitt Moroney (msr) [6'15]; ed Brown; rec Royal Abbey of Fontevraud 12/1996. Hyperion stereo digital CDA 66551–7 (7 cds 1999).
7.   Martin Souter (hist virg) [6'14]; rec Hill Music Room Ashmolean Museum Oxford Classical Communications [stereo digital] CCLCD 832 (cd 2003).

Pavan and Galliard in C minor, no 2
4.   Colin Tilney (virg) [6'46]; rec St Isidore Church St Isidore Québec 11/1993. Dorian stereo digital DOR 90195 (cd 1994).
5.   Davitt Moroney (msr) [6'47]; ed Brown; rec Royal Abbey of Fontevraud 12/1996. Hyperion stereo digital CDA 66551–7 (7 cds 1999).

Pavan and Galliard in D minor, no 1
3.   Ton Koopman (hpsc) [6'59]; rec Maria Minor Utrecht 12/1986. Capricio stereo digital 10211 (cd 1988).

4.   Davitt Moroney (hpsc) [6'47]; ed Brown; rec Royal Abbey of Fontevraud
      2/1997. Hyperion stereo digital CDA 66551–7 (7 cds 1999).
5.   Peter Watchorn (hpsc) [6'37]; ed Brown; rec St Stephen's Episcopal
      Church Belvedere 2/2/2001. Musica Omnia stereo digital MO 0104
      (3 cds 2001).

Pavan and Galliard in F, no 1, Bray
3.   Davitt Moroney (hpsc) [6'09]; ed Brown; rec Royal Abbey of Fontevraud
      2/1997. Hyperion stereo digital CDA 66551–7 (7 cds 1999).

Pavan and Galliard in F, no 2, Ph Tregian
9.   Louise Bagger (hpsc) [5'14]; rec Studio Dufay Leverett 1993. Lyrichord
      stereo digital LEMS 8015 (cd 1995).
10.   Skip Sempé (hpsc) [6'05]; rec Temple de l'Ascension Paris 3/1997.
      Audivis stereo digital E 8611 (cd 1997).
11.   Davitt Moroney (msr) [6'47]; ed Brown; rec Royal Abbey of Fontevraud
      12/1996. Hyperion stereo digital CDA 66551–7 (7 cds 1999).
12.   Aapo Hakkinen (hist hpsc) 7'03; ed Brown; rec Brussels 6/1999. Alba
      stereo digital ABCD 148 (cd 2000).
13.   Peter Watchorn (hpsc) [7'36]; ed Brown; rec Southern Vermont College Old
      Bennington 6/1998. Musica Omnia stereo digital MO 0104 (3 cds 2001).
14.   Andreas Staier (hpsc) [6'41]; ed Brown; rec DeutschlandRadio Cologne
      8/2001. Teldec stereo digital 0927422052 (cd 2001).

Pavan and Galliard in G, no 2
4.   Davitt Moroney (hpsc) [4'39]; ed Brown; rec Royal Abbey of Fontevraud
      12/1996. Hyperion stereo digital CDA 66551–7 (7 cds 1999).

Pavan and Galliard in G, no 3
4.   Davitt Moroney (hpsc) [5'50]; ed Brown; rec Royal Abbey of Fontevraud
      2/1997. Hyperion stereo digital CDA 66551–7 (7 cds 1999).

Pavan and Galliard in G, no 4
4.   Davitt Moroney (msr) [4'02]; ed Brown; rec Royal Abbey of Fontevraud
      12/1996. Hyperion stereo digital CDA 66551–7 (7 cds 1999).

Pavan and Galliard in G minor, no 2, Sir William Petre
6.   Talent DOM 291022 (cd 1996).
9.   Laurent Stewart (hpsc) 7'21; rec Chateau de Vicq Pas-de-Calais 11/1994.
      Pierre Verany stereo digital PV 795051 (cd 1995).
10.   Sophie Yates (virg) [6'14]; rec Forde Abbey 4/1994. Chandos stereo
      digital CHAN 0574 (cd 1995).

11. Davitt Moroney (hpsc) [6'35]; ed Brown; rec Royal Abbey of Fontevraud 2/1997. Hyperion stereo digital CDA 66551–7 (7 cds 1999).
12. Peter Watchorn (hpsc) [7'31]; ed Brown; rec St Stephen's Episcopal Church Belvedere 2/2/2001. Musica Omnia stereo digital MO 0104 (3 cds 2001).

*Pavan and Galliard in G minor, no 2, Sir William Petre: Pavan
*1. Sophie Yates (hpsc) [4'09]; rec Forde Abbey 25/8/1996. Chandos stereo digital CHAN 0609 (cd 1997).
*2. Skip Sempé (msr) [5'09]; rec Temple de St Marcel Paris 3/2001. Naive stereo digital E 8841 (cd 2002) [Lady Nevell's Book version].

Pavan and Galliard in G minor, no 3
 4. Davitt Moroney (msr) [3'57]; ed Brown; rec Royal Abbey of Fontevraud 12/1996. Hyperion stereo digital CDA 66551–7 (7 cds 1999).
 5. Skip Sempé (virg) [3'10]; ed Brown rec Temple St Marcel Paris 3/2001. Naive stereo digital E 8841 (cd 2002).

Pavan and two Galliards in A minor, no 2, The Earl of Salisbury
4+. Geoffrey Coffin (org) [nt]; ed Graves. Foxglove stereo digital FOX 031CD [cd 1991].
 6. Martin Souter (hpsc) [3'42]; rec Greenacre Studios Oxford 1996. Isis stereo digital CD 020 (cd 1996).
 7. David Leigh (hist hpsc) [5'12]; [ed Brown] rec [Leigh's house] Charlbury Oxfordshire 10/1998. Acanthus [stereo digital] 94010 (cd 1998).
 8. Davitt Moroney (msr) [4'56]; ed Brown; rec Royal Abbey of Fontevraud 12/1996. Hyperion stereo digital CDA 66551–7 (7 cds 1999).

*Pavan and two Galliards in A minor, no 2, The Earl of Salisbury: Pavan
*13. IMP 3036701752 (cd 1987).
*14. Skip Sempé (virg) 1'29; rec Temple St Marcel Paris 3/2001. Naive stereo digital E 8841 (cd 2002) [Parthenia version].

Pavan in A minor, no 4
 5. Skip Sempé (hpsc) 4'50; rec Temple de l'Ascension Paris 3/1997. Audiovis stereo digital E 8611 (cd 1997).
 6. Davitt Moromey (msr) 4'56; ed Brown; rec Royal Abbey of Fontevraud 12/1996. Hyperion stereo digital CDA 66551–7 (7cds 1999).

Pavan in G, no 6, Canon 2 in 1
 3. Davitt Moroney (msr) 4'49; ed Brown; rec Royal Abbey of Fontevraud 12/1996. Hyperion stereo digital CDA 66551–7 (7 cds 1999); CDA 66558 (cd 2001).

Pavan in G, no 8
2.   Davitt Moroney (msr) 3'07; ed Brown; rec Royal Abbey of Fontevraud 12/1996. Hyperion stereo digital CDA 66551–7 (7 cds 1999).

Quadran Pavan and Galliard
3.   Davitt Moroney (hpsc) [13'10]; ed Brown; rec Royal Abbey of Fontevraud 2/1997. Hyperion stereo digital CDA 66551–7 (7 cds 1999).
4.   Aapo Hakkinen (hist hpsc) 13'34; ed Brown; rec Brussels 6/1999. Alba stereo digital ABCD 148 (cd 2000).

Other dances, descriptive music and arrangements

Alman in C
1.   Davitt Moroney (hpsc) 2'10; ed Brown; rec Royal Abbey of Fontevraud 2/1997. Hyperion stereo digital CDA 66551–7 (7 cds 1999).
2.   Aapo Hakkinen (hist hpsc) 2'11; ed Brown; rec Brussels 6/1999. Alba stereo digital ABCD 148 (cd 2000).

Alman in G
2.   Laurent Stewart (hpsc) 1'06; rec Chateau de Vicq Pas-de-Calais 11/1994. Pierre Verany stereo digital PV 795051 (cd 1995).
3.   Davitt Moroney (msr) 1'20; ed Brown; rec Royal Abbey of Fontevraud 12/1996. Hyperion stereo digital CDA 66551–7 (7 cds 1999).
4.   Andreas Staier (hpsc) 0'55; ed Brown; rec DeutschlandRadio Cologne 8/2001. Teldec stereo digital 0927422052 (cd 2001).

Alman in G minor
5.   Davitt Moroney (hpsc) 1'22; ed Brown; rec Royal Abbey of Fontevraud 2/1997. Hyperion stereo digital CDA 66551–7 (7 cds 1999).

Coranto in C
3.   Gary Cooper (virg) [nt]; rec 1995. Philips stereo digital 4466874 (mc), 4466872 (cd 1997).
4.   Davitt Moroney (hpsc) 1'10; ed Brown; rec Ingatestone Hall Essex 3/1992. Hyperion stereo digital CDA 66551–7 (7 cds 1999).

Galliard (Harding, arr Byrd)
4.   Sophie Yates (virg) 2'27; rec Forde Abbey 4/1994. Chandos stereo digital CHAN 0574 (cd 1995).
5.   Davitt Moroney (msr) 2'57; ed Brown; rec Royal Abbey of Fontevraud 12/1996. Hyperion stereo digital CDA 66551–7 (7 cds 1999).

In Nomine (Parsons, arr. attrib. Byrd)
2.   Davitt Moroney (cha org) 2'51; ed Brown; rec Ingatestone Hall Essex 3/1992. Hyperion stereo digital CDA 66551–7 (7 cds 1999).

Jig in A minor
7.   Davitt Moroney (msr) 1'06; ed Brown; rec Royal Abbey of Fontevraud 12/1996. Hyperion stereo digital CDA 66551–7 (7 cds 1999).

Lachrymae Pavan (Dowland, arr. Byrd)
3.   rec 1977. L'Oiseau-Lyre 4525632 [12 cds nd].
8.   Sophie Yates (virg) 5'14; rec Forde Abbey 4/1994. Chandos stereo digital CHAN 0574 (cd 1995).
9.   Martin Souter (hpsc) 5'37; rec Greenacre Studios Oxford 1996. Isis stereo digital CD 020 (cd 1996).
10. David Leigh (hist hpsc) 7'19; [ed Brown] rec [Leigh's house] Charlbury Oxfordshire 10/1998. Acanthus [stereo digital] 94010 (cd 1998).
11. Davitt Moroney (msr) 5'58; ed Brown; rec Royal Abbey of Fontevraud 12/1996. Hyperion stereo digital CDA 66551–7 (7 cds 1999).
12. Aapo Hakkinen (hist hpsc) 7'23; ed Brown; rec Brussels 6/1999. Alba stereo digital ABCD 148 (cd 2000).
13. Byron Schenkman (hpsc) [nt]. Centaur stereo digital CRC 2638 (cd 2003).

Lavolta in G minor, no 1, Lady Morley
4.   Sophie Yates (virg) 1'22; rec Forde Abbey 17/11/1994. Chandos stereo digital CHAN 0578 (cd 1995).
5.   Davitt Moroney (hpsc) 1'28; ed Brown; rec Royal Abbey of Fontevraud 12/1996. Hyperion stereo digital CDA 66551–7 (7 cds 1999).

Lavolta in G minor, no 2
13. Laurent Stewart (hpsc) 1'04; Chateau de Vicq Pas-de-Calais 11/1994. Pierre Verany stereo digital PV 795051 (cd 1995).
14. Davitt Moroney (hpsc) 1'24; ed Brown; rec Royal Abbey of Fontevraud 12/1996. Hyperion stereo digital CDA 66551–7 (7 cds 1999).
15. Peter Watchorn (hpsc) 2'28; rec Southern Vermont College Old Bennington 6/1998. Musica Omnia stereo digital MO 0104 (3 cds 2001).
16. Andreas Staier (hpsc) 1'06; ed Brown; rec DeutschlandRadio Cologne 8/2001. Teldec stereo digital 0927422052 (cd 2001).

Monsieur's Alman in C
1.   Davitt Moroney (hpsc) 2'09; ed Brown; rec Royal Abbey of Fontevraud 2/1997. Hyperion stereo digital CDA 66551–7 (7 cds 1999).

Monsieur's Alman in G, no 1
2.   Davitt Moroney (hpsc) 3'48; ed Brown; rec Royal Abbey of Fontevraud
      2/1997. Hyperion stereo digital CDA 66551–7 (7 cds 1999).

Monsieur's Alman in G, no 2
2.   John Whitelaw (hpsc) [5'35]. Talent stereo digital DOM 291022 (cd
      1996).
3.   Davitt Moroney (hpsc) 6'06; ed Brown; rec Royal Abbey of Fontevraud
      2/1997. Hyperion stereo digital CDA 66551–7 (7 cds 1999).

O quam gloriosum
1.   Davitt Moroney (msr) 7'03; ed Brown; rec Ingatestone Hall Essex. 3/1992.
      Hyperion stereo digital CDA 66551–7 (7 cds 1999); CDA 66558 (cd 2001).

Pavan and Galliard, Delight (Johnson, arr Byrd)
3.   Davitt Moroney (hpsc) [6'56]; ed Brown; rec Royal Abbey of Fontevraud
      2/1997. Hyperion stereo digital CDA 66551–7 (7 cds 1999).

*Pavan and Galliard, Delight (Johnston, arr Byrd): Galliard
*1.   Davitt Moroney (hpsc) 1'46; ed Brown; rec Royal Abbey of Fontevraud
      2/1997. Hyperion stereo digital CDA 66558 (cd 2001) [from 3].

Piper's Galliard (Dowland, arr Byrd?)
1.   Davitt Moroney (hpsc) 2'26; ed Brown; rec Royal Abbey of Fontevraud
      2/1997. Hyperion stereo digital CDA 66551–7 (7 cds 1999).

The Barley Break
2.   Colin Tilney (virg) 9'56; rec St Isidore Church St Isidore Québec 11/1993.
      Dorian stereo digital DOR 90195 (cd 1994).
3.   Sophie Yates (virg) 7'47; rec Forde Abbey 4/1994. Chandos stereo digital
      CHAN 0574 (cd 1995).
4.   Davitt Moroney (hpsc) 8'20; ed Brown; rec Royal Abbey of Fontevraud
      2/1997. Hyperion stereo digital CDA 66551–7 (7 cds 1999).

The Battle
3.   Davitt Moroney (msr) 12'50; ed Brown; rec Royal Abbey of Fontevraud
      2/1997. Hyperion stereo digital CDA 66551–7 (7 cds 1999).

*The Battle: The soldiers' summons; The marh of footmen; The march of horse-
      men; The trumpets; The march to the fight
*5.   Bob van Asperen (hpsc) 6'41; rec St Lawrence's & St Vincent's Church
      Backenmoor Germany 10/1998. Aeolus stereo digital AE 10014 (cd 1998).

*The Battle: The Irish march
*6   Skip Sempé (hpsc) 1'37; rec Temple de l'Ascension Paris 3/1997. Audio-
        vis stereo digital E 8611 (cd 1997).

*The Battle: The trumpets
*7.   Davitt Moroney (msr) 1'24; ed Brown; rec Royal Abbey of Fontevraud
        2/1997. Hyperion stereo digital CDA 66558 (cd 2001) [from 3].

The Galliard for the Victory
   4.   Bob van Asperen (hpsc) 1'47; rec St Lawrence's & St Vincent's Church
        Backenmoor Germany 10/1998. Aeolus stereo digital AE 10014
        (cd 1998).
   5.   Davitt Moroney (msr) 1'59; ed Brown; rec Royal Abbey of Fontevraud
        2/1997. Hyperion stereo digital CDA 66551–7 (7 cds 1999); CDA 66558
        (cd 2001).

The Galliard Jig
   3.   Davitt Moroney (hpsc) 2'03; ed Brown; rec Royal Abbey of Fontevraud
        12/1996. Hyperion stereo digital CDA 66551–7 (7 cds 1999).

The Ghost
   2.   Davitt Moroney (hpsc) 2'58; ed Brown; rec Royal Abbey of Fontevraud
        12/1996. Hyperion stereo digital CDA 66551–7 (7 cds 1999).

The March before the Battle, or The Earl of Oxford's March
   3.   Davitt Moroney (msr) 4'12; ed Brown; rec Royal Abbey of Fontevraud
        2/1997. Hyperion stereo digital CDA 66551–7 (7 cds 1999).
   4.   Sophie Yates (virg) 3'13; rec Forde Abbey 5/2002. Chandos stereo digital
        CHAN 0699 (cd 2003) [Fitzwilliam Virginal Book version].

The Queen's Alman
   12. Sophie Yates (hpsc) 3'24; rec Forde Abbey 25/8/1996. Chandos stereo
        digital CHAN 0609 (cd 1997).
   13. Davitt Moroney (msr) 3'00; ed Brown; rec Royal Abbey of Fontevraud
        12/1996. Hyperion stereo digital CDA 66551–7 (7 cds 1999).
   14. Christopher Stembridge (hist org) 3'46; rec Church of the Ospedaletto
        Venice 5/1999. Quilisma stereo digital QUIL 302 (cd 2000).
   15. Andreas Staier (hpsc) 3'09; ed Brown; rec DeutschlandRadio Cologne
        8/2001. Teldec stereo digital 0927422052 (cd 2001).
   16. Sophie Yates (virg) 3'07; rec Forde Abbey 5/2002. Chandos stereo digital
        CHAN 0699 (cd 2003).

Three French Corantos
3.   Davitt Moroney (hpsc) [2'36]; ed Brown; rec Ingatestone Hall Essex
      31992. Hyperion stereo digital CDA 66551–7 (7 cds 1999).

*Three French Corantos: First French Coranto, Third French Coranto
*1.   Laurent Stewart (hpsc) [1'43]; rec Chateau de Vicq Pas-d-Calais 11/1994.
      Pierre Verany stereo digital PV 795051 (cd 1995).
*2.   Skip Sempé (hpsc) [1'46]; rec Temple de l'Ascension Paris 3/1997.
      Audiovis stereo digital E 8611 (cd 1997).

Doubtful works

Christ rising again (EECM 13)
1.   Tallis Scholars/Peter Phillips [nt]. Gimell stereo digital CDGIM 007 (cd
      1986).
2.   Chapelle du Roi/Alistair Dixon 4'39; rec St Jude-on-the-Hill Church
      Hampstead 7/2000. Signum stereo digital SIGCD 022 (cd 2003).

Fantasia à 4 in D minor, no 2
1.   New York Consort of Viols 1'38; rec Studio Dufay Leverett 1993. Lyri-
      chord stereo digital LEMS 8015 (cd 1995).

Lullaby [Keyboard adaptation] (EK 53)
2.   Aapo Hakkinen (hist hpsc) 4'59; ed Brown; rec Brussels 6/1999. Alba
      stereo digital ABCD 148 (cd 2000).

Medley (BK 112)
1.   John Whitelaw (hpsc) [5'07]. Talent stereo digital DOM 291022 (cd
      1996).

Pavan and Galliard in C (EK 10)
1.   Davitt Moroney (hpsc) [2'55]; ed Brown; rec Royal Abbey of Fontevraud
      2/1997. Hyperion stereo digital CDA 66551–7 (7 cds 1999).

The day delayed
1.   Ines Villanueva (s), Jaye-Consort Berlin 3'00; rec Kapelle Klein-Glien-
      icke concert 7/2/2001. Jaye-Consort Berlin stereo digital 'Farewell all
      ioyes' (cd 2001).

Michael Greenhalgh was for several years principal lecturer in Information
Management at Thames Valley University London and Director of its MA, MSc,
and Postgraduate Diploma courses. He has been a regular reviewer for music
periodicals: *Records and Recording* (1972–78), *International Music Guide*

(1979–82), *Cassette Scrutiny* (1981–82), and *Sound Scrutiny* (1983–86). In 1975 he gained an MLitt from Oxford University for a thesis on Dryden and Purcell's King Arthur. In 1980 he was awarded a Fellowship of the Library Association for his complete discography of Purcell. Among other publications are short monographs on Purcell (1982) and Vaughan Williams's symphonies (1987), as well as a complete discography of Gibbons (1999).

A NOTE ON RECOMMENDED RECORDINGS

RICHARD TURBET

Historically informed performances have become the norm for recordings of early music. Even some modern performances on anachronistic instruments show signs of an awareness of scholarly research. Mutual suspicion and ignorance at times remain between performers and scholars, but many recordings can supplement and support musicological research, and vice versa. There are three articles by RT within Byrd literature in which archival and current recordings are recommended: 1993Tm, 1994Tm, and 2002Tr. Also, some recordings mentioned in Chapter 6 of the first edition have been transferred to compact disc. The three finest are the performance of the Mass for Five Voices by the Choir of St John's College, Cambridge, now on 7243 5 74220 2 in the Classics for Pleasure label on the EMI label; Quink's version of *Ave verum corpus*—still the finest ever made—on Etcetera KTC 1031; and soprano Lorna Anderson's penetrating interpretation, sung in contemporary Scots and accompanied by the Scottish Early Music Consort, of *In angel's weeds,* a (probably contrafacted) lament for Mary Queen of Scots, on Chandos CHAN 0529. Some more compact discs are recommended in chapter A-VI of 1994Tt. Also, in every issue of *Annual Byrd newsletter,* there was a column noting "Significant new recordings." In 1993Mb, John Milsom made a plea for a more comprehensive coverage of Byrd's music on disc, specifically in authentic performances, praising the way in which some discs already released had shown the right approach. It is gratifying that, within a decade, suitable artists and recording companies subsequently responded, leaving only the English-texted music in need of the attention advocated by Milsom.

In addition to the recordings featured in these articles, there are a few that slipped through the net. The best performance on disc of a Byrd mass is on RRC 1226, a recent reissue on the Regis label by Pro Cantione Antiqua, who sing the Mass for Four Voices (T 1) at low pitch with religious intensity and musical awareness. (The disc is recommended in 1994Tm on account of a penetrating performance of one of Byrd's motets, *Domine non sum dignus,* T 49.) On *Songs and sonnets: music for voice and viols* (Meridian CDE 84271, recorded, like another well-chosen anthology mainly of Byrd's consort pieces—Duo DUOCD 89027—in the ideal acoustic of St. Edward the Confessor's Church, Mottingham, London), clarity and vivacity inform Concordia's performances of most of Byrd's instrumental repertory in five parts, qualities that the soprano Rachel Platt complements in a broad range of Byrd's consort songs. Nowhere is this more evident than in her mesmerizing empathy with the words of *Constant Penelope,* one of the great performances of Byrd's music on disc.

The Byrd edition, the admirable and ambitious recording of all Byrd's Latin music by The Cardinall's Musick, conducted by Andrew Carwood and using editions by David Skinner, continues on the renamed Gaudeamus label, formerly ASV. In the world of commercial recording, events are more volatile and change more quickly than in the world of publishing. Despite the aspirations expressed at its launch, the project will not now embrace the Anglican music performed with a male choir including trebles, nor the secular vocal music, nor the instrumental music. Nevertheless, it is a tribute to the high quality sustained throughout the project that each performance of every item of Latin music, and of the few items of consort music played by the Frideswide Consort, can be recommended. The project has continually added to the recorded repertory of Byrd's music, as is apparent from the discography, and from the number of subsequent premieres noted below.

Byrd's secular vocal music continues to appear piecemeal, with usually individual premieres, particularly of songs, scattered across various recordings, but the instrumental music has been recorded in its entirety, on two outstanding projects noted in 2002Tr.

Individual recordings can move into and out of availability several times during the course of several years. The definitive accompanied recording of the *Great Service* (T 197) by the Choir of King's College, Cambridge, listed on page 226 of 1992Gb, is a worthy successor to the classic unaccompanied recording by the Choir of St. Thomas Church, New York, which is listed immediately above it. Both versions are historically valid. The Cambridge version benefits from being available on compact disc as well as LP and has the added advantage of having been performed from a new unpublished edition by James Wrightson rather than from the worthy but by then outdated edition of Fellowes. Whether or not it is commercially available at any given time, it remains the essential focus for reference to Byrd's Anglican music.

RECORDED PREMIERES OF BYRD'S MUSIC SINCE 2003

RICHARD TURBET

Since the completion of Michael Greenhalgh's discography, and before the completion of the entire *Guide,* some hitherto unrecorded pieces by Byrd received their premiere recordings.

On *William Byrd: All in a garden green: keyboard works & two songs* (Helikon HCD 1048) baritone Niles Danielsen, accompanied by Oliver Hirsh playing the chamber organ, sings *My soul oppressed* (T 218) and *Truce for a time* (T 350). Two premieres have been recorded for the label Harmonia Mundi USA

(HMU 907383) on a disc of Byrd's songs and consort music, one from either category: *He that all earthly pleasure scorns* (T 340), and the reconstructed third Fantasia in four parts (T 383). The singer is the soprano Emma Kirkby, accompanied by the viol consort Fretwork, which also plays the fantasia and the rest of the instrumental works.

The ninth volume of *The William Byrd edition,* entitled *O sacrum convivium* (CD GAU 332) was released on the Gaudeamus label in 2004, and contained no fewer than six recorded premieres, all from the second book of *Gradualia*: *Jesu nostra redemptio* (T 137), *Dominus in Sina* (T 145), *Ascendit Deus* (T 146), *O rex gloriae* (T 148), *Spiritus Domini* (T 149), and *Alleluia. Emitte spiritum* (T 150).

A disc of *Cantiones* from 1589 and 1591 performed by the Choir of Trinity College, Cambridge, conducted by Richard Marlow, and released by Chandos, includes the first recording of *Quis est homo* (T 36).

On the ensemble's eponymous disc, Cantiones Renovatae has made the first recordings of *Lord in Thy Wrath Reprove Me Not* (T 224) and *Prostrate O Lord* (T 242) in versions reconstructed from Paston sources (Meden Recordings, unnumbered CD).

A new recording of the complete *Great Service* has been made by the Choir of Westminster Abbey for the Hyperion label; new to disc is the anthem *How long shall mine enemies* (T 201).

5

Annual Byrd Newsletter 1995–2004: History and Indexes

Annual Byrd newsletter is the only periodical devoted to an early English composer. Indeed, it is the only periodical devoted to a British composer earlier than Elgar.

In 1994, I conceived the idea for what became *Annual Byrd newsletter*. Before the publication of John Harley's monograph about Byrd (1997Hw) with its remarkable biographical discoveries, it was presumed that Byrd had been born in 1543 or late 1542. Since the putative quatercentenary of his birth had been overshadowed by the continuing World War II, his presumed 450th anniversary was celebrated all the more. I had already written the first edition of the present volume (1987Tw) and had incorporated a supplement into *Tudor music: a research and information guide* (1994Tt). In a subsequent article "Byrd at 450" (1994Tb), I endeavored to list and, where appropriate, annotate all subsequent writings about Byrd during 1993, continuing from the *terminus ad quem* of *Tudor music* at the end of 1992, adding any earlier items previously overlooked, and setting out all the articles celebrating his anniversary.

It was at this stage that I sought some means of continuing to disseminate news of rediscovered and new writings about Byrd. I also envisaged news of recordings, notes and queries, and short articles. Having investigated and rejected the idea of a separate publication, I decided that a supplement to an existing periodical would be the best medium. I approached Clifford Bartlett, whom I had already met through the International Association of Music Libraries. He had given me sound advice in the past when I was seeking a publisher for what became *Byrd studies* (1992B) and was now founder, editor, and publisher of

the monthly *Early music review.* With characteristic aplomb he took my suggestion on board. We do not know (yet) *precisely* when Byrd was born, but we know
he died on 4 July 1623, so I planned to publish the Byrd supplement within each
July issue of *Early music review.* However, as all the material was assembled in
good time, Clifford decided to launch it with the June issue. The working title
was "Annual Byrd supplement." I had earlier suggested "newsletter" as an alternative but it was Clifford who settled on *Annual Byrd newsletter* as appropriate,
despite the fact that it was physically a yellow-papered supplement within the
plain white paper of his *Review.*

The first issue set the basic pattern for all ten. An editorial call to arms was
followed by "New writings," a list, annotated where appropriate, of the previous
year's publications devoted to Byrd, or containing significant information about
him. These have all been subsumed within Chapters 2 and 3. There followed intimations of new, continuing, and forthcoming research about Byrd. Recordings
came next: first, reviews of discs sent for review; and, second, references to all
recordings of significance, such as premieres, important reissues, or discs that
consist entirely or substantially of Byrd's music. It was a point of principle not to
pass any evaluative comment on discs not submitted for review. All recordings of
Byrd's music up to the end of 2003 are in Michael Greenhalgh's three discographies: 1992GRb, 1996Gb, and Chapter 4.

The succeeding section was entitled merely "Miscellany," and every effort
was made to range as widely as possible in providing information about Byrd
that fitted nowhere else: recent broadcasts, corrections to published writings,
explanations, amplifications, elucidations, ruminations, and observations. This
section, with the editorial, is indexed in this Chapter.

The music supplement could crop up anywhere within the *Newsletter* or even
in the surrounding *Early music review,* depending on the exigencies of space and
layout. The music was usually but not always by or attributed to Byrd, and could
be newly published, a new discovery, a facsimile or illustrating an article.
Another peripatetic but occasional series was "Meanings," in which people from
a variety of musical backgrounds—composing, librarianship, teaching, and performing—wrote in a paragraph or two what Byrd's music means to them. All the
supplements and contributors to "Meanings" are listed in this chapter.

The final section of the *Newsletter* was given over to the articles. Usually
these were commissioned by the editor, although an encouraging proportion
were suggested or offered by their authors. I envisaged articles too short or otherwise unsuitable for the mainstream musicological journals, perhaps offshoots of
previous or continuing research that could not be fitted into the major narrative,
or a particular idea an author wished to explore. Some authors were neither
musicologists nor musicians. Every article has extended our knowledge or understanding of Byrd. Each one is included in chapters 2 and 3, as are those more
substantial miscellanea that acquired their own titles and which contain some
significant information about Byrd.

To summarize: "Miscellany" and the editorial are indexed together in this chapter. "Meanings" and the music supplements are both listed in this chapter. Every item listed in the *Newsletter* among "New writings" is subsumed within Chapters 2 and 3. Every headed article and miscellaneum is listed and annotated in Chapters 2 and 3, respectively.

In 2003 I took the decision to discontinue *Annual Byrd newsletter.* Clifford Bartlett announced plans to reorganize *Early music review* after number 100, May 2004; this, albeit brought forward by a month, would coincide with the tenth issue of the *Newsletter,* another round figure. Also, work was advancing on the present volume, which would subsume material destined for any following issue. The future for such material, which for a decade found its home in the *Newsletter,* is discussed in Chapter 6. Within its chosen sphere, *Annual Byrd newsletter* has achieved what had been envisaged for it. Byrd has had far too little written about him in relation to his status and the quality of his music, and the *Newsletter* increased the quantity of enlightening and informative articles. The international breadth of correspondence sent to the editor and the number of citations of the *Newsletter* in books and articles confirm that the contents of the *Newsletter* have increased awareness of Byrd and his music.

1. INDEX TO MISCELLANY AND EDITORIALS

(Newsletter number/page)

2. MUSIC SUPPLEMENTS

"W. Byrd—Fantasia a 4 no. 3."
Early music review 11 (1995): 6–7.
Note: See K in list of editions, Chapter 1.

"Haec est dies (attrib. William Byrd)."
Annual Byrd newsletter 2 (1996): 6–7.
Note: For commentary, see *Early music review* 21 (1996): 16.

"W. Sterndale Bennett—Fugue on Byrd's 'Bow thine ear.'"
Annual Byrd newsletter 3 (1997): 12.

"Coste: He that hath my commandments."
Early music review 41 (1998): 11–12.

"A hymn set by Mr Byrd 1570."
Annual Byrd newsletter 5 (1999): 12.
Note: Facsimile of spurious *Glory be to God,* 1774: see PS in list of editions
    in Chapter 1, *supra.*

"Jubilate for Mr Bird's Service."
Early music review 61 (2000): 14–17.
Note: Eighteenth-century arrangement of Benedictus from *Short Service;* for
    commentary, see *Annual Byrd newsletter* 6 (2000): 12.

"Paduana a William Byrde" and "Galliarda. William Byrde."
Annual Byrd newsletter 7 (2001): 16–20.
Note: Transcription of *Tenth pavan and galliard* from New German tablature.

"Non nobis."
Annual Byrd newsletter 8 (2002): 11.
Note: Facsimile of arrangement by James Oswald of spurious round: see adja-
    cent article, page 10.

"Byrd *Look and bow down.*"
Early music news 91 (2003): 28 and *Diary:* 35.
Note: Facsimile of surviving fragments. (The *Diary* is a separate, and sepa-
    rately paginated, supplement to *Early music review.*)

"Aspice Domine (a6)" Philip van Wilder.
Annual Byrd newsletter 10 (2004): 27–28.
Note: Full text of the two surviving parts.

3. MEANINGS

Jonathan Bielby	8 (2002): 5.
James MacMillan	4 (1998): 5.
Colin Matthews	5 (1999): 4.
David Matthews	6 (2000): 5–6.
Roger Bevan Williams	7 (2001): 4–5.
Susi Woodhouse	9 (2003): 5–6.

4. ARTICLES NOT DEVOTED TO BYRD

Harley, John. "Orlando Gibbons's supposed doctorate." 7 (2001): 6.

Notes evidence in support of Nathaniel Giles being the recipient of the doctorate, not Gibbons.

Smith, D. J. "Further light on Peter Philips." 3 (1997): 8–9.

Reports on the researches of Erik Duverger and of Godelieve Spiessens which uncovered many new facts about Philips's life.

Turbet, Richard. "Music of Orlando Gibbons in early printed editions: a supplement." 8 (2002): 10.

Original article: "Orlando Gibbons: music in early editions 1625–1925," *Fontes artis musicae* 47 (2000): 42–47.

6

Not a Conclusion

The equivalent chapter in the first edition of this book scattergunned a number of suggestions for further research about Byrd. It is gratifying to observe that the majority have, in some form or other, been taken up. Meanwhile, to repeat a passage from the first paragraph of that chapter, since this "is a chapter about ideas and insights, it is less academic in its trappings than the rest of the monograph aspires to be." Only one electronic resource for Byrd is mentioned in this chapter because otherwise there are none that add to existing knowledge or understanding of his life or music. So, what next for Byrd literature? In the context of the present volume, the answer is that although *Annual Byrd newsletter* has ceased, an annual column entitled "Byrd on a wire" will continue without a break in each June issue of *Early music review*, the host to the *Newsletter* throughout its existence.

During 2004 several projects devoted to Byrd were known to be in progress but were unlikely to reach fruition before the end of that year. (Realistically, there is the possibility that some might never reach it, though one completed project of major significance, originally given a date of publication as late 2004 subsequently postponed to early 2005, has been included in the checklist and the annotated bibliography.) Nevertheless, it is assumed that those consulting this *Guide* would expect to be alerted to projects that are in progress at the time of writing. Some projects may have reached publication before the *Guide*, while others may still be pending, but in any event their existences or otherwise can be investigated, both by contemporary readers and by posterity.

Five books are known to be in various stages of development. *William Byrd's modal practice* by John Harley is scheduled for publication by Ashgate on 20 May 2005. *William Byrd's six-part fantasias in G minor* by Richard

Rastall has been accepted for publication by the same publisher. The third book is a planned collection of writings by, and as memorial to, the late Philip Brett, edited by Joseph Kerman and Davitt Moroney. Entitled *William Byrd and his contemporaries*, it includes an introduction "Traditionalist and innovator: aspects of William Byrd," 1981Bh, 1972BRw, "2002: thoughts on William Byrd," and his prefaces to A 5-7b, as well as published articles on Tallis, Paston, Whitney, Weelkes and Gibbons. It is to be published by the University of California Press in 2006. The complete *Annual Byrd newsletter* is planned for publication by King's Music late in 2005, and Kerry McCarthy's *Byrd as reader*, based upon her doctoral thesis "Byrd as exegete: his Gradualia in context" (Stanford University, 2002) has been accepted for publication by Routledge.

It has already been noted (in Chapter 2) that Philip Brett died before he could make a start on "The anthems, Services and songs of William Byrd," which would have been volume 2 of the series *The music of William Byrd* (For volumes 1 and 3 see 1981Km and 1978Nc). A conference entitled "The English-texted music of William Byrd" held at the University of Leeds, 11 September 2004, was devoted to a review of present-day scholarship, and the repertory that would have been discussed in Philip Brett's contribution to the intended trilogy. This was a historic event in that it was the first conference to be devoted to Byrd and his music. The proceedings consisted of "Byrd's English-texted music: a review of published research" by RT, "Sacred or domestic: criteria for identification of the initial destinations of Byrd's music to vernacular texts" by Roger Bowers, "William Byrd and Sir John Petre's cultural circle in the 1580s" by David Mateer, and "William Byrd's B1, the succession, Diana, Oriana and the Essex revolt: political readings and new interpretations" by Jeremy Smith, a version of which is to be published in the *Journal of the American Musicological Society*. A comprehensive report was compiled by Kerry McCarthy, for publication in *Early music*. This brings into the public domain, via these papers, many hitherto unpublished ideas, which expand, and in some cases disrupt, existing thinking on topics such as Byrd's social circle and the origins of certain of Byrd's compositions with English sacred texts. As a result of the conference, and particularly of its concluding round-table, chaired by the organizer of the conference, Richard Rastall, and led by Kerry McCarthy plus those who gave the papers, further progress may be expected on the creation of a body of writing (including a related website) on Byrd's English-texted music, to replace the planned volume by the late Philip Brett. This could amount to a single volume; two volumes, one each on the Anglican music and the songs; a sequence of articles; or a series of shorter monographs, no fewer than three, no more than eight.

The International William Byrd Conference, with an especial emphasis on the other categories of Byrd's music, Latin-texted and instrumental, is planned by Kerry McCarthy for Duke University, Durham NC, 17-19 November 2005.

Other projects that are intended for eventual publication as articles include the following:

"An unknown keyboard piece by Byrd in a Dutch source?" by Pieter Dirksen;

"What's the point?: contrapuntal techniques in Byrd's pavans and galliards" by Davitt Moroney. A development of the author's lecture–recital given at the reception in the British Museum to celebrate the seventieth birthday of Oliver Neighbour in 1993, this paper was given on 18 April 2004 during the Dutch Harpsichord Society's Festival of Virginals, Delft, 16-18 April 2004, the proceedings of which are intended for publication;

"The *Clarifica me* settings of Tallis and Byrd: friendly emulation or friendly competition?" by Rachelle Taylor and Frauke Jurgensen. This paper was given at the Symposium of Early English Keyboards, University of Aberdeen, 15–17 April 2005;

"Byrd's musical recusancy" by David Trendell, which is based substantially on T 22, T 24, T 50 and responds from the first and second *Cantiones*;

"Composer of the month: William Byrd" by Jeremy Summerly, for *BBC music magazine* (January 2005);

"New evidence of William Byrd's aristocratic Catholic friends" by David Crankshaw, cited in footnotes 2, 5 and 8 of 2002Bw;

"Collaborative voice in the 1575 Tallis-Byrd *Cantiones*" by Kerry McCarthy;

"Greatness thrust upon 'em: Services by Byrd and others reconsidered" in which RT apostacizes concerning much of what he wrote in 1990Tg, 1992Tg and 1995Ty, is scheduled for publication in *Musical times* during 2005;

Instrumentale Konzeptionen in der Virginalmusik von William Byrd by Martin Klotz for Tutzing: Schneider, 2005.

"Playing Elizabeth's tune: the Tallis Scholars sing William Byrd", a DVD on Ginsell GIMDN 902, scheduled for 2004.

Only one electronic resource is adding information about Byrd that is not available in print. This is the Christ Church Library music catalogue, University of Oxford, the work of John Milsom at www.chch.ox.ac.uk/library/public/music. Provenance entries for holdings of the original printed editions of Byrd's music are being expanded to include the names of their owners during Byrd's lifetime and the emerging details of owners' backgrounds.

That takes care of disseminating information about Byrd literature as it was and is now, but whatever shall be next for the literature itself? What should that literature be about? It could well be on a subject that has been covered already. Many individual works or groups of works from the Baroque onwards have had several articles and more than one book written about them. The *Gradualia* are a fertile soùrce for research into structure, organization, theology and compositional technique, both as a collection and as individual pieces, and there is much of a similar vein to be written about the *Cantiones*. In the continuing absence of the final volume, numbered two, of the series *The music of William Byrd*, mentioned above, there is a pressing need for extensive and radical studies of Byrd's Anglican music and of his songs. Nevertheless, the two volumes already published in the series should not be regarded as full stops nor as impediments to further monographs on the specific aspects of Byrd's *oeuvre*, which they cover.

Byrd's recusancy is a fact, but so is his loyal service to Queen Elizabeth. How did he resolve these two apparently warring elements — one covert, the other overt — in his music? Perhaps the first word of the previous sentence is redundant. Psychological or spiritual, as well as musicological, investigation might reveal some pointers. Tensions may have been worked out in the instrumental music. What Byrd composed made sense at the time, and makes sense four centuries later, but what was that "sense"? Even during the nadir of his reputation for two hundred years after his death, it was never quite lost while being sustained by the likes of Barnard and Boyce, and, perhaps even more significantly, by the likes of Gainsborough. It is a secure technique, yet in a volatile period, and something made sense sufficiently for Byrd's music to continue resonating with undiminished integrity. The William Byrd Festival continues annually in Portland, OR, and on 6 July 2004 the William Byrd Memorial Recital, sung by the Stondon Singers under Justin Doyle, resumed its annual sequence at the Church of St Peter and St Paul, Stondon Massey, Essex after a break of a year in which priority was given to celebrating the golden jubilee of Her Majesty Queen Elizabeth II's coronation. The works performed were T 4, T 31, T 47, T 90 and T 92. On 12 July 2005 T 197f and T 197g will be performed. On 12 July 2005 T 197f and T 197g will be performed. In *Gerald Finzi: his life and music* (Woodbridge: Boydell, September 2005) Diana McVeagh notes on page 27 that the composer quotes T 8 in his "motet" *Up to those bright and gladsome hills* (London: Stainer and Bell, 1925).

Byrd's biography requires continued research. The records of many City churches in London have been lost, and among such records are those from the parishes in which the Byrd family is thought to have lived. Nevertheless many records remain to be consulted in the Public Record Office, the Guildhall and other such repositories in London and elsewhere, and there is the possibility that some documents relevant to Byrd have come to light but have not been recognised, by those reading them, as being of potential interest to those others who are researching Byrd.

Knowledge of Byrd's social circle and family circle continues to grow, yet little by way of pattern or cohesion has emerged. There is a need continually to expand these researches yet at the same time to juxtapose all these contacts, in the hope that a catalyst will emerge who or which will assist in placing all these relationships in context.

Of comparable interest and importance is Byrd's cultural circle. We have some idea of his relationships with fellow musicians thanks to dedications and observations made by pupils. Knowledge of working relationships within the Chapel Royal remains a blank, likewise working practices. The suspicion remains that Byrd followed his two brothers to St Paul's for at least part of his early education, perhaps as a chorister or even a vicar choral, but whether he had a stint at the Chapel Royal some time before going to Lincoln Cathedral, as well as after returning from it, remains another secret that requires unlocking. His relationship with the contemporary literary culture is a little clearer. He had contact – perhaps tenuous, perhaps intimate – with Sidney and his circle, including Watson. It is now known, thanks to a recent feat of consummate literary detection, that Shakespeare mentions Byrd. Frustratingly it is impossible at present to know whether the reverse applies. Byrd never set any of Shakespeare's words to music, and it is easier for a poet or dramatist overtly to refer to a composer than it is for a composer, other than setting a writer's words, to refer even covertly to a poet or dramatist. Nevertheless such contact continues to surface, and Byrd's known socializing with the family of George Herbert prompts the thought as to whether there may have been also some contact with the ubiquitous John Donne. While the fact of such contacts is of some interest, the real significance for Byrd as a creative artist lies in the consequences, if these can be uncovered.

The beginning of the revival of Byrd's music can conveniently be pinpointed to 1840 and the publications of the Musical Antiquarian Society. Nevertheless such events do not emerge from a vacuum, and their effects can take a long time to percolate into the prevailing culture. A handful of his pieces were published individually or in small groups during the early and mid-nineteenth century, and placing these in the context of the survival since his death of his music in manuscript and print, as well as placing it alongside the music of his contemporaries, both English and foreign, that survived and was revived similarly, would add to understanding of the "early music" revival. Several of Byrd's works survive fragmentarily. Rediscovery or recognition of missing parts, or even of additional fragments of already fragmentary works, would be invaluable, especially if such rediscoveries rendered such pieces playable, thereby effectively adding new works to the Byrd repertory. This is much easier said than done, but it is worth noting that there are no fewer than ten songs, which survive incomplete and unperformable, plus some Anglican music. Entire works may yet be rediscovered, and attributions to Byrd of anonymous pieces should continue judiciously to be made.

Although this is the final chapter in the present *Guide*, it is not a conclusion. The scope for research and thought about Byrd's music is unlimited and endless. The continuous evolution of ideas brings forth opportunities for new approaches, while the profundity, variety and extent of his compositions mean that any part of it can be researched and discussed repeatedly. Much remains to be discovered about his life. To control such information beneficially, there is a need to organize and disseminate continually all published knowledge about Byrd, by way of bibliographies and discographies. Not a conclusion; in fact, a continuum.

Index

Warner, S.T 1922Wb
Weaver, G. 2003Wc
Wesley, S. 1826Wp, 1923Ws
Westover, C. II.Ww, 1993Ww
Westrup, J. 1943Ww, 1961Wb
Whitfield, J. 1923WHw
Whittaker, W.G. VI.app, X.app, 1941Wb, 1942Wb
Whymper, F. 1891Ww
Willan, H. III.Ww, 1943WIw
William Byrd Festival 1998W
Williams, S. X.app.
Wilson, R. XII.WIa
Winch, N. 1987Ww

Wood, A. I.WOa, 1987WOa
Woodward, D. 1985Ww
Worrall, E. 1971Wc
Wortham, H. 1923WOw
Woudhuysen, H. VII.Wm
Wright, N.F. 1957Ww
Wulstan, D. II.app, IV.Wb, IV.Wby, 1992Wb, 1996Wb

Z

Zimmerman, F. VII.app, 1959Za